# Teenagers, Sexual Health Information and the Digital Age

# Teenagers, Sexual Health Information and the Digital Age

KERRY MCKELLAR, BSC, MRES, PHD
Department of Psychology
Northumbria University
Newcastle, UK

ELIZABETH SILLENCE, BSC (HONS), MSC, PHD
Department of Psychology
Northumbria University
Newcastle, UK

Teenagers, Sexual Health Information and the Digital Age  ISBN: 978-0-12-816969-8
**Copyright © 2020 Elsevier Inc. All rights reserved.**

No part of this publication may be reproduced or transmitted in any form or by any means, electronic or mechanical, including photocopying, recording, or any information storage and retrieval system, without permission in writing from the publisher. Details on how to seek permission, further information about the Publisher's permissions policies and our arrangements with organizations such as the Copyright Clearance Center and the Copyright Licensing Agency, can be found at our website: www.elsevier.com/permissions.

This book and the individual contributions contained in it are protected under copyright by the Publisher (other than as may be noted herein).

---

**Notices**

Practitioners and researchers must always rely on their own experience and knowledge in evaluating and using any information, methods, compounds or experiments described herein. Because of rapid advances in the medical sciences, in particular, independent verification of diagnoses and drug dosages should be made. To the fullest extent of the law, no responsibility is assumed by Elsevier, authors, editors or contributors for any injury and/or damage to persons or property as a matter of products liability, negligence or otherwise, or from any use or operation of any methods, products, instructions, or ideas contained in the material herein.

---

*Publisher:* Stacy Masucci
*Acquisition Editor:* Kattie Washington
*Editorial Project Manager:* Samantha Allard
*Production Project Manager:* Kiruthika Govindaraju
*Cover Designer:* Alan Studholme

# Acknowledgments

I would first like to thank Elizabeth Sillence (coauthor) whose feedback, advice, and support is always valued and appreciated. Also, to Michael Smith, who supervised five of the studies presented in this book, and provided support and guidance throughout. In addition, without the funding from Northumbria University, the studies presented in this book would not have been possible.

A special mention to Kayleigh Richardson, who collected the data presented in chapter 9; her hard work and determination was shown throughout her MRes project. A particular thank you as well to all current and past colleagues in PaCT lab for their valuable feedback and advice. I would also like to thank all of the schools and youth groups who have participated in the studies presented in this book. This research would not have been possible without the cooperation and support from the staff, pupils, and parents.

Also, I would like to thank my husband, David McKellar, for his patience, proofreading, and editing skills.

Finally, to you, the reader, I hope you find this book an enjoyable read.

**Kerry McKellar**

# Contents

1 Introduction, *1*

2 Current Research on Sexual Health and Teenagers, *5*

3 Sexual Health Education in and Outside of Schools and Digital Sexual Health Interventions, *25*

4 Sexual Health Professional Views of Sexual Health Education, *41*

5 Ethical Issues When Researching Sexual Health With Teenagers, *55*

6 Teenagers' Views of Sexual Health Education, *69*

7 Predictors of Risky Behaviors for Female Teenagers, *79*

8 Teenagers' Views of Sexual Health Education Websites and Apps, *99*

9 Students' Views of Sexual Health Apps, *113*

10 A Brief Online Self-affirmation Intervention to Promote Safe sex Intentions, *123*

11 Reflections, *135*

REFERENCES, *141*

INDEX, *153*

# CHAPTER 1

# Introduction

## CHAPTER OUTLINE

Introduction ................................................. 1
Contributions of this Book.......................... 2
  Current Research on Sexual Health and
  Teenagers (Chapter 2) ........................................ 2
  Sexual Health Education in Schools and Digital
  Interventions (Chapter 3) ..................................... 3
  Sexual Health Professional Views of Sexual
  Health Education (Chapter 4) .............................. 3
  Ethical Issues When Researching Teenagers
  and Sexual Health (Chapter 5) ........................... 3
  Teenagers' Views of Sexual Health Education
  (Chapter 6) ............................................................ 3

  Predictors of Risky Sexual Behaviors for Female
  Teenagers (Chapter 7) ......................................... 3
  Teenagers' Views of Sexual Health Education
  Websites and Apps (Chapter 8) .......................... 4
  Students' Views of Sexual Health
  Apps (Chapter 9)................................................... 4
  A Brief Online Self-affirmation Intervention to
  Promote Safe sex Intentions (Chapter 10)............ 4
  Reflections and Conclusions (Chapter 11) .......... 4

## ABSTRACT

This chapter provides an overview of the contributions of this book. In this book, we aim to highlight current research on teenagers, sexual health, and the digital age. Teenagers are surrounded by information about sexual health, and access to digital technology has made it possible to envisage exciting opportunities for innovative and creative ways of providing teenagers with reliable information in a confidential manner. However, the online environment also poses challenges for teenagers, parents, and health practitioners with access to unreliable, misleading and potentially dangerous information. This book examines the current information landscape for teenagers. It examines the online resources available including games and digital interventions and highlights current issues such as sexting and pornography. Information needs and provision will be examined, and existing sexual health interventions and digital interventions will be discussed, gathering both teenagers' and sexual health professionals' views on these services. In addition to a review of the current literature on sexual health and teenagers, the book examines groups of teenagers particularly vulnerable to risky sex and asks what are the predictors of

these behaviours and what can be done to address the behaviours. This book will also provide reflections and practical advice on the ethical issues associated with research in this context. This chapter provides an overview of the contributions of each of the following chapters.

## KEYWORDS

Digital sexual health interventions; Teenagers; Sexual health; Sexual health intervention programs.

## INTRODUCTION

First sexual initiation is a normal and expected aspect of adolescent development (Heywood, Patrick, Smith, & Pitts, 2015). However, risky sexual behaviors are also prevalent among teenagers. In the UK, teenagers are becoming sexually active at an earlier age (Mercer et al., 2010). A large survey in Britain found that although the average age of first heterosexual intercourse was 16, nearly a quarter of girls had sex before they were 16. Furthermore, half of the girls said they wish they had waited longer to have sex, and were twice

Teenagers, Sexual Health Information and the Digital Age. https://doi.org/10.1016/B978-0-12-816969-8.00001-1
Copyright © 2020 Elsevier Inc. All rights reserved.

as likely to say this if they were under age 15 at first sexual initiation (FPA, 2016).

It is important to reduce teenage risk taking, as the consequences of teenage sexual risk taking are unplanned pregnancies and sexually transmitted infections (STIs). Teenage pregnancy rates in the UK have shown a downward trend in the last decade and are currently at the lowest level since records began. Despite this, the UK continues to have one of the highest rates of teenage conceptions in Western Europe (ONS, 2014). One of the reasons for the reduction in teenage pregnancy is that contraception use is improving in this age group. A recent survey found a small reduction in the overall number of new STIs in the teenage population; however, overall levels remained very high (Health Protection Report, 2017). Teenage abortion rates have not decreased, although the rise is only slight, 0.6% since 2014 (FPA, 2016).

There are many teenage sexual health intervention programs in the UK. General practitioners and school nurses offer free and confidential services for teenagers across the country (Baxter, 2010), and teenagers have widespread access to free contraceptives. However, teenagers generally do not report using these services and often report reluctance to use these because of worries about confidentiality and feeling judged (Iyer & Baxter-MacGregor, 2010). In addition, teenagers believe it is embarrassing to discuss sexual health with sexual health professionals and parents (Buhi, 2013). Therefore, despite the confidential and free sexual health services available, teenagers are still reluctant to use them. This may be one of the reasons that there is still a high number of unplanned pregnancies and STIs in the teenage population.

Teenagers are known for their early adoption of the Internet, and teenagers report that the Internet is their primary source when seeking health information (Gray & Klein, 2006), likely because of the anonymity it affords. Discussing sex with teachers, parents, or even friends is considered embarrassing in a society that problematizes teenage sexuality (Kendall & Funk, 2012; Moran, 2000). The Internet is an appealing source of sexual health information because teens can access the information without the embarrassment of anyone finding out (Kanuga & Rosenfeld, 2004). Therefore, it is worthwhile to consider current digital interventions and whether technology is contributing to teenage sexual health knowledge.

## CONTRIBUTIONS OF THIS BOOK

In this book, we aim to highlight current research on teenagers, sexual health, and the digital age. Teenagers are surrounded by information about sexual health, and access to digital technology has made it possible to envisage exciting opportunities for innovative and creative ways of providing teenagers with reliable information in a confidential manner. However, the online environment also poses challenges for teenagers, parents, and health practitioners with access to unreliable, misleading, and potentially dangerous information. Examining our teenagers' information needs and existing levels of knowledge is important, but we also need to understand how they engage with and evaluate sexual health information both offline and in a digital context so that we can improve the provision of useful information.

This book examines the current information landscape for teenagers. It examines the online resources available including digital interventions and highlights current issues such as sexting and pornography. Information needs and provision are examined, and existing sexual health interventions and digital interventions are discussed, gathering both teenagers' and sexual health professionals' views on these services. In addition to a review of the current literature on sexual health and teenagers, this book examines groups of teenagers particularly vulnerable to risky sex and asks what are the predictors of these behaviors and what can be done to address the behaviors. Our own research studies presented throughout this book are conducted within the North East England in the UK, with low socioeconomic status (SES) female teenagers, as we identified that these were a high-risk group for unplanned teenage pregnancies and STIs. However, teenage sexual risk taking, unplanned pregnancies, and STIs are issues facing many countries. The background literature explores teenage sexual risk taking from a worldwide perspective, and the ideas discussed within this book are generalizable beyond the UK and to non-SES populations. This book also provides reflections and practical advice on the ethical issues associated with research in this context.

Overall, the book comprises 11 chapters, with Chapters 2−11 outlined below.

## Current Research on Sexual Health and Teenagers (Chapter 2)

Chapter 2 provides current literature around teenager's sexual health. The chapter is split into five sections: (1) an overview of teenage sexual health and consideration of risky sexual behaviors; (2) an overview of the main theoretical models in the literature; (3) an examination of the predictors of risky sexual behaviors; (4) an overview of sexual health issues in the digital world; and finally (5) the particular issues associated with females from low SES areas. Taken together, these sections provide an overview of current research on sexual health and teenagers.

## Sexual Health Education in Schools and Digital Interventions (Chapter 3)

Chapter 3 presents an overview of the research on commonly cited sexual health intervention programs. This chapter is in three sections to provide greater clarity of the research literature. The first section provides an overview of sexual health education within schools, the second section provides an overview of external sexual health intervention programs, and the final section considers digital sexual interventions.

## Sexual Health Professional Views of Sexual Health Education (Chapter 4)

Chapter 4 presents a qualitative study exploring sexual health professionals' views of female teenagers' sexual health information seeking practices and barriers and reexamines the sexual health predictors suggested by previous literature. The focus on sexual health professionals is important given their position as key stakeholders in implementing sexual health interventions, yet their views are largely absent from the literature. The barriers identified were "environment and family," "society and media," "peer influences," "self-esteem," and "moving forward with intervention programs." In terms of the sexual health predictors, sexual health professionals ranked 33 of the 57 identified as key predictors in the extant literature as highly important, thus supporting previous research. Some of the barriers identified were consistent with previous research, while others were particularly novel. Interestingly, sexual health professionals identified self-esteem as a highly important factor influencing teenagers' likelihood to seek sexual health information, while also being an important predictor of risky sexual behaviors. Yet, limited evidence for self-esteem has been found in previous quantitative studies. This suggests that going forward, sexual health interventions that build self-esteem and address socioeconomic stigma may encourage adolescents to feel confident to make their own informed sexual health decisions.

## Ethical Issues When Researching Teenagers and Sexual Health (Chapter 5)

Chapter 5 considers the importance of ethical issues when conducting sexual health research with teenagers. The chapter is divided into four sections. Section 1 discusses the importance and background of ethics. Section 2 considers existing ethical guidelines and Section 3 provides a consideration of our own personal experiences of the ethical issues encountered in sexual health research. The final section draws together the key issues and provides guidance on how to implement ethical procedures when researching sexual health with teenagers.

## Teenagers' Views of Sexual Health Education (Chapter 6)

Chapter 6 discusses a qualitative study designed to explore low SES female teenagers' sexual health knowledge and information sources. The study utilized a 4-week diary produced three themes: (1) *Can I ask you a question? (2) The social consequences of sex; (3) Information sources.* The first two themes explored teenagers lack of knowledge and misunderstandings around the biological and social experiences of sexual health. The third theme explored the limited ways in which teenagers encounter sexual health information currently despite their desire to understand more. The findings of this study highlight the juxtaposition between teenagers' lack of understanding about the biological and social aspects of sex and at the same time their curiosity and thirst for knowledge. This point was emphasized in the teenagers' use of the diaries as a confidential way of seeking sexual health information. This study concluded that teenagers do not have access to reliable sexual health information, and have very limited sexual health knowledge, but are thinking about sex. Furthermore, teenagers from low SES areas do not have any strategies for actively seeking sexual information, and as such sexual health practitioners need to think more creatively about how to provide teenagers with access to reliable sexual health information in a convenient and confidential way.

## Predictors of Risky Sexual Behaviors for Female Teenagers (Chapter 7)

Chapter 7 discusses a quantitative study that aimed to investigate the predictors of early sexual behavior and intentions to have sex for low SES female teenagers. A large online questionnaire was administered to 318 low SES female teenagers measuring the high-risk predictors found from Chapters 4 and 6 and current literature. The analysis showed that higher sensation seeking and more high-quality sexual health information, lower self-esteem, lower delayed gratification, and lower sexual health knowledge significantly predict early sex before age 16. Further, the analysis showed that higher peer pressure and higher pornography use significantly predict intention to have sex in the next year. By contrast, none of the predictors significantly predicted intention to have safe sex in the next year. Therefore, this study provided further evidence for an intervention that targets both self-esteem and reliable sexual health information. In addition, sexual health information sources should focus on a wide range of sexual health issues including peer pressure and pornography.

## Teenagers' Views of Sexual Health Education Websites and Apps (Chapter 8)

Chapter 8 investigates female teenagers' views of current sexual health websites and mobile apps. This research aimed to explore whether Internet-based sexual health resources via websites and mobiles apps are meeting teenagers' sexual health needs and to explore, for the first time, teenagers' perceptions of the design features of sexual health mobile apps. Twenty-three female participants aged 13−16 years either viewed six existing sexual health websites or three existing sexual health mobile apps chosen to be representative of the range and variety currently available. Participants then took part in focus groups evaluating each of the websites and mobile apps. The findings indicate that adolescents currently use their phones to access sexual health information due to ease of access and privacy. However, none of the adolescents were aware of sexual health apps. Participants believed apps should have similar design features to websites but apps should contain an appropriate interactive element paired with accurate sexual health information. At the moment, female adolescents are not using sexual health mobile apps, they believe they are more convenient and private compared with websites, yet they trust sexual health websites more than mobile apps.

## Students' Views of Sexual Health Apps (Chapter 9)

Chapter 9 explores the current literature on menstrual tracking apps and considers students' views of menstrual tracking apps. Three female students were asked to download and use the app 'moody month' for 8 weeks and then take part in an interview exploring their experiences and perceptions of using the app. We found three key themes explained users' experiences of the app: reliable information, ease of use, trust and privacy. Users liked that they had access to reliable information about the menstrual cycle in an accessible and convenient way, and they realized that they did not know a lot about the menstrual cycle. Participants

found the app easy to use and trusted the information. Overall, participants believed it was suitable for younger adolescents and that teenagers would benefit from learning more about the menstrual cycle.

## A Brief Online Self-affirmation Intervention to Promote Safe sex Intentions (Chapter 10)

Chapter 10 discusses our research evaluating a self-affirmation and sexual health intervention for low SES female teenagers aged 13−16 years. A self-affirmation intervention was chosen because of its links with self-esteem. Self-esteem has been found to be a highly important predictor of early sexual initiation in our earlier studies (described in Chapters 3 and 7). A sexual health website was used to deliver the sexual health information as it was perceived to be reliable by teenagers in the study described in Chapter 8. The website included information about all areas of sexual health, including peer pressure and pornography, which were identified as important predictors of risky sexual behavior. The results showed that the self-affirmation intervention significantly increased self-esteem for the self-affirmed group compared with the nonaffirmed group. In addition, the self-affirmed group had significantly higher intentions to have safe sex postintervention and at a 1 week follow-up compared with the nonaffirmed group. However, there were no significant postintervention differences in sexual health knowledge between the self-affirmed and nonaffirmed groups.

## Reflections and Conclusions (Chapter 11)

The final chapter moves onto some final reflections and conclusions. It provides a summary and conclusion based on each of our studies presented throughout the book and an overview and summary of the main research literature. Finally, future research ideas and design implications for moving forward with online self-esteem and sexual health intervention programs are discussed.

# CHAPTER 2

# Current Research on Sexual Health and Teenagers

## CHAPTER OUTLINE

Sexual Health and Defining Risky Sexual Behaviors ..................................................... 5
Theoretical Models of Risky Sexual Behavior ...... 7
  The Theory of Planned Behavior .......................... 7
    *Health belief model*................................... 8
    *Problem behavior theory* ......................... 9
Predictors of Risky Sexual Behaviors ................. 11
  Parental and Peer Influences ........................... 13
  The Self ...................................................... 14
  Personality ................................................. 16
  Situational Factors ...................................... 16
  External Factors .......................................... 17
Digital World Issues ............................................ 18
  Pornography ............................................... 18

Sexting ............................................................ 18
  *What is "sexting"?* ...................................... 18
  *Prevalence of "sexting"?* ......................... 18
  *Teenagers' views of sexting*................... 19
  *Professional's views of sexting* .............. 20
  *Sexting and risky sexual behavior*.......... 21
  *Best practices—guidelines from research*................................................. 21
Spotlight on: Female Teenagers from low SES Areas ............................................................... 21
  *Pressure, coercion, and consent* ........... 21
Chapter Summary.............................................. 23

## ABSTRACT

This chapter examines the literature around teenagers' sexual health. The chapter is split into five sections to provide greater clarity around the research problem. The first section provides an overview of teenage sexual health and discusses the different definitions of risky sexual behaviors. The second section provides an overview of the main theoretical models that are discussed in the literature, while the third section examines the predictors of risky sexual behaviors. The fourth section discusses sexual health issues in the digital world, and the final section focuses specifically on the issue of females from low socioeconomic status areas, as discussed briefly in the previous chapter, is the target group for our own research. Taken together, these sections provide an overview of the current research on sexual health and teenagers.

## KEYWORDS

Digital health interventions; Sexual health; Sexual health education; Sexual health interventions; Teenagers.

## SEXUAL HEALTH AND DEFINING RISKY SEXUAL BEHAVIORS

The term, sexual health, is frequently used in the applied context of sexual education and health promotion; according to the current working definition from the World Health Organization, sexual health is

*...a state of physical, emotional, mental and social well-being in relation sexuality; it is not merely the absence of disease, dysfunction or infirmity. Sexual health requires a positive and respectful approach to sexuality and sexual relationships, as well as the possibility of having pleasurable and safe sexual experiences, free of coercion, discrimination and violence. For sexual health to be attained and maintained, the sexual rights of all persons must be respected, protected and fulfilled.*

WHO (2006), P. 6

First sexual initiation is a normal and expected aspect of adolescent development, which usually takes place during adolescence or young adulthood (Heywood, Patrick, Smith, & Pitts, 2015) and marks the beginning of an individual's sexual and reproductive life. The majority of these first sexual connections are with the opposite sex (Diamond, 2004; Diamond & Lucas, 2004; Horne & Zimmer-Gembeck, 2005).

Teenagers, Sexual Health Information and the Digital Age. https://doi.org/10.1016/B978-0-12-816969-8.00002-3
Copyright © 2020 Elsevier Inc. All rights reserved.

Healthy teenage sexuality is defined as teenagers accepting their bodies, gender identity, and sexual orientation; communicating effectively with family, peers, and partners, as well as possessing accurate knowledge of sexual health, understanding the risks, responsibilities, and outcomes of sexual actions, possessing skills needed to take action to reduce their risk, knowing how to access and seek sexual health information, and forming and maintaining healthy relationships (Department of Health, 2011). Healthy teenage sexuality is central to well-being and entails active exploration of identity, values, goals, and behavior (Halpern, 2010). Healthy and positive attitudes toward sexual health are significantly associated with better general overall health for teenagers (Hensel, Nance, & Fortenberry, 2016).

However, risky sexual behaviors are also prevalent among teenagers. The number of pregnancies and prevalence of sexually transmitted infections (STIs) in the teenage population are still high despite the development of numerous sexual health intervention programs (Health Protection Agency, 2010).

Teenage sexual risk-taking has been conceptualized in various ways:

- Early age at first intercourse (Heywood et al., 2015)
- Multiple sexual partners (Kuortti & Kosunen, 2009; Valois, Kammermann, & Drane, 1997a)
- Type of partner or length of relationship (Potard, Courtois, & Rusch, 2008)
- Frequency of intercourse (Valois, Kammermann, & Drane, 1997b)
- Consistency of condom use (Morrison et al., 2009)
- Sexual intercourse and alcohol/drug use (Brown & Vanable, 2007)

Consequently, there are various ways that sexual risk-taking has been measured, and while these can be considered an aspect of risk-taking, it has been argued that these do not measure the construct, as sexual risk-taking usually involves a combination of these behaviors (Casey & Beadnell, 2010). For example, inconsistent condom use is less of a risk with one partner if they do not have an STI; however, inconsistent condom use becomes a greater risk with multiple sexual partners. Furthermore, there are contrasting findings in the literature. Stone and Ingham (2003) found condom use but not number of partners to be a significant predictor of STIs. In contrast, Beadnell et al. (2005) found number of partners but not condom use to be a significant predictor of STIs.

Much of this research is correlational and has not established cause and effect. Further research has sought to establish causality using longitudinal designs, and subsequent research has found that early age of sexual intercourse is associated with poorer social environmental factors, such as poor connections with family and peer pressure (Crockett, Bingham, & Chopak, 1996; McBride & Paikoff, 2003; Whitbeck, Yoder, Hoyt, & Conger, 1999). Siebenbruner and Zimmer-Gembeck, (2007) reviewed published longitudinal studies and found that early sexual intercourse, before the age of 16 years, is more likely to lead to other sexual risk behavior, such as higher number of sexual partners and inconsistent contraception use.

Analysis from the first National Sexual Attitudes and Lifestyles (NATSAL) survey found a decline in age at first intercourse and a significant increase in condom use among the youngest age cohort (Wellings, Wadsworth, & Johnson, 1994). Findings from the second NATSAL survey found a significant association between early first intercourse and early pregnancy, but not experience of STIs (Johnson, Mercer, Erens, & Copas, 2001). Finally, early sexual intercourse, before the age of 16 years, is associated with other sexual risk-taking behaviors which can result in unplanned pregnancies and STIs (McClelland, 2012; Magnusson, Masho, & Lapane, 2012).

Therefore, it is difficult to define risky sexual behaviors for teenagers, and there is not a clear definition of risky sexual behavior in the literature. Teenagers engage in many different sexual behaviors, and it is difficult to understand which behaviors are deemed risky (Heywood et al., 2015). In general, behaviors are deemed risky if the negative consequences outweigh the positives (Moore & Gullone, 1996; Gullone, Moore, Moss & Boyd, 2000). Consequently, many explanations of risky behaviors have focused on STIs or unplanned pregnancies. However, these only measure one construct of the behavior and do not account for the entirety of the behavior. Whereas early sexual intercourse before the age of 16 years has been found to lead to other risk-taking behaviors. It has consistently been found as a significant risky sexual behavior for female teenagers (Greenberg, Magder, & Aral, 1992; Vasilenko, Kugler, & Rice, 2016), and across different cultures (Belgrave & Marin, 2000; Day, 1992). Consequently, early sexual intercourse before the age of 16 years may provide a stronger definition of risky sexual behaviors for teenagers because it leads to other negative consequences.

In this book, risky sexual behaviors are defined as early sexual intercourse before the age of 16 years, unless otherwise stated.

# THEORETICAL MODELS OF RISKY SEXUAL BEHAVIOR

This next section provides an overview of three theoretical models that are frequently discussed in the literature in relation to sexual health. The first two, theory of planned behavior (TPB) (Ajzen, 1991) and the health belief model (HBM) (Hochbaum & Rosenstock, 1952), are often used in health psychology to provide a theoretical explanation of sexual health and sexual behaviors. The third model, the theory of problem behavior (PBT) (Jessor, 2001; Jessor & Jessor, 1977a), is a commonly used model in explaining adolescent risk behavior. These three models are examined because each model has previously been linked with adolescents and sexual health issues (Armitage & Conner, 2001; Brown, DiClemente & Reynolds, 1991; Tschannm, Adler, Milstein, Gurvey & Ellen, 2002; Whitaker & Miller, 2000). It is worth noting that other models, such as the self-regulation theory (Kanfer, 1970) and the subjective culture and interpersonal relations theory (Triandis, 1977), have also been used to help understand adolescent risk behaviors. However, there is less evidence that these models can significantly aid understanding of adolescent risky sexual behaviors and so detailed examination of these models is not made in this section.

## The Theory of Planned Behavior

The TPB (Ajzen, 1991), previously the theory of reasoned action (Ajzen & Fishbein, 1980), is one of the most prominent models of behavior in the health psychology literature. The TPB has clearly defined constructs and has consistently accounted for large predictive validity when compared with other models of health behavior (Ajzen, 1991; Conner & Armitage, 1998). The TPB extends beyond the theory of reasoned action to include the concept of perceived behavioral control, as the theory of reasoned action was restricted to predicting volitional behaviors (Ajzen, 2011; Lawton, Conner, & McEachan, 2009). This model proposes that behavior is determined by behavioral intention, which is a measure of a person's motivation to engage in particular behaviors. Intentions are determined by three constructs, *attitudes, subjective norms, and perceived behavioral control* (Ajzen, 1991). *Attitudes* are a person's beliefs about the expected costs or rewards of a particular behavior in a global positive or negative evaluation of behavior. *Subjective norms* are a person's beliefs about the social pressure they feel from their social group. *Perceived behavioral control* is a global summary of specific beliefs about the ease or difficulty of performing a behavior. Consequently, people intend to engage in behaviors that they evaluate positively (*attitude*), observe within their social group (*subjective norm*), and believe it is achievable (*perceived behavioral control*). A schematic representation of the model is shown in Fig. 2.1.

The TPB has successfully explained a broad array of health behaviors (Armitage & Conner, 2001; Godin & Kok, 1996; Hatherall, Ingham, Stone, & McEachran, 2007; Rivis & Sheeran, 2003), including the use of condoms in sexual health (Albarracín, Johnson, Fishbein, & Muellerleile, 2001). A meta-analysis found that people are more likely to use condoms if they have previously formed intentions to use condoms, and these intentions derive from *attitudes, subjective norms,* and *perceived behavioral control* (Albarracín et al., 2001; Gerrard, Gibbons, & Bushman, 1996). Interventions aimed at sexual behavior underpinned by TPB have had successful results. Jemmott and Jemmott, (2000) examined 36 controlled interventions and those that had theoretically prescribed cognitive mediators of behavior change, including knowledge, beliefs, intention, and self-efficacy, were most effective. Interventions that

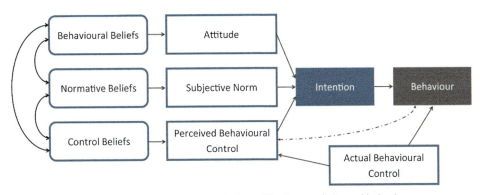

FIG. 2.1 A schematic representation of the theory of planned behavior.

had greater effects on cognitive mediators were found to have greater effects on behavior, including condom use and sexual abstinence. A more recent meta-analysis (Tyson, Covey, & Rosenthal, 2014) that examined a broad view of interventions aimed at all types of STIs and pregnancies in heterosexual individuals found that the TPB provides a valuable framework for designing interventions to change heterosexual sexual risk behavior.

However, there has been controversy in literature, as teenagers usually engage in unplanned, spontaneous sex. Therefore it is questionable as to whether TPB can explain teenage sexual behavior (Moore, 1995). However, the empirical evidence suggests that these cognitions also predict teenagers' sexual behavior (Jemmott, & Hacker, 1991; Gillmore et al., 2002; Morrison, Baker, & Gillmore, 1998). Gillmore et al. (2002) found support for the theory as a model of the cognitive processes underlying teenagers' decisions to have sex. They found that sexual intercourse was associated with intentions to have sex and intentions were associated with general attitudes and social norms. There were no significant differences between males and females. This was in line with Morrison et al., (1998) who found that condom use among teenagers related more to attitudes than norms, and the most predictive outcome beliefs were beliefs about potential negative effects on intimacy rather than the efficacy of condoms to prevent pregnancy or STIs. Research has also found that both attitudes and perceived norms predict teenage sexual initiation (Bongardt & Reitz, 2015; Zimmer-Gembeck & Helfand, 2008).

Another criticism of the TPB is that it has failed to recognize the emotional aspect of safe sex (Norton, Bogart, & Cecil, 2005). Extending the TPB to include affective attitudes has enhanced the effectiveness of safe sex interventions (Ferrer, Klein, & Persoskie, 2016). Furthermore, safe sex interventions underpinned by TPB concentrate on one behavior, yet safe sex for adolescents should involve a series of linked behaviors, for example, condom use and fewer sexual partners; TPB interventions that have focused on more than one behavior have been more effective (Moore, Dahl, & Gorn, 2006). Taken as a whole, and despite the criticisms discussed here, these studies suggest that the TPB can aid understanding of teenage sexual behavior.

### Health belief model

The Health Belief Model (HBM) is another extensively researched model of health behavior (Hochbaum & Rosenstock, 1952). The HBM attempts to predict health-related behavior in terms of certain belief patterns. A person's motivation to undertake a health behavior can be divided into three categories: *individual perceptions, modifying factors,* and *likelihood of action. Individual perceptions* are factors that affect the perception of illness and with the importance of health to the individual, perceived susceptibility, and perceived severity. *Modifying factors* include demographic variables, perceived threat, and cues to action. *The likelihood of action* is the perceived benefits minus the perceived barriers of taking the recommended health action. The combination of these factors causes a response that often manifests into the likelihood of that behavior occurring (Janz & Becker, 1984; Rosenstock & Strecher, 1988).

The HBM proposes that the perception of a personal health behavior threat is influenced by at least three factors, general health values, which include interest and concern about health; specific health beliefs about vulnerability to a particular health threat; and beliefs about the consequences of the health problem (Hochbaum & Rosenstock, 1952). If a person perceives a threat to their health, is consecutively cued to action, and their perceived benefits outweigh the perceived barriers, then they are likely to undertake the recommended preventive health action. A schematic representation of the model is shown in Fig. 2.2.

The HBM has been used to aid understanding in sexual risk-taking behavior among various age (Brown, DiClemente, & Reynolds, 1991) and cultural groups (Lin, Simoni, & Zemon, 2005). Numerous studies have examined the capacity of the HBM to predict whether sexually active adolescents and young adults will use protection against STIs during sexual or oral intercourse and found support for HBM in understanding safe sex behaviors (Brown et al., 1991; Laraque, Mclean, & Brown-Peterside, 1997; Lin et al., 2005). HBM has been found to account for 43% of the variance in safe sex intentions in young adolescents (Petosa & Jackson,1991). Furthermore, Downing-Matibag and Geisinger (2012) demonstrated that the HBM can serve as a useful framework for understanding sexual risk-taking during casual hookups, as adolescents' assessments of their own and peers' susceptibility to STIs are often misinformed and situational characteristics, such as spontaneity, undermine adolescents' sexual self-efficacy.

However, there are issues with using the HBM and meta-analyses have found mixed results of its effectiveness (Carpenter, 2010; Taylor, 2006). In a UK review of research utilizing HBM there was no evidence that HBM-based interventions have contributed positively to overall improved health outcomes in the United Kingdom (Taylor, 2006). Furthermore, a meta-analysis

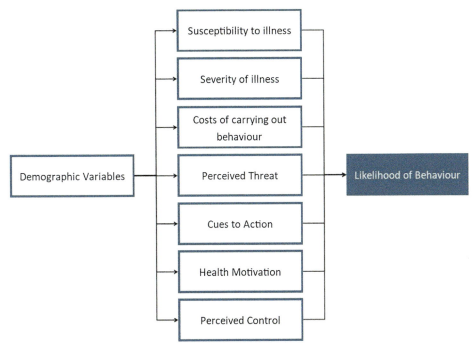

FIG. 2.2 A schematic representation of the Health Belief Model.

of 18 studies found perceived barriers and perceived benefits to be the strongest predictors of behavior, but perceived severity was weak (Carpenter, 2010). Carpenter (2010) suggested that future research should examine possible mediation and moderation between the core components of the HBM, than to explore direct effects. However, another meta-analysis of 18 studies investigated interventions based on the HBM to improve health adherence, with 83% of these studies reporting improved adherence and 39% of studies showing moderate to large effect sizes. Yet only six of the studies included explored the model in its entirety (Jones, Smith, & Llewellyn, 2014). Health adherence to teenagers attending routine STI screenings and taking oral contraception pills has been reported as an issue, and as discussed above, the HBM can assist in understanding adolescents' safe sex intentions (Goyal, Witt, Gerber, Hayes, & Zaoutis, 2013). Therefore, despite the criticisms discussed here, there is evidence that the HBM can assist in understanding sexual risk-taking behavior in teenagers.

## Problem behavior theory

Problem behavior theory (PBT) is a social-psychological framework that helps to explain the development and nature of problem behaviors, for example, risky sex or alcohol use (Jessor & Jessor, 1977a; Jessor, 2001). Jessor (1987) described problem behavior as any behavior that deviates from both social and legal norms. The model comprises three systems of psychosocial influences: personality system (all social cognitions, personal values, expectations, beliefs, and values), perceived environmental system (family and peer expectations), and the behavior system (problem and conventional behavioral structures that work in opposition to each other). Demographic and socialization variables affect the personality and perceived environmental systems and have an indirect impact on behavior. The personality and perceived environment systems are viewed as proximal or more direct determinants of behavior than are demographic and socialization variables.

The three systems of the PBT each utilize different variables that either influence the problem (such as risky sex) to occur or decrease the likelihood of the behavior taking place. For each individual, when predicting a problem behavior, the conventional-unconventional behaviors of the individual are taken into consideration (Donovan, Jessor, & Costa, 1991). Donovan et al. (1991) defined conventional behaviors as actions that are socially approved behaviors; while unconventional behaviors are defined as any behavior that deviates from social norms. By analyzing conventional-unconventional behaviors in each of the three psychosocial systems in an individual, it allows a prediction on future behaviors to be made. A schematic representation of the original model is shown in Fig. 2.3.

Early research has supported this theory as multiple factors as a cluster can influence risky sexual behaviors. Protective factors such as self-esteem and cognition may play important roles in teenage decision-making and are embedded within social and community contexts (Norman & Turner, 1993). Teenagers with low self-

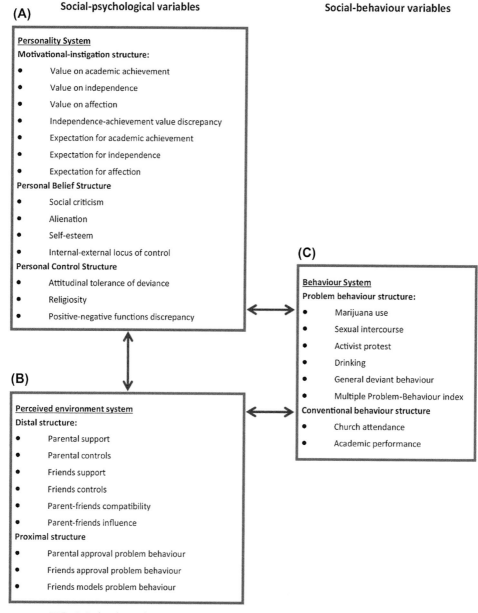

FIG. 2.3 A schematic representation of the original problem behavior theory model.

esteem may become sexually active at an early age to help fill a void left by feelings of inadequacy and fear of failure (Bloom, 1990). This cluster of behaviors has also carried into recent research; teenagers who engage in earlier alcohol use significantly predicted risky sex with multiple partners with inconsistent condom use (Mason, Hitch, & Kosterman, 2010). Furthermore, social norms are all related to sexual risk behavior and cluster together; risky sexual behaviors in older adolescents can be predicted by higher sensation seeking (personality), lack of communication with parents (perceived environment), and engagement in alcohol use (behavioral factors) (Whitaker & Miller, 2015).

However, most studies investigating PBT have only accounted for one of the three systems, or looked at the three systems individually (Davis, 2002). This means it is difficult to predict future behavior, if all three systems are not investigated together. PBT also does not work for all cultures (Deutsch, Slutske, Heath, Madden, & Martin, 2014). The basis of this theory is that it works for all groups who engage in deviant behavior; however, research and development of this theory was originally conducted in a community composed of white individuals with middle-class backgrounds (Jessor, 2001). Therefore, it is difficult to generalize the theory to other subcultures. Despite this, the PBT has been shown to account for variation in a number of different problem behaviors, and can help explain risky sexual behaviors for teenagers.

## PREDICTORS OF RISKY SEXUAL BEHAVIORS

There is a rich literature around the predictors of risky sexual behaviors in teenagers. The key predictors are discussed in this section and are split into five subsections to provide greater clarity with respect to how these cluster together into larger categories. The subsections are parental and peer influences, self-influences, personality, situational factors, and external factors. For a full overview of key studies exploring the factors see Table 2.1.

**TABLE 2.1**
**Overview of Predictors, Participants, and Behaviors Found in Previous Research.**

| Group | Factor | Literature | Participants | Behavior |
|---|---|---|---|---|
| Peers | Peer pressure | (Gillmore et al., 2002) | Males and females 14–16 years | Earlier sexual initiation |
| | Social norms | (Skinner, Smith, Fenwick, Fyfe, & Hendriks, 2008) | Females 14–19 years | Intention to have sex |
| | Age of partner | (Vanoss Marín et al., 2000) | Males and females 16–18 years | Early sexual initiation |
| | Peers approval of sex | (Baumer & South, 2001; Robinson, 1998). | Male and females 10–18 years | Early sexual initiation Higher number of sexual partners |
| | Coercion from sexual partners | (Skinner et al., 2008) | Females 14–19 years | Intention to have sex |
| | Conforming to peer norms | (Gillmore et al., 2002) | Males and females 14–16 years | Intention to have sex |
| | Social support | (Mazzaferro et al., 2006) | Females 13–16 years | Likelihood of STIs |
| | Peer communication | (Busse et al., 2010) | Males and females 14–16 years | Intention to have sex |
| Parents | Negative parenting | (Guilamo-Ramos, Bouris, Lee, McCarthy, Michael, Pitt-Barnes, & Dittus, 2012) | 11–18 years Males and females | Age at first intercourse |
| | Role models | (Guilamo-Ramos et al., 2012) | 11–18 years Males and females | Age at first intercourse |
| | Education and social class of parent | (Manning, Longmore, & Giordano, 1995) | 13–17 years Males and females | Age at first intercourse and higher number of partners |
| | Parental attitudes toward sex | (Dittus & Jaccard, 2000) | 12–16 years Males and females | Early sexual intercourse and contraception use |
| | Family support | (Hyde et al., 2013) | 12–16 years Males and females | Earlier sexual intercourse |

*Continued*

## TABLE 2.1
## Overview of Predictors, Participants, and Behaviors Found in Previous Research.—cont'd

| Group | Factor | Literature | Participants | Behavior |
|---|---|---|---|---|
| | Parental influences and monitoring | (Wight & Fullerton, 2013) | Review of parental sexual health interventions | Knowledge and behavior improved after parental interventions |
| | Younger parents | (Manning et al., 1995) | 13–17 years Males and females | Age at first intercourse and higher number of partners |
| | Lone parents | (Guilamo-Ramos, Bouris, Lee, McCarthy, Michael, Pitt-Barnes, & Dittus, 2012) | 11–18 years Males and females | Age at first intercourse |
| Self | Self-esteem | (McGee and Williams 2000) | 11–16 years males and females | Earlier sexual behavior and condom use |
| | Self-efficacy | (Dilorio, 2001) | Review—teenagers | Earlier sexual behavior |
| | No direction | (Buhi & Goodson, 2007) | Systematic review—adolescents | Earlier sexual behavior |
| | Low aspirations | (Pearson, Child, & Carmon, 2011) | Review—adolescents | Earlier sexual behavior |
| | Connectedness | (Markham et al., 2010) | Review—teenagers | Protective against sexual risk-taking |
| | Self-standards | (Dilorio et al., 2000) | Review—teenagers | Earlier sexual behavior |
| | Beliefs and attitudes toward sex | (Sieverding, Adler, Witt, & Ellen, 2005) | Male and female teenagers (mean age 15 years) | Less sexual initiation |
| | Depression | (Brawner et al., 2012) | Females aged 13–19 years | Higher frequency of having sex, higher number of partners, more alcohol and drug use |
| | Belief in the future | (Gavin et al., (2010) | Systematic review—teenagers | Less teen pregnancy and STIs |
| | Self-determination | (Gavin et al., 2010) | Systematic review—teenagers | Less teen pregnancy and STIs |
| | Body image | (Schooler, 2012) | Females 14–17 years | Condom use |
| | Low school aspirations and performance | (Wheeler, 2010a) | Adolescents | Sexual initiation |
| Personality | Big-five | (Bogg & Roberts, 2004; Hoyle et al., 2000) | Teenagers males and females | Higher number of sexual partners and more unprotected sex |
| | Sensation seeking | (Hoyle, Fejfar & Miller, 2000). | Teenagers males and females | Earlier sexual initiation |
| | Impulsivity | (Hoyle, Fejfar & Miller, 2000). | Teenagers males and females | Higher number of sexual partners and more unprotected sex |
| | Self-regulation | (Rafaelli & Crockett, 2003) | 14–16 years males and females | Greater number of sexual partners |
| | Delayed gratification | (Zayas, Mischel & Pandey, 2014) | 13–18 years males and females | Higher account of unprotected sex |
| Situational factors | Spontaneous sex | (Buhi & Goodson, 2007a) | Systematic review—adolescents | Condom use |
| | Alcohol | (Ritchwood et al., 2015) | Systematic review—teenagers | Unprotected sex, number of sexual partners, drug use. |

# CHAPTER 2 Current Research on Sexual Health and Teenagers

**TABLE 2.1**
**Overview of Predictors, Participants, and Behaviors Found in Previous Research.—cont'd**

| Group | Factor | Literature | Participants | Behavior |
|---|---|---|---|---|
| | Drug use | (Brawner et al. 2012) | Females aged 13–19 years | Higher frequency of having sex, higher number of partners, more alcohol use. STIs |
| | Not considering the long-term implications | (Rothspan & Read, 1996) | Males and females—teenagers | |
| | More egocentric thinking | (Catania et al., 1989) | Female adolescents | STIs |
| | Boredom | (Buhi & Goodson, 2007) | Systematic review—adolescents | Earlier sexual behaviors |
| | Time spent alone at home | (Resnicow et al., 2001) | Systematic review—adolescents | Earlier sexual behaviors |
| | Lack of awareness | (Buhi & Goodson, 2007) | Systematic review—adolescents | Earlier sexual behaviors and condom use |
| | Sexual abuse | (Valle et al., 2009) | Males and females— 15–16 years | Earlier sexual behavior |
| | Early physical intimacy experiences | (Pearson et al., 2011) | Review—adolescents | Earlier sexual behavior |
| | Low awareness of contraception | (Lader, 2009) | Review—adolescents | STIs, pregnancy, and earlier sexual behavior. |
| External factors | Media | (Brown et al., 2006) | Males and females 12–14 years | Earlier sexual behavior |
| | Culture | (Karakiewicz, Bhojani, Neugut, Shariat, Jeldres, Graefen, & Kattan, 2008) | Review—adolescents | STIs |
| | Age of puberty | (De Genna, Larkby, & Cornelius, 2011) | Pregnant teenagers— 12–18 years | Earlier sexual behavior, unplanned pregnancy |

## Parental and Peer Influences

One of the main factors known to predict sexual risk-taking in teenagers is parental influences. Communication with parents is important. Teenagers who talk to their parents have better knowledge and attitudes toward sex and are likely to delay first sexual initiation (Guzmán & Schlehofer-Sutton, 2003; Wight & Fullerton, 2013). However, there are significant gender differences. Males who talk to their parents about sex, report inconsistent condom use, whereas females who are comfortable talking to their parents report consistent condom use (Hyde et al., 2013). Also, teenagers who live with both parents have better contraception use than teenagers who live with one or a stepparent (Manning, Longmore, & Giordano, 2000). Parental support is also important. Perceived maternal or paternal disapproval for engaging in sexual intercourse is associated with better sexual behavior outcomes (Aronowitz & Rennells, 2005; Jaccard, Dodge, & Dittus, 2002; Sr & Nagy, 2000) and high family and parental

support is associated with less risky behaviors (Bobakova, Geckova, Klein, van Dijk, & Reijneveld, 2013; Coley, Votruba-Drzal, & Schindler, 2009). Females' parental warmth and emotional connection is linked with fewer sexual partners and greater condom use (Abrego, 2011; Noll, Haralson, & Butler, 2011; Zimmer-Gembeck, 2011). Therefore, parents can develop capacity for positive, healthy attitudes toward sexual health with a comfortable and supportive environment. This is further enhanced by promoting skills and values that build autonomy and encourage sex only within a relationship (Parkes, Henderson, Wight, & Nixon, 2011).

In contrast, some research has also found no link between parental attitudes, support, and teenagers' sexual health. Resnicow et al. (2001) found no relationship between control strictness and frequency of sex and sexual partners. Also, research has found increased family and parental support has no effect on risky sexual behaviors (Benda & Corwyn, 1996; Lammers, Ireland,

Resnick, & Blum, 2000; Sionéan et al., 2002). Therefore, evidence relating to associations between parent-teen relationships is somewhat mixed. A reason for these mixed findings might be because of inconsistencies with respect to the extent to which parents talk to their children about sexual health. Yun et al. (2012) found that even though parents believe it is important to speak to children about sexual health, only 8.3% discussed it very often and 37.2% discussed it sometimes. In addition, qualitative research has found that parents delay speaking to teenagers about sex as they believe that this is covered by sex education at school, furthermore parents worry that speaking about sex may encourage sexual activity (Hyde et al., 2013). Also, while some parents believed they had covered all areas of sexual health, talks only focused on the consequences of risky sex and parents had limited conversations about safe sex (Hyde et al., 2013). Therefore, there are inconsistencies, and it is difficult to assess how much parents talk to their children about sex and whether they are covering all areas of sexual health. Quantitative data may reveal that parents report covering sexual health talks, yet qualitative research has identified that some parents are only covering basic issues.

Lack of communication with parents may cause adolescents to turn to other sources for advice and guidance such as peers. Parental influences are known to interact with peer influences so that teenagers whose mothers are more open about sexual activity can decrease peer influence (Ajilore, 2015). Also, social norms and peer pressure are more likely when parents have not previously discussed sex or condoms with their child (Whitaker & Miller, 2000). There are a few reasons why peers may influence risky sexual behaviors. Teenagers may engage in risk-taking because they believe the behavior will enhance their popularity if it matches the social norms of their peer group, especially if the behavior is reinforced by their peers, or if the behavior contributes to a favorable self-identity (Brechwald & Prinstein, 2011). Peers also influence sexual activity through dissemination of information or misinformation about sexual health and the formation of intention to engage in sexual activity (Blume & Durlauf, 2005; Cawley & Ruhm, 2011).

Perceived peer attitudes toward sex are consistently identified in the literature as being important to teenagers in forming their own attitudes. Teenagers who believe their friends have pro-childbearing attitudes are more likely to have earlier sexual initiation and a higher number of sexual partners (Baumer & South, 2001; Robinson, 1998). Also, permissiveness of peers is related to higher frequency of unprotected sex (Potard

et al., 2008). By contrast teenagers who believe their peers have less favorable attitudes toward sex are more likely to be sexually abstinent (Sr & Nagy, 2000) or delay sexual initiation (Santelli, Kaiser, et al., 2004). Furthermore social norms and peer pressure are important, as believing peers have had sex is associated with intention to have sex (Gillmore et al., 2002; Kinsman, Romer, & Furstenberg, 1998) and early sexual initiation (Skinner, Smith, Fenwick, Fyfe, & Hendriks, 2008; Vanoss Marín et al., 2000). Peer communication is therefore highly important, as how teenagers discuss sexual health with their peers influences their future sexual health decisions (Busse, Fishbein, Bleakley, & Hennessy, 2010). Also, teenagers are likely to date people in their peer groups and be more pressured into alcohol and substance use leading to riskier situations and behavior (Allen, Porter, & McFarland, 2006). A link has been observed between alcohol use and sexual initiation, especially with an older partner. Teenagers with older partners are more likely to have early initiation and more unwanted sexual advances (Marín et al., 2000). Therefore, peer attitudes, communication, social norms, and peer pressure have big influences on sexual decisions.

## The Self

There are also self-factors that have been found to be important in predicting risky sexual behaviors. Some self-factors have been consistently and significantly linked with risk-taking behaviors, for example, self-efficacy (Resnicow et al., 2001), having no direction in life (Buhi & Goodson, 2007), connectedness (Markham et al., 2010), self-standards (Dilorio, Dudley, Soet, Watkins, & Maibach, 2000), belief in the future (Gavin, Catalano, David-Ferdon, Gloppen, & Markham, 2010), and self-determination (Gavin et al., 2010). However, some self factors have proved more contentious, for example self-esteem.

Self-esteem is an assessment of one's self-worth that is a component of the self-schema (Rosenberg, Schooler, & Schoenbach, 1995). Self-esteem can be measured in two ways, global self-esteem is the overall assessment of self-worth (Rosenberg et al., 1995) and domain-specific is assessment of self-worth in a certain context (McGee & Williams, 2000). Rosenberg et al. (1995) proposed that individuals who display higher self-esteem value the self more and demonstrate more confidence than a person with low self-esteem. Female teenagers are less likely to report having high self-esteem compared with male teenagers (Birndorf, Ryan, Auinger, & Aten, 2005). However, a teenager's self-esteem is more fragile to social comparison during the developmental stage (Harter & Whitesell, 2003) and decreases around the age of 12 years (Simmons & Rosenberg, 1975). Self-esteem gradually increases in later adolescence around the age of 17 years and becomes more positive as freedom, personal authority, and role-taking abilities increase (Harter & Whitesell, 2003). Therefore, in younger adolescents, self-esteem has been associated with higher risk engagement because it increases or maintains self-esteem or reduces the threat of having low self-esteem (Crocker & Park, 2004).

As self-esteem is linked with risk engagement it has been investigated with risky sexual behaviors. There have been significant links found between self-esteem and risky sexual behaviors (Cole, 1997). In longitudinal research, it has been found that self-esteem predicts risky behavior (Donnellan & Trzesniewski, 2005). McGee and Williams, (2000) measured self-esteem at ages 9 and 13 years and then followed up on risk behaviors at age 15 years and found that self-esteem was linked with multiple risk-taking behaviors, including sexual risk-taking. However, a systematic review by Goodson, Buhi, and Dunsmore (2006) found no association between self-esteem and sexual behaviors, attitudes, or intentions. This may be explained by the context in which that self-esteem develops. Boden and Horwood (2006) found that while there were significant links between lower self-esteem and unprotected sex, greater number of sexual partners and greater risk of an unplanned pregnancy between the ages of 15 and 25 years, this link was nonsignificant when taking socioeconomic status (SES) background, family, and individual characteristics into account. Therefore, self-esteem may be dependent upon how it develops and interacts with other predictors.

Research that has investigated self-esteem in conjunction with these factors has found significant results, yet with small effect sizes. Laflin, Wang, and Barry (2008) followed teenagers from virgin to nonvirgin status and found that academic achievement and lower self-esteem significantly predicted early sexual initiation in both males and females. However, while religiosity, self-efficacy, and self-esteem were significant predictors for males, only peer pressure, age, family, and self-esteem were significant predictors for females. Therefore, there may be important differences in the interplay of self-esteem and other factors for males and females.

Also, in older female adolescents it has been found that self-esteem may reduce the likelihood of unprotected sex, whereas multivariate analysis indicated that being employed or in school may play a protective role with respect to number of sex partners (Tevendale, Lightfoot, & Slocum, 2008). Furthermore, adolescent girls with higher alcohol use, lower religiosity, and higher self-esteem may reflect a nonconventional profile overall, of which sexual transitions are just a part (Ronis & Sullivan, 2011). Taken together, this suggests that self-esteem is difficult to measure and needs to be considered alongside multiple factors.

Parents have an important role in self-esteem development, and by fostering high-quality relationships parents can enhance their child's self-esteem and consequently sexual relationships (Boislard, Van de Bongardt, & Blais, 2016). Therefore, there has been a lot of research on self-esteem and risky sexual behaviors, with contrasting results. It is difficult to generalize self-esteem findings as there have been significant differences between younger and older adolescents as well as between males and females. It is also important to consider how self-esteem develops and interplays with other factors. Because of this, it is difficult to draw a firm conclusion with respect to how self-esteem influences the sexual behaviors of young teenagers.

Self-efficacy, however, has consistently been found to be a significant predictor of risky sexual behaviors. High levels of self-efficacy have been associated with resisting peer pressure, safer sex, delaying initiation, and avoiding risky sexual behaviors (Ludwig & Pittman, 1999; Resnicow et al., 2001; Sionéan et al., 2002). Furthermore, it has been found that self-efficacy can predict intended and actual condom use (Baele, Dusseldorp, & Maes, 2001). This may be because of the perceived benefits of protected sex rather than the threat of unprotected sex (Parsons, Halkitis, Bimbi, & Borkowski, 2000). It has been suggested that self-efficacy can explain 18%–45% of the variance in condom use; however, there are significant gender differences, and self-efficacy may be more important in condom use for males than females (Farmer & Meston, 2006). Therefore, self-efficacy has continually been highlighted as a highly important factor in predicating risky sexual behaviors, but may be more important for males than females in condom usage.

Three self-factors that are often linked together in predicting risky sexual behaviors are school performance, body image, and depression (Perry, Braun, & Cantu, 2014). School performance has consistently been linked with risky sexual behaviors, with lower school performance linked with more vaginal sex and earlier sexual initiation (Perry et al., 2014; Wheeler, 2010a). Also a number of studies have found significant relationships between body dissatisfaction and lowered condom use self-efficacy with young female teenagers

(Gillen, Lefkowitz, & Shearer, 2006; Salazar & Crosby, 2005; Watson, Matheny, & Gagné, 2013). Furthermore, depressed adolescents are more likely to be sexually active than nondepressed adolescents (Brawner, 2012), and depression is longitudinally linked with increased risky sexual behavior, including greater number of partners (Mazzaferro, Murray, Ness, & Bass, 2006; Spencer, Zimet, Aalsma, & Orr, 2002), condom nonuse (Mazzaferro et al., 2006; Noar, Clark, Cole, & Liza Lustria, 2009), and age at first sexual intercourse (Skinner, Robinson, Smith, Chenoa, & Robbins, 2015).

## Personality

The link between individual personality traits and sexual risk-taking is well documented and two large systematic reviews have indicated that there is a consistent link between the big five personality traits and risky sexual behaviors in teenagers (Bogg & Roberts, 2004; Hoyle, Fejfar, & Miller, 2000). Teenagers with higher levels of extraversion engage in more sexual behaviors and report a higher number of partners and a higher number of accounts of unprotected sex (Bogg & Roberts, 2004; Eysenck, 1976; Hoyle et al., 2000; Miller, Lynam, Zimmerman, & Logan, 2004; Raynor & Levine, 2009; Schmitt, 2004) This may be because extraverts may seek more stimulation as they may have less cortical arousal (Eysenck, 1976). Conscientiousness has been negatively associated with sexual risk-taking for unprotected sex and neuroticism is weakly associated with number of partners and unprotected sex (Hoyle, Fejfar & Miller, 2000). In addition, Miller and Lynam (2003) found low agreeableness, low openness to experience, and high extraversion are significantly related to multiple high risk sexual behaviors. Linking with peers it has been found that adolescents tend to make friendships based on dissimilarity in agreeableness, and similarity in gender and sexual intention (Baams, Overbeek, & Bongardt, 2015). This may help explain why peer pressure is such a big influence (Santelli, Kaiser, et al., 2004).

Furthermore, sensation seeking, characterized by a greater need for exciting experiences, thrill seeking and novelty (Zuckerman, Buchsbaum, & Murphy, 1980), and impulsivity, characterized by decision-making with little or no thought or planning (Donohew et al., 2000) are well documented as predicting earlier initiation, a greater number of partners, and unprotected sex (Hoyle, Fejfar, & Miller, 2000). Individual differences in self-regulation have recently been suggested to explain engagement in risky activities. Zayas, Mischel and Pandey (2014) identified that health, social, and academic outcomes can be predicted by delayed gratification—the ability to wait for larger delayed rewards, while resisting smaller immediate ones. Magar, Phillips, and Hosie (2008) found that poor cognitive self-regulation and emotional regulation is linked with greater participation in risky behaviors. Similarly, Raffaelli and Crockett (2003) found that self-regulation was associated with a greater number of partners after becoming sexually active, but had no effect on sexual initiation. Quinn and Fromme (2010) found that an interaction between self-regulation sensation seeking and heavy drinking; in low sensation seeking, self-regulation buffered against the effects of heavy drinking. This may be because internalizing such social values can enhance mechanisms of self-control and reduce problem behaviors such as unprotected sex to peer pressure (Reyna & Wilhelms, 2016). Therefore, there has been support for individual personality traits predicting sexual risk-taking and these link with peer groups, as teenagers tend to make friends based on similar personality traits.

## Situational Factors

Situational factors also have an effect on risky sexual behaviors and as previously mentioned, alcohol is an important predictor linked with other factors such as peer pressure (Marín et al., 2000) and self-esteem (Ronis & Sullivan, 2011). Multiple systematic reviews have found that alcohol and marijuana use is significantly related to a higher number of partners and higher incidents of unprotected sex (Brawner, 2012; Ritchwood, Ford, DeCoster, & Sutton, 2015; Tapert, Aarons, Sedlar, & Brown, 2001). Furthermore, early age at first alcohol use is significantly linked with multiple partners, unprotected sex, and unplanned pregnancies (Stueve & O'donnell, 2005). Qualitative research suggests that under the influence of alcohol, teenagers are not too shy to have sex but remain embarrassed to talk about condom use (Hammarlund & Lundgren, 2008). In addition, teenagers often use alcohol as an excuse for socially unacceptable behavior, especially if it goes against social and peer norms (Hopkins, Lyons, & Coleman, 2004).

Another important situational factor found in the literature is physical and sexual abuse. A 30-year longitudinal study investigating physically and sexually abused children (aged 1−11 years) matched with nonmaltreated children and followed into adulthood found that maltreated children were more likely to report early sexual initiation, engage in prostitution, and have higher incidence of STIs in middle adulthood (Wilson & Widom, 2008). Systematic reviews have also found that childhood sexual abuse is a significant risk factor for unplanned pregnancies, depression, and alcohol use in older adolescence (Hipwell, Keenan, Loeber, & Battista, 2010). In comparison to other factors, systematic reviews have found that the long-term impact of childhood sexual abuse on sexual health problems are similar for both males and females (Dube, Anda, Whitfield, & Brown, 2005). Therefore, it is a consistent finding that childhood sexual abuse has a significant impact on risky sexual behaviors in teenagers and these are similar for both males and females.

## External Factors

One important external factor identified in the literature is the mass media. The mass media can have an effect on teenagers' sexual attitudes. For example, teenagers who saw risky sex displayed in the media had significantly higher permissive attitudes than teenagers who had never been exposed to sex in the media (Braun-Courville & Rojas, 2009). There are also significant cultural and gender differences with respect to the extent that media exposure can influence sexual attitudes and behavior. For example, Brown, L'Engle, Pardun, and Guo (2006) investigated white and black adolescents aged between 12 and 14 years old and found that exposure to sexual content in music, films, television, and magazines accelerated white adolescents' sexual activity, whereas black adolescents were more influenced by parents than the media. Longitudinal studies have shown that exposure to risky sex in the mass media predicted less progressive gender role attitudes, more permissive sexual norms, and having oral sex and sexual intercourse two years later for males. For females, early exposure to risky sex in the mass media predicted subsequently less progressive gender role attitudes and having oral sex and sexual intercourse (Brown & L'Engle, 2009). Therefore, the mass media has important implications for the formation of teenagers' sexual attitudes and behaviors; however, it is difficult to generalize studies due to important gender and cultural differences.

Age of puberty has also been considered in the literature. It has been established that early puberty is associated with early sexual intercourse and teenage pregnancy (Deardorff, Gonzales, & Christopher, 2005; Downing & Bellis, 2009). In a longitudinal study on pregnant female teenagers (aged 12−18 years old) it was found that early puberty was associated with early sex and teenage pregnancy, especially if their mother had also gone through early puberty (De Genna, Larkby, & Cornelius, 2011). A reason that early puberty may increase early sexual initiation is that during puberty there are hormonal changes that encourage sensation-seeking and stimulate sexual interest (Gardner & Steinberg, 2005; Halpern, 2006). This may particularly be an issue for vulnerable teenagers as the prefrontal cortex develops at a much slower rate than secondary sex characteristics (Blume & Durlauf, 2005), therefore females that experience puberty earlier may be more influenced by social influences and their emotions and are less likely to be able to inhibit risky behaviors (Steinberg, 2005). This may also be an issue because they may look older than their peers. However, research has found that while early puberty was associated with earlier sex for males, it was not significantly related in females (Bingham & Crockett, 1996). Also, in a large Australian study it was found that girls who had early puberty were equally likely to have sex before age 16 years than girls who had not had early puberty (Marino, Skinner, Doherty, & Rosenthal, 2013). Therefore, age of puberty has found contrasting results in previous research and may not be a risk factor for female teenagers, and may only be important for males. However, research has shown that the strength of associations and mixed results may be based on the method used to classify pubertal timing (Negriff, Fung, & Trickett, 2008). It is difficult therefore to draw a conclusion on how pubertal timing influences sexual behaviors.

Linking with the PBT (Jessor & Jessor, 1977b) discussed above, relationships have been observed between adolescent sexual activity and involvement in other problem behaviors (Crockett, Raffaelli, & Shen, 2006). Delinquency and problem behaviors have been associated with earlier age at first sexual intercourse (Skinner et al., 2015) and with age of puberty, as early maturing adolescents may actively seek out opportunities to engage in risky behaviors including sexual risk-taking (Negriff, Susman, & Trickett, 2011). Longitudinal studies indicate that early sexual activity is a risk for delinquency one year later (Armour & Haynie, 2007); other studies report that delinquency is also associated with higher sexual initiation (Caminis, Henrich, & Ruchkin, 2007). Therefore, it is clear that teenage risky sexual behaviors tend to cluster around other risk-taking behaviors.

As discussed in this section, there are a range of predictors of risky sexual behaviors, with some consistent predictors (for example, alcohol use) and other nonconsistent predictors (for example, self-esteem) found across the literature. Further, there are known differences for males and females. Most of the predictors have been studied across different populations and the mixed findings may be due to different characteristics of the sample. There has also been a range of definitions and different study designs used for risky sexual behaviors. For an overview of the key predictors see Table 2.1.

## DIGITAL WORLD ISSUES

This section summarizes sexual health in the digital world, specifically covering pornography use and sexting. There is an extensive body of research on pornography use, and it is beyond the scope of this chapter to include a comprehensive review. Instead, a number of key papers and reviews are discussed. This section also covers recent research on sexting behaviors, as well as research on perceptions and attitudes toward sexting behaviors, from both teenagers, parents, and professionals. Recommendations and best practice guidelines are also discussed.

### Pornography

Pornography has been defined as professionally produced or user-generated videos and pictures intended to sexually arouse the watcher (Peter & Valkenburg, 2011). This usually includes people performing sexual activities with clearly exposed genitals. Most pornography is accessed via the Internet, and due to the proliferation of smartphone use and ease of access of the Internet, pornography use among adolescents has increased (Kyriaki et al. 2018). Teens use both smartphones and computers for pornography use. Teenagers aged 13−18 years report using their smartphone predominately for Internet access, but those who use computers more were more likely to intentionally view pornography (Ryan, Beckert, Rhodes & Mitchell, 2017).

There has been extensive research on teenagers and pornography use because of concerns that it may have adverse consequences (Flood, 2009). Peter and Valkenburg (2016) carried out a large review of 20 years of pornography research, between 1995 and 2015 on the prevalence, predictors, and implications of teens pornography use. Comparing both qualitative and quantitative studies, they found that prevalence rates varied greatly, but teenagers who viewed pornography more frequently were male, at a more advanced pubertal stage were sensation seekers with weak or troubled family relationships. Pornography use was also associated with more permissive sexual attitudes and tended to be linked with stronger gender-stereotypical sexual beliefs. There were also links with sexual behavior; higher pornography use was linked with occurrence of sexual intercourse and greater experience of casual sex behavior.

Koletic (2017) carried out a further review that examined longitudinal studies on pornography use

and teenagers. The results showed that viewing pornography does have an effect on teens' sexual behavior, sexual norms and attitudes, gender attitudes, self-esteem, sexual satisfaction, uncertainty, and preoccupancy. Randall and Langlias (2018) further examined qualitative data on virgins and nonvirgins and found that pornography use provided unrealistic sex expectations which had negative effects on teenage development, which was particularly an issue for teenagers who had not yet engaged in any sexual activity.

Teenagers are now growing up in a world where pornography and sexually explicit material is readily available. From large-scale reviews of the research it appears that pornography use is having a significant effect on teenagers' attitudes toward sex and their sexual behaviors. Sexual health education programs will need to ensure they are incorporating information on pornography use so that teenagers can appropriately navigate through a platform that may cause confusion and potentially have adverse ramifications.

### Sexting
#### What is "sexting"?
In recent years a new trend of sexualized text communication has emerged, sexting (a combination of the words sex and texting). The term sexting was first publically used in 2005 as a term to describe the practice of sending nude photos through mobile phones (Roberts, 2005). The term "sexting" can be broadly understood as using mobile phones or other electronic devices to send self-generated sexually explicit messages, images, or videos (Lenhart, 2009; NSPCC, 2018; The National Campaign, 2008; Ostrager, 2010). Due to the advancement and proliferation of smartphone use, it is easier than ever to take and distribute these self-made sexualized photos. However, it is important to note any sexualized photos that are exchanged which are not self-produced (e.g., Internet pornography) are not classed as sexting (Doring, 2014). Sexting, however, can cover a range of behaviors, from "experimental" (explorative and romantic) to more "aggravated" (abusive and exploitative) (Wolak & Finkelhor 2011).

#### Prevalence of "sexting"?
The prevalence of sexting varies greatly depending on how it is defined and the population being assessed. One issue with research on sexting behaviors is teenagers, especially in English-speaking countries, do not use the term "sexting" preferring to use terms such as "nudes" or "pornos" (Albury, 2015; Ringrose et al., 2013). Therefore, in self-report questionnaire studies where the term "sexting" has not been defined,

teenagers may not identify with the term. Also, there is not one clear uniform definition of sexting, which limits generalizability between studies (Englander & McCoy, 2018). The definition of sexting has varied on three constructs:
(1) The degree of nudity included in the pictures (semi-nude versus nude);
(2) The degree of sexuality required for inclusion (some studies only ask about nudity, while others examine pictures, video, and/or text depicting sexual acts);
(3) The modality of communication (text, photos, or videos).

Sending sexually explicit photographs in comparison to sexually suggestive messages tends to affect risk perception and prevalence scores (Barrense-Dias et al. 2017; (Drouin, Vogel & Stills, 2013), yet in some surveys these two elements have been measured as a single behavior.

In an American survey, 20% of teenagers (aged 13–19 years) and 33% of young adults (aged 20–26 years) had engaged in sexting behaviors (Sex and Tech, 2008). Whereas, the teen online and wireless safety survey, found 61% of 16–18 years olds had engaged in sexting behaviors compared with 39% of 13–15 year olds (Cox communications, 2009). In both of these surveys sexting behaviors was measured as one construct, both sexually suggestive texts and sexually explicit images together, rather than separately. More recent meta-analyses on sexting behaviors found that the prevalence of sexting ranged from 1% to 60% due to these discrepancies in defining sexting (Barrense-Dias et al. 2017).

Age may also be a contributing factor in prevalence. Temple et al. (2012) found that older teenagers were more likely to send nude photos than younger teenagers; only 9% of younger teenagers reported sending nude pictures, compared with 27% of older teenagers. Yet, 24% of younger teenagers and 65% of older teenagers reported receiving a nude picture. Crimmins and Seigfried-Spellar (2014) found 61% of undergraduate students (19–23 years) had reported engaging in sexting behaviors. A more recent US survey with 12–18 year olds found 17% both sent and received sexts, and 24% only received sexts (Rice, Craddock et al., 2018).

In the United Kingdom, one survey found that 40% of teenagers knew a peer who had engaged in sexting, but engaging in sexting themselves was not measured (Phippen, 2009). Also, NSPCC reports that there was a 28% increase in calls to Childline in 2012/13 that mentioned sexting than in 2011/12; this is nearly one every day (NSPCC, 2014). Thus, it appears sexting

behaviors are on the rise; however, the inconsistency in terminology and measurements between previous studies makes comparability between studies difficult. However, across all studies it appears sexting is most prevalent among older teenagers and young adults.

In the Sex and Tech survey (2008), 51% of teenage girls and 18% of teenage boys had felt pressure to send nude photos. Lenhart (2009) found that teenage girls often report feeling pressure to send sexualized photos of themselves and it appears that pressure from a partner or a friend is an important driver in the decision to send a sexual image (Cox communications, 2009).

Two large systematic reviews of the sexting prevalence literature have been conducted. Klettke et al. (2014) concluded that sexting is not rare, and age is positively correlated with increased involvement in sexting. Prevalence rates were very inconsistent, the frequency of sexting ranged from 5% of the population to 44% or more, and there were no clear conclusions on the differences between male and female prevalence. Madigan et al. (2018) conducted a more recent meta-analysis of 39 studies on sexting prevalence. The results similarly concluded that older teenagers were more likely to engage in sexting, and that prevalence appears to be increasing over time; and that much more sexting occurs on mobile devices than computers. There was also a growing body of evidence of nonconsensual sexting, yet not enough research had been conducted on this to make any firm conclusions.

### Teenagers' views of sexting

A qualitative study with teenagers and young adults (aged 15–20 years) found that female teenagers felt pressure to send nude photos, whereas males felt more pressure from peers to share or pass on nude photos they had received themselves (Englander, 2012). Therefore, female teenagers feel significant pressure to send nude photos, and male teenagers feel pressure to show their peers photos they have received. This poses a problem as those who felt pressure to send a nude photo reported being twice as likely to regret sending the photo than those who felt no pressure to send the photo (Englander, 2012). Also, those who engaged in sexting because they wanted to were more likely to rate sexting as something that is fun and enjoyable (Englander, 2012). Thus, it is important that teenagers are not being pressured or coerced into sexting, as this could lead to unhappiness and regret with their behaviors.

Geqirtz-Meydan, Mitchell and Rothman (2018) conducted a survey with 1560 10–17 year olds' attitudes toward sexting and found the majority of their participants believed sexting was a crime. However, participants who had engaged in sexting themselves were less likely to consider sexting a crime, and did not believe that sexting would hurt their chances of getting a job, hurt friendships, romantic relationships, or their relationship with their family. Boys and older teens held more favorable attitudes toward sexting than girls and younger teens. Boys were also less likely to say that they would report sexting to authorities and less likely to say that they would talk to their friends in order to prevent them from sexting. Teenagers who reported substance use, had engaged in sexual intercourse, and used pornography were less likely to think sexting would hurt friendships or relationships, or say they would report sexting than teens not involved in these activities.

Previous research has also found that teens who are in a relationship and are sexually active are more likely to engage in sexting behaviors (Delevi & Weisskitch, 2013; Drouin & Landgraf, 2012). According to the Pew Research Center (2009) sharing sexually suggestive messages and sexualized photos can be part of a normal, healthy sexual relationship. Sexting can be used as a way to be sexually romantic in a relationship (Mitchell et al. 2012). Thus, sexting behaviors with a romantic partner can lead to many benefits and have a positive impact on the relationship. There are also less associated risks when sexting with a romantic partner as it is less likely the photos will be publically disseminated, and less risk of negative feelings after sexting (Dir, Coskunpinar, Steiner, Cyders, 2013). However, a limitation with the previous relationship and sexting questionnaires employed is that they have not measured who individuals are sexting with; it is important to explore whether individuals are sexting with romantic or nonromantic partners, as committed relationships are less common than casual and cheating relationships among teenagers (Grello, Welsh & Harper 2006; Regan & Dreyer, 1999). Half of the teenagers in both the studies by Grello et al. and Regan and Dreier had engaged in casual sex, and one-fifth of these had a partner at the current time. As sexting with a nonromantic partner lacks intimacy and commitment, there is a higher chance that the photos will be publically disseminated, which could lead to embarrassment and regret (Simon & Daneback, 2013).

Due to previous research not investigating who individuals were sexting with, we conducted our own case study of older teenagers in 2014, to see if there were any differences between those who send nude photos to romantic and nonromantic partners. We found that pressure and happiness with sexting behaviors were associated with sending nude photos to romantic partners, while pressure, multiple sexual partners, and high levels of extraversion were associated with sending nude photos to nonromantic partners (see Table 2.2).

### Professional's views of sexting

As sexting has captured a great deal of media attention, it has caused concerns for parents, educators, and law enforcement officials. The interpretation of sexting is that it represents a high-risk sexualized media behavior and the young Internet generation are ignoring its harmful consequences (Draper, 2012; Hua, 2012). Much of the previous research has examined the legal consequences of sexting, and whether teenagers should be arrested for child pornography (Sacco, Argudin, Maguire & Tallon, 2010; Wolak, Finkelhor & Mitchell, 2012). In England any sexually explicit images of minors under age 16 years are considered child pornography, even if they created the images themselves (West, 2008). However, there can be negative consequences of sexting at any age. If an explicit photo is publically disseminated, it can lead to cyberbullying,

| TABLE 2.2 Our Own Case Study Examining Older Teenagers Sending Nude Photos to Romantic Versus Nonromantic Partners. | |
|---|---|
| | **Case study** |
| Aims | Identify the factors between senders and nonsenders of nude photos to romantic and nonromantic partners. |
| Method | A total 68 females (63.6%) and 39 males, aged 18 years, completed three online questionnaires, measuring; pressure to engage in sexting, general happiness with sexting behaviors, risky sexual behaviors, and the big five personality traits. |
| Results | A higher percentage of participants were sending nude photos to romantic partners (44.9%) compared with nonromantic partners (15.0%). Senders to both romantic and nonromantic partners felt significantly more pressure to send nude photos compared with nonsenders; however, only senders to nonromantic partners felt significantly less happy with their sexting behaviors. Senders to nonromantic partners were significantly more extraverted than nonsenders. |

embarrassment, and public humiliation for the individual (Ryan, 2010). Significant media attention has been devoted to a number of cases of teenagers and young adults who have committed suicide after sexts had become public, and they were ridiculed and harassed by their peers (Agomuoh, 2012; Celizic, 2009; Inbar, 2009). Furthermore, Mitchell et al. (2012) found 21% of older teenagers and young adults who appeared in sexually explicit images reported feeling extremely upset, or embarrassed as a result, and 25% of those who received images reported feeling very upset.

Beharry et al. (2018) examined prevalence of sexting among pregnant and parenting teens and health professionals' knowledge about their teenager patients' sexting behaviors. Beharry found that 53% of teens reported that they had been asked to send a sext to someone, and 16% reported sending one. Whereas 60% reported having been sent a sext without asking for one. The health professionals who completed the survey could correctly define "sexting" and 72% estimated that less than half of their adolescent patients were involved in sexting behaviors. Therefore, there is a discrepancy between the actual prevalence of sexting and healthcare providers' estimated prevalence. This discrepancy means that healthcare providers are not routinely discussing sexting behaviors with teenagers, or including them in any educational guidelines. This highlights how important it is to find the true prevalence of sexting behaviors with any target teenage population.

### Sexting and risky sexual behavior

There have been links between sexting behaviors and risky sexual behaviors. Research has found individuals who engage in sexting behaviors are twice as likely to report having multiple partners and unprotected sex, compared with adolescents who do not engage in sexting behaviors (Benotsch, Snipes, Martin & Bull, 2013; Henderson, De Zwart, Lindsay & Phillips, 2010). Furthermore, those who engage in sexting are more likely to report recent substance use and 31.8% of participants reported having sex with a new partner for the first time after sexting with that person (Benotsh, 2012). Dir Cyders and Coskunpinar (2013) found sexting is a partial mediator in the relationship between alcohol use and hookups (a casual sexual encounter with no plans to become romantically involved) among adolescents. Therefore, sexting could be used as a way of initiating sex with a partner. In addition, those who engage in sexting are more likely to take other sexual risks. According to Crimmins and Seigfried-Spellar (2014), individuals who have had unprotected sex were 4.5 times

more likely to sext; individuals who viewed pornography were 4 times more likely to sext; and individuals who had engaged in web-based video chatting with strangers were 2.4 times more likely to sext.

However, research findings on risky sexual health and sexting have been mixed. Fergusson and Haugen (2010) found sexting was not associated with any sexual risk-taking behaviors, apart from failure to use contraceptives when not seeking to become pregnant. Furthermore, Gordon-Messer, Bauermeister, Grodzinski and Zimmerman (2013) found no link between sexting behaviors and riskier sexual health for young adults. The mixed research findings on sexting and risky sexual behavior may reflect the definitions used to define sexting and the populations assessed.

### Best practices—guidelines from research

- Sexting has become part of the teen sexual landscape; it is not rare behavior, although it may not lead directly to STIs and pregnancy, there are potential damaging ramifications of sexting, such as loss of privacy, reputation, and possible criminal prosecution. As such, sexting should be included in more comprehensive sexual health education programs.
- Currently, the emphasis is on the legal and criminalized side of sexting and cyber safety. While this is important, adults should also talk to teenagers about sexting in a noncriminalized way to highlight that there may also be social and relationship consequences.
- It is also important that any health professionals are determining the real prevalence of sexting among that population, rather than relying on previous statistics, and including discussion around sexting with teenagers.
- It is also important that professionals are providing information/education to parents about teenagers' use of technology, focusing on the benefits of new technologies for teenagers, along with the associated risks.

## Spotlight on: Female Teenagers from low SES Areas
### Pressure, coercion, and consent

Having identified some of the pressures teenagers are under to engage in risky sex and sexual behaviors, it is worth spending a little time focusing on a particularly vulnerable group—female teenagers from low SES areas. Previous studies have identified that female teenagers from low SES areas are more likely to feel pressure to engage in earlier sexual intercourse (Nahom et al.,

2001), and the majority of teenagers report regretting the age they started having sex (Meier, 2007). Early intercourse for female teenagers can lead to negative influences on females' psychological well-being and their reproductive health (Olesen et al., 2012). Negative sexual health outcomes include an increased risk of STIs (Kaestle, Halpern, & Miller, 2005), unplanned pregnancies (Finer & Philbin, 2013), and increased number of sexual partners (Sanjose, Cortés, & Méndez, 2008). In addition, female teenagers are more likely to engage in general health risk behaviors if they have an earlier age of first intercourse, such as alcohol and drug use (Kellam, Wang, Mackenzie, & Brown, 2014).

There are consequences of teenage pregnancies on the mother and baby, as teenage mothers are more likely to be disadvantaged than women who have children past teenage years (Bissell, 2000). Teenage mothers usually face many disadvantages arising from the families and communities in which they live; they may have lower incomes, poorer support systems, and weaker school systems which all contribute uniquely to poorer overall health outcomes (Hoffman & Maynard, 2008). In terms of health issues, teenage mothers are at an increased risk for preterm delivery and low birth weight (Chen et al., 2007). Many studies report an increased risk of fetal death, and infants born to teenage mothers have an increased tendency to have a lower birth weight, be born premature, have poorer cognitive development, lower educational attainment, more frequent criminal activity, higher risk of abuse, neglect, abandonment, and behavioral problems during childhood (Dahinten, Shapka, & Willms, 2007; Jolly, Sebire, Harris, & Robinson, 2000). In terms of social and emotional impact, a large qualitative study conducted in the United Kingdom with pregnant teenagers found teenagers felt they were "on the road to social death", as there is a lot of stigma around teenage pregnancy and teens reported that they lost contact with friends (Whitehead, 2001). There are many negative psychological and health consequences for the mother and baby.

It is important that female teenagers have access to sexual health information and an appropriate sexual health intervention program before they become sexually active. Females with increased sexual health knowledge are more likely to delay first sexual initiation and have greater confidence in using condoms (McElderry & Omar, 2003; Weinstein, Walsh, & Ward, 2008). It is critically important that teenagers are targeted with reliable information because teenagers report concern for negative consequences of sexual behavior (Hagan,

Shaw, & Duncan, 2007). Ideally, teenagers should receive information that is medically accurate and is reinforced from multiple sources (Martino, Elliott, Corona, & Kanouse, 2008). Thus, early information may help protect against and delay earlier sexual initiation. As mentioned earlier, earlier initiation leads to unplanned pregnancies and STIs (Heywood et al., 2011).

Also, research has demonstrated that differences exist between girls from a lower SES area and girls from a higher SES area, in regards to sexual health and access to appropriate sexual health information. SES, measured by parental education and parental income, is associated with many measures of health status (Santelli, Lowry, & Brener, 2000; Sieverding, Adler, Witt, & Ellen, 2005). Previous research has shown that females from lower SES areas engage in sexual activity at a younger age, and have higher rates of underage pregnancies and STIs compared with teenagers from higher SES areas (Karakiewicz, Bhojani, Neugut, Shariat, Jeldres, Graefen, & Kattan, 2008; Langille, Hughes, Murphy, & Rigby, 2005). Additionally girls from a lower SES area whose sister or mother had had a teenage birth are significantly more likely to experience a teenage pregnancy (East, Reyes, & Horn, 2007). High education and social class of parents are associated with greater contraception use (Abma, Driscoll, & Moore, 1998; Manning, 2000). One reason for this may be because there has been a decline in comprehensive sexual health programs in low SES areas (Santelli, Lindberg, & Finer, 2007). Thus, it is difficult for low SES female teenagers to access reliable sexual health information.

It should be emphasized that although the factors discussed in this chapter increase the chances of an individual engaging in sexual risk-taking, nearly all teenagers and young people experience pressures of some kind to have sex which places them at risk for pregnancy or STIs (Kirby & Laris, 2009). Our own studies have focussed on females from low SES backgrounds given that they may be at relatively greater risk of many of the predictors of risky sexual behaviors that may increase the likelihood of having an unplanned pregnancy or STI (Finer & Philbin, 2013). It is important that interventions are targeted at specific groups of individuals, in order to identify interventions that appropriately meet their needs (Kreuter, Lukwago, Bucholtz, Clark, & Sanders-Thompson, 2003). The background literature discussed explores teenage sexual risk-taking from a worldwide perspective, and the predictors discussed within this book are generalizable to other teenage populations.

## Chapter Summary

This chapter has provided an overview of the current literature on sexual health in low SES female teenagers. An extensive list of predictors of risky sexual behaviors has been identified, including parents, peers, self-factors, personality, situational factors, and external factors. The chapter has also highlighted some of the key issues around sexual health in the digital age, including pornography use and sexting behaviors. The following chapter outlines current sexual health interventions within schools, the community, and current digital interventions.

# CHAPTER 3

# Sexual Health Education in and Outside of Schools and Digital Sexual Health Interventions

## CHAPTER OUTLINE

Current School-Based Interventions in the United Kingdom..................................................25
    Outside of the United Kingdom .........................27
Current Sexual Health Interventions Outside of Schools ...................................................27
Digital Sexual Health Interventions .....................29
    Benefits of the Internet for Health Information ...29
    How do Teenagers Seek Online Health Information?.......................................................30
    Issues With Using the Internet for Health Information ...................................................31

*Trust* ...........................................................31
*Privacy* ........................................................32
Current Online Sexual Health Interventions........33
    *Sexual health websites* ...........................34
    *Social networking sites* ..........................35
    *Text messaging*......................................36
    *Sexual health mobile apps* ....................38
Chapter Summary................................................39

## ABSTRACT

This chapter presents an overview of the research on sexual health intervention programs. There are many different sexual health interventions programs and it is beyond the scope of this chapter to discuss them all, so we provide an overview of some of the most commonly cited intervention programs. This chapter is separated into three sections to provide greater clarity of the research literature. The first section provides an overview of sexual health education within schools, the second section provides an overview of external sexual health intervention programs, and the final section considers digital sexual interventions. Patton, Sawyer, Santelli, Ross, and Afifi (2016) highlight that digital technologies show the greatest potential for improving health outcomes for teenagers. It has been identified that teenagers do not like speaking about sex, therefore for sexual health interventions, online delivery may help reduce the embarrassment teenagers often report when discussing sexual health (Bailey et al., 2015). In addition, online interventions offer a low-cost solution to sexual health, making it a suitable method for low socioeconomic status (SES) areas.

## KEYWORDS

Digital health interventions; Online sexual health interventions; School-based sexual health education; Sexual health; Sexual health education; Sexual health interventions; Teenagers.

## CURRENT SCHOOL-BASED INTERVENTIONS IN THE UNITED KINGDOM

Sex and Relationship Education (SRE) is a nonassessed subject within British schools and as such remains inconsistent (UK Department of Education and Employment, 2000, pp. 1–34). Currently it is only compulsory for local authority maintained schools to teach basic biology and reproduction. Academies and free schools (local authority maintained schools) do not have to teach this, as they do not have to follow the national curriculum. In a 2002 review, it was found that over a third of SRE in schools was outdated and needed improving (OfSTED, 2002). An example of the narrow perspective of current SRE was highlighted by a recent study that found 4 out of 10 schoolgirls in England aged 14–17 years reported having experienced

Teenagers, Sexual Health Information and the Digital Age. https://doi.org/10.1016/B978-0-12-816969-8.00003-5
Copyright © 2020 Elsevier Inc. All rights reserved.

sexual coercion (Barter et al., 2016), yet the girls did not understand coercion as they are currently not taught basic information such as consent. SRE in schools is provided primarily by teachers (Westwood, 2007), yet teachers often report having insufficient sexual health knowledge about STIs and emergency contraception to effectively teach the subject (Westwood & Mullan, 2007). Sexual health professionals have better knowledge of SRE; however, pupils have less positive attitudes toward them as they do not see them frequently (Westwood & Mullan, 2009). As teachers do not have sufficient knowledge to teach SRE, it is not clear what sexual information teenagers are provided with and SRE remains inconsistent.

However, this is due to change in 2020, with the introduction of Relationships and Sex Education (RSE) which will be compulsory for all secondary schools, including academies and maintained schools (Schulkind, Hurst, Biggart, & Bowsher, 2015; Sellgren, 2017). Currently SRE is only compulsory from ages 11 years upwards for local authority maintained schools. Whereas academies and free schools do not have to teach this. This is because academies and free schools do not have to follow the National curriculum. This is concerning as only 31% of schools are local authority maintained, and therefore, the majority of schools in England have inconsistent sex education which is not regulated.

However, even though SRE is compulsory in local authority maintained schools, it is not assessed and therefore, is also inconsistent in these schools. The only information that schools are required to teach is basic sex education such as puberty, reproduction, menstrual cycle, and the reproductive system (UK Department of Education and Employment, 2000, pp. 1–34). This information does not reflect the complex and broad array of sexual health issues. In a recent 2017 review it was found that even though there have been changes in attitudes toward gender and sexuality, such as increased gender equality (Mercer, Tanton, Prah, 2013), the United Kingdom's SRE provision was still outdated as the Government had not issued any new guidance on sex education in the previous 17 years (Pound, 2017). There are guidelines on what schools should cover; however, as guidelines these are not compulsory to include. The current guidelines are *to teach about responsibilities of parenthood as well as sexual intercourse, to focus on boys and girls, to build self-esteem, to discuss responsibility and consequences of one's actions in relation to sex and parenthood, to include information about different contraception methods, to use teenage mothers and fathers as educators, to provide a clear argument for delaying sex and resisting peer pressure, to link sex education with other risky behaviors such as drugs, alcohol, smoking, and lastly to ensure young people understand the law and consent* (UK Department of Education and Employment, 2000, pp. 1–34).

This is due to change for the 2020 academic year, and it has been proposed that all secondary schools, including academies and maintained schools, will have to teach RSE (Gov UK Legislation, 2017). This will be age-appropriate information and will start with a focus on relationships in primary schools, and move to RSE in secondary schools. The full guidelines of this proposed change are not fully confirmed; however, it is known that all schools will have to have a written policy on sex education and make this available to parents for free (Long, 2017). This will encourage parents to discuss sex education with their children as they will know what sexual health education their children are currently being taught. In addition, it will be compulsory to cover different types of relationships including strangers, friends, intimate relationships, consent and healthy relationships, well-being and mental health, safety online, sex and sexuality, sexual health in the context of relationships, healthy bodies, healthy minds, self-esteem, mental health resilience, and economic well-being (Long, 2017). There will also be a push for RSE in the modern world, which will include information on meeting strangers online and sexting (Gov UK, 2017). There will also be a move to improve awareness of the risks of sharing nude images and pornography use (House of Parliament, 2018). All schools will be inspected to ensure schools are providing the full statutory curriculum.

One of the issues identified with current SRE is that teachers conducting these sessions do not usually have the correct training and have insufficient knowledge about STIs and emergency contraception to effectively deliver these sessions (Westwood & Mullan, 2007). Sexual health professionals are ideally placed to provide SRE but are not easily accessible in the eyes of teenagers and so are viewed in a less positive light than other potential sources of information (Westwood & Mullan, 2009). Even though some schools have a school nurse, most low SES schools are under-resourced and teenagers are not able to access the school nurse for sexual health questions (France, 2014). Therefore, while primarily sex education is provided by schools, due to the inconsistencies and the fact that it is due to undergo a change, it is also important to review sexual health interventions outside of schools (Table 3.1).

**TABLE 3.1**
**Overview of Sexual Health Education in UK Schools.**

**Summary Points**

- Sex and Relationship Education is a nonassessed subject within British schools and remains inconsistent
- Due to change to Relationships and Sex Education in September 2020.
- Aims to increase knowledge about sexual risk and help reduce teenage pregnancies. Include attitudes toward relationships, self-esteem, and raising awareness of sexting and pornography use.
- Currently not clear what impact this will have on schools and sexual health education in England.

## Outside of the United Kingdom

The coverage of sexual health education in schools globally varies greatly. A review of Australian programs found that school-based education programs were trusted by students but focused too heavily on the biological aspects of sex rather than the social aspects of sexual relationships, such as intimacy and love (Johnson et al., 2016). In Germany, reviews have found that school-based sexual health education does not cover enough inclusive sexuality such as lesbian, gay, bisexual and transgender (LGBT) issues (Geganfurtner & Genhardt, 2017). Therefore, even though sex education is important for teenagers and is regarded as a trusted source of information, it remains inconsistent in schools globally. Also, in the United States there is a prevalence of abstinence-only over comprehensive sexual education compared to the United Kingdom and Australia (Goodson & Buhi, 2011; Ott & Santelli, 2007a; Santelli et al., 2017). There continues to be significant controversy over the use of abstinence-only and abstinence-plus education. Researchers and practitioners argue that abstinence-only programs do not allow adolescents to be fully informed and aware of contraception and STIs (Walsh-Buhi, Maness & Mahony 2016). Programs should focus on discussing abstinence as an option based on personal choice (in conjunction with comprehensive sexual education), rather than relying heavily on a moral message that abstaining from sex is the "correct" thing to do (Bruess & Schroeder, 2013; Santelli et al.2017). Thus, sexual health education varies greatly in schools and globally, and there is no clear consensus on which educational method works best for teenagers. However, there have been arguments that a more holistic approach, covering all areas of sexual health education, may have the best outcomes for promoting positive sexual health attitudes and providing teenagers with sexual health knowledge to make their own decisions.

## CURRENT SEXUAL HEALTH INTERVENTIONS OUTSIDE OF SCHOOLS

There are also sexual health interventions aimed at teenagers that operate externally outside of schools. Ingram and Salmon (2007) reviewed the "no worries clinics". These are sexual health clinics designed for teenagers inside existing GP surgeries and health clinics. These clinics are in the South West of England and cover all areas of sexual health advice and screening. Ingram and Salmon concluded that teenagers who attended these clinics felt more confident about sex, were informed about sex, and reported less intention to take risks.

There are also the adolescent pregnancy prevention clinics, which are privately funded clinics for adolescents and young adults (Yoost, Hertweck, & Barnett, 2014). These clinics provide female family planning and sexual education to females aged 11−24 years. They concentrate on contraception methods and sexual health information and work on building a positive relationship between the patient and healthcare provider so that confidential information and advice can be sought. A review of these clinics found that they had a significant influence on knowledge and sexual intentions in younger adolescents 11−16 years. However, they had less of an effect on older adolescents.

Even though these clinics are more effective for younger adolescents, the majority of younger adolescents do not feel comfortable accessing these types of clinics and worry about confidentiality and judgment when visiting (Mulholland & Wersch, 2007). The biggest worries for teens are confidentiality and anonymity as well as staff members being unfriendly or critical (Iyer & Baxter-MacGregor, 2010). Also, teenagers are only likely to access these clinics when they are already sexually active (Jones & Biddlecom, 2011). Only a third of young people use a service prior to having sex for the first time (Stone & Ingham, 2002). As early sex is linked with more risky behaviors

(Zimmer-Gembeck & Helfand, 2008), it is important to target teens at age-appropriate times. While drop-in clinics are effective, there also needs to be a way to ensure that teens can feel comfortable accessing information before they become sexually active. Ingram and Salmon (2010) found that delivering services within schools and communities makes them more accessible. However, many low SES schools and areas cannot afford to have these types of drop-in services available.

The recommended standard for sexual health provision in the United Kingdom is to provide individuals with safe sex information and access to free contraceptives (Recommended standards for sexual health services, 2011), and for teenagers to have access to free contraceptives throughout the United Kingdom. Yet as mentioned, many teenagers are uncomfortable visiting sexual health professionals. Previous sexual health interventions that have been underpinned by theoretical models such as the theory of planned behavior have tried to increase the number of teenagers visiting sexual health clinics. The Department of Education in the United Kingdom ran a national campaign called "Sex. Worth Talking About" (SWTA) (Goodwin, Smith, Davies, & Perry, 2011). Although this campaign was not based on the TPB, it was developed from extensive evidence of the role of health communication on behavior change (Brown, Burton, Nikolin, & Crooks, 2012; NHS Choices, 2012). This intervention was aimed at sexually active adolescents under the age of 25 years, using posters and television advertisements (Ajzen, 2006). Brief health messages were provided in speech bubbles, which directed the reader to a website with further contraception information. Research investigating the impact of the campaign found that the number of young adolescents requesting sexual health appointments increased (NHS Choices, 2012). Therefore, brief messages can have an impact on changing behavior, but the content of the message (DiClemente, Marinilli, & Singh, 2001), and mode of delivery, need to be carefully considered (Abraham & Michie, 2008). Using this approach, teenagers are encouraged to make informed decisions about health behaviors, and be aware of negative consequences of not performing these behaviors (Broadstock & Michie, 2000). However, nudging a person to change their behavior by increasing their knowledge about safe sex and providing free condoms only has a modest effect on changing an individual's behavior (Ajzen, 2011; Marteau, 2011).

Another intervention widely discussed in the literature is the Positive Youth Development (PYD) program. The aim of PYD programs is to provide teenagers with the confidence to be able to refuse sex or practise safer sexual behaviors (Gavin, Catalano, David-Ferdon, Gloppen, & Markham, 2010). This is achieved by helping teenagers strengthen their relationships and skills and develop a more positive view about their future (Mji, 2016; Turner, 2017). PYD programs aim to provide a holistic view of adolescent development that reinforces skills needed for safer sex (Schwartz et al., 2010). Bonding and relationships are an important part of PYD programs and the atmosphere is supportive so that the program staff and teenagers can connect and a sense of belonging with the other program participants can be achieved (Eccles & Gootman, 2007). In this format, prosocial behaviors are encouraged and peer pressure toward problem behaviors is minimized, with positive and safe behaviors being actively promoted.

There have been mixed results from PYD programs. There have been significant gender differences, with male students reporting less sexual intercourse and more condom use after a PYD program, but no significant differences in sexual behavior for females (Clark, Miller, Nagy, Avery, & Roth, 2005; Flay, Graumlich, & Segawa, 2004). However, another study found that female participants were significantly less likely to have sex or get pregnant than the control group, yet there were no differences for males (Quinn & Fromme, 2010). A further study found similar results with no significant differences for males but females were significantly less likely than controls to have sex under pressure, to have ever had sex, and to have a pregnancy or birth. Female participants were also significantly more likely to use hormonal contraception than those in the control group, but the groups did not differ significantly on condom use (Philliber, Kaye, Herrling, & West, 2002). Furthermore in a longitudinal study on PYD youth, PYD teens were significantly less likely to be parents at age 20 years than the control group (Campbell, Ramey, & Pungello, 2002). A further two studies found no significant differences on sexual behavior and pregnancy rates between the PYD teens and control group (Melchior, 1998; Piper, Moberg, & King, 2000). However, a large systematic review of the literature concluded that overall PYD programs do significantly improve condom use and frequency of sex (Gavin et al., 2010).

One of the reasons for these contrasting results might be the definitions used to describe PYD programs. PYD programs have many different definitions developed by academic researchers, program providers, and funding organizations who have worked in the area. A literature review of PYD programs identified

CHAPTER 3 Sexual Health Education in and Outside of Schools **29**

15 different definitions; ranging from specific goal setting to spirituality and volunteer work (Catalano, Berglund, & Ryan, 2004). It is difficult to assess how these programs work due to the definitional differences. It is also difficult to assess whether each program is targeting the same behaviors and skills. Consequently, it is not clear if all of the programs discussed are actually PYD programs.

PYD programs tend to last for an entire school year or longer, so that teens have adequate time to benefit from the program (Gavin et al., 2010). Because of their heavy emphasis on human resources and length of program, they have a large upfront cost (Schulman & Davies, 2007) often rendering them inaccessible to low SES areas.

There are also interventions with parents that aim to improve the sexual health of their children, as research has shown that parental communication is important in shaping teenager's early sexual health attitudes. Wight and Fullterton (2013) reviewed 44 programs that involved parents, to evaluate if these types of interventions were effective in improving teenagers' sexual health. It was concluded that parent-child interaction and teenagers' sexual health knowledge and attitudes did improve, but sexual behavior outcomes only improved in half the studies. However, Wight and Fullterton (2013) noted that the review was limited by lack of rigorous evaluations, therefore, while parental communication is important for shaping teenagers' sexual health knowledge and attitudes, further research needs to establish when and how parents should discuss sexual health with their children. A further review of parent-based sexual health education programs found that parental involvement did increase parent-teenager communication about sexual health (Santa, Markham & Mullen, 2015). However, the researchers highlighted that there are clear gaps in the range of programs published, often missing out sexual minority youths, grandparents, and faith-based services, and further research is needed before any firm conclusions are made (Table 3.2).

## DIGITAL SEXUAL HEALTH INTERVENTIONS
### Benefits of the Internet for Health Information

Teenagers are known for their early adoption of the Internet and mobile technology (Fox & Jones, 2009; Lenhart, Purcell, Smith, & Zickhur, 2010; Rideout, Foehr, & Roberts, 2010). In a 2017 survey it was found that 99% of teenagers had recently used the Internet (ONS, 2017), and according to the 2015 Pew Research Center report, 92% of adolescents report going online daily (Lenhart, 2015). Teenagers report that the Internet is their primary source when seeking health information (Gray & Klein, 2006). This may be because of the anonymity it affords. Discussing sex with teachers, parents, or even friends is considered embarrassing in a society that problematizes teenage sexuality (Kendall & Funk, 2012 ). Teenagers noted the Internet is an appealing source of sexual health information because they can access the information without the embarrassment of their parents finding out (Kanuga & Rosenfeld, 2004). In contrast, the Internet is perceived as a more private and anonymous place. Therefore, teenagers may feel more comfortable seeking and accessing sexual health information through the Internet.

There are many appeals of using the Internet to deliver a health intervention such as its ability to deliver timely information, convenience for the user as it can be completed anywhere, reduction of stigma for sensitive issues, and there is increased user and supplier control of the intervention (Griffiths, Lindenmeyer, & Powell, 2006). Another main appeal of using the Internet to deliver health information is its low cost (Michael & Cheuvront, 1998; Napolitano, Fotheringham, & Tate, 2003). It is an effective method when working with low SES or hard-to-reach populations, such as teenagers. As long as they have access to the Internet, then high quality and interactive sexual health information (a sensitive issue) can be delivered

---

**TABLE 3.2**
**Summary Points of Sexual Health Education Delivered Outside of Schools.**

**Summary Points**

- There is an extensive list of sexual health interventions aimed at teenagers discussed in the literature, but it is still unclear which approach is the most effective.
- Most programs are costly and long-lasting and may not be appropriate for all teenagers (for example, those from a low socioeconomic area)
- It may be useful to involve a component of parental communication in helping to shape teenagers' early sexual health attitudes.

to them. Research has found that low SES teenagers are more likely to search for health information online than high SES teenagers (Madden, Lenhart, Cortesi, Smith, & Beaton, 2013). One of the reasons for this is that low SES teenagers have less access to physical health services.

Teenagers are interested and enthusiastic about digital technology to enhance sexual health education and are happy to use the Internet to search for sexual health information (Selkie, Benson, & Moreno, 2011). Simon and Daneback (2013) qualitatively observed that teenagers report engaging with sex information online and are interested in a number of topics, including sexually transmitted infections and pregnancy. Even though teenagers thought the quality of some sexual health websites was lacking, teenagers believed it was a suitable source for information.

A systematic review of Internet interventions for teenagers found that using tailored messaging and reminders to perform positive health behaviors, along with an incentives-based approach, was successful at eliciting behavior change (Crutzen, 2010). Therefore, there is potential to use new media and mobile technology to communicate effectively with teenagers about sexual health (Levine, 2011). Teenagers are familiar with the Internet and use it every day. Paired with reliable behavior change techniques, the Internet appears to be successful for delivering sexual education. However, due to the increasing volume of Internet-based resources, it is important teenagers can navigate, select, and evaluate health information online (Table 3.3).

## How do Teenagers Seek Online Health Information?

Teenagers, like adults, struggle finding relevant health information online because of the sheer volume of websites retrieved by most search engines. This is often resolved by teenagers confining their interest to the first few results (Hansen, Derry, & Resnick,

2003). Also teenagers have noted that while they enjoy using the Internet as a source of information, they are often unable to locate satisfactory information for a specific query (Zeng & Parmanto, 2004; Bickmore, Utami, Matsuyama & Passche-Orlow, 2016). Teenagers believe that high-quality information does exist on the Internet, but they are insufficiently skilled to find it (Skinner, Biscope, & Poland, 2003).

Teenagers often begin their searches on Google, or other search engines; however, the vast number of results generated makes it difficult to determine a site's credibility (Gray, Klein, Noyce, & Sesselberg, 2005; Hameed & Swar, 2016). When using search engines online to answer health-related questions, teenagers tend to choose between the first nine results, without searching further (Hansen, Derry, & Resnick, 2003). Thus, adolescents' use of the Internet to search for health information may be limited in relation to their search heuristics and tactics; this behavior is not dissimilar to adults.

Wartella, Rideout, and Montague (2016) found even though teenagers usually use Google to direct them to health information, younger teens (13−15 year olds) also use novel online sources such as "YouTube" for health information or websites specifically for teens. In addition, girls were more likely than boys to use actual medical websites for health information. Girls in particular noted that using a novel source like YouTube is more interesting than using traditional websites. Generally, teens tend to be quite passive when searching for health information online, unless they specifically have a health issue (Wartella et al., 2016) This may link with teenagers feeling that they have insufficient skills to locate specific information (Skinner et al., 2003), and may need more guidance when searching for health information online.

Teenagers are using the Internet for a wide range of health topics including sensitive issues such as sexual health and researchers have investigated the topics

---

**TABLE 3.3**
**Summary Points of the Benefits of Using the Internet for Sexual Health Information.**

**Summary Points**

- The Internet is perceived as an anonymous and confidential modality for searching for sexual health information.
- The Internet delivers timely information, convenience for the user, and reduction of stigma for sensitive issues.
- Low cost and so suitable for teenagers from low socioeconomic areas that may not have access to external sexual health services.

# CHAPTER 3 Sexual Health Education in and Outside of Schools

that teenagers search for online. A focus group study with teenagers indicated that they search for a wide range of health topics on the Internet, including sexual health, relationships, specific medical conditions, violence, body image, and nutrition (Skinner et al., 2003). There is a vast amount of information available on the Internet regarding sexual health (Keller, Labelle, & Karimi, 2002; Von Rosen & Von Rosen, 2017), including online health sources specifically geared toward teenage users that allow teenagers to seek advice and reassurance on sensitive topics. These websites serve as anonymous online venues that foster peer acceptance (Mitchell, Patrick, & Heywood, 2014). Other reasons teenagers use the Internet for sexual health information include low cost of access, accessibility of health information without having to speak to a provider face to face, and teenagers report that peers are friendly and helpful online (Yager & O'Keefe, 2012). Evidence suggests that teenagers appreciate the efficiency and immediacy of health information online and that they can interactively access personalized information (Gardner & Davis, 2014; Third, Bellerose, Dawkins, Keltie, & Pihl, 2014).

Willingness to search for sensitive health information online differs by age and gender. Girls, especially older girls, are far more likely to search for sensitive health topics online, whereas, younger boys (ages 12–13 years) were the least likely to search for sensitive health topics (Lenhart et al., 2010). As stated above, girls are also more likely to use actual medical and novel websites when seeking health information (Wartella et al., 2016). However, while girls are happy to use the Internet to seek sexual health information, they may be hindered by poor search techniques (Holstrom, 2015). Research has recommended using key terms that teenagers are familiar with in order to make it easier for teenagers to locate reliable sexual health websites (Holstrom, 2015) (Table 3.4).

## Issues With Using the Internet for Health Information

While teenagers are happy to use the Internet for health information, they still worry about the privacy and credibility of sexual health information online (Gray et al., 2005; Jones, Biddlecom, 2011; Lenhart, 2015). Therefore, trust and privacy issues with online sexual health information are discussed in the following section.

### *Trust*

With the proliferation of sexual health information available on the Internet, it is key to understand *if* and *how* teenagers trust online information. There are many factors that influence trust in eHealth (Beldad, De Jong, & Steehouder, 2010). Online trust is important to teenagers. Veinot, Campbell, Kruger, Grodzinski, and Franzen (2011) found that when teenagers (14–24 year olds) investigated eHealth sites, they had concerns about design recommendations and trust, especially around condom- and STI-related information. Trust is important because it acts as a mechanism to counter concerns about uncertainty and risk (Kim, 2016). As sexual health is a sensitive issue, the risks are quite high and so trust is an issue.

Researchers have investigated the factors that increase trust in online health websites. Users have a rapid screening process for rejecting sites that they do not trust, based on poor design appeal, sites with adverts, pop-up surveys, or sites that were poorly laid out (Silence, Briggs, Fishwick, & Harris, 2004). After this initial judgment, users then evaluate trust based on a more careful evaluation of the website and content (Sillence et al., 2004). Individuals trust websites that are unbiased and have information that is supported by an original source, or have frequently asked questions or hints and tips. In summary, people make initial rapid judgments of trust and then evaluate websites more carefully. More recent research has supported these

---

**TABLE 3.4**
**Summary Points of How Teenagers Search for Health Information Online.**

**Summary Points**

- Searches often begin on search engines (e.g., Google); however, the vast number of results generated makes it difficult to determine a site's credibility.
- Teens search for a wide range of health topics on the Internet, including sexual health, relationships, specific medical conditions, violence, and body image.
- There are sex differences, girls, especially older girls, are far more likely to search for uncomfortable health topics online, whereas younger boys (ages 12–13 years) are least likely to search for sensitive health topics.

findings noting that trust is based on well-known brands, reliable content, credibility, ease of use, recommendation from trusted others, usefulness, and verification of sources (Rowley, Johnson, & Sbaffi, 2015).

Even though the majority of past studies have been conducted with adult users, trust factors appear to be similar for teenage users. Starling and Cheshire (2016) conducted a qualitative study on how teenagers search for and evaluate online sexual health information. Participants initially based judgments on first impression and ease of use of websites. Advertisements and pop-ups were also part of the process for deciding about particular sites. Generally, teenagers preferred professional layouts and believed these were more credible, and preferred websites that were shown first on search engines. Mendes, Abreu, Vilar-Correia, and Borlido-Santos (2016) highlighted that teenagers often rank health websites based on whether they believe the information is trustworthy and prioritize those at the top of the search engine list. Teenagers, like adults have a rapid judgment system for trust, basing it on the design and usability of websites.

Individuals also make judgments based on who has authored and produced the information (Sillence, Briggs, Harris, & Fishwick, 2007). Medical expertise can be conveyed explicitly or by association with a health organization. Reputation is also important with information seekers trusting in the benevolence of charity websites and the expertise of the author. In addition to the information produced by healthcare professionals, the Internet now allows "lay experts" to share their health experiences online. User-generated content exists in online health communities such as forums, blogs, and social networking sites. Peer resources can vary enormously, making it more difficult to assess whether or not the information and the author can be deemed trustworthy. People seek out like-minded individuals to provide support and reinforce preexisting views (Sillence et al., 2010). Those giving the information and advice develop ways to portray their competence and trustworthiness online, so that others take their advice. Therefore, trust is influenced by information that users feel is personalized and similar to them. This is important to teenagers, especially females as even though they use professional medical websites, they prefer user-generated resources such as the videos found on YouTube (Wartella et al., 2016). However, studies have found that user-generated content through vlogs such as YouTube often have misleading and inaccurate information (Liu, Huh, Neogi, Inkpen, & Pratt, 2013). Therefore, teenagers may need more guidance on how to trust information from a variety of different sources.

Familiarization and time spent using the Internet also impacts upon trust. Zhang (2013) found that people believe that it is important to use websites that are trustworthy and have high-quality information; however, they are also inclined to use sources that they are familiar and comfortable with. Metzger, Flanagin, Macarthur and Eysenbach (2008) found that those who are highly proficient with the web have lower perceptions of risks in online transactions, and are happier to use the Internet. However, Aiken and Boush (2006) found although users' trust increases in the early stages of Internet experiences, at higher levels trust declines, especially when something goes wrong. They found that familiarization with the website or provider was more important for trust than experience of the Internet. Teenagers are highly proficient Internet users and are happy to use unfamiliar websites (Garside, 2014), therefore, it is likely they may have experienced technical issues with websites and may have lower levels of trust (Table 3.5).

### Privacy

We know that teenagers like to use online sources for sexual health information because of the privacy it affords (Buhi, Daley, Oberne, & Smith, 2010). Despite this, teenagers still have privacy concerns. Privacy in general is a complex issue, lacking a single,

---

**TABLE 3.5**
**Summary Points of Trust Issues When Using the Internet for Sexual Health Information.**

**Summary Points**

- Trust is defined as well-intentioned, truthful, and unbiased information.
- Users have a rapid screening process for rejecting sites that they do not trust, based on poor design appeal, sites with adverts, pop-up surveys, or sites that are poorly laid out. After this initial judgment, users then evaluate trust based on a more careful evaluation of the website and content.
- Trust is influenced by information that users feel is personalized and similar to them

straightforward definition. In relation to digital domains, the majority of research has centered on privacy within e-commerce (Buchanan, Paine, & Joinson, 2007); however, given the sensitive nature of health information, there are overlapping themes. Several types of privacy are relevant to digital interventions (Little & Briggs, 2006), and three types of privacy concern congruent with teenagers are discussed here, parental privacy concerns, user privacy concerns in the virtual world, and user privacy concerns in the physical world.

While parents are supportive of teenagers searching for sexual health information online (Gaskin, Bruce, & Anoshiravani, 2016), the nature of online interaction can make it easy to collect information from teenagers without parental involvement or awareness (Montgomery, 2000). Thus, there are growing parental concerns about privacy. Parents worry about teenagers disclosing personal or sensitive information online which may constitute an invasion of privacy (Turow, 2001b). Also, parents worry that teenagers may access inappropriate information when searching for sexual health advice (Scheff, 2013; Turow, 2001a). In a survey, 81% of parents were concerned about their child's online behavior, with 46% being "very" concerned (Zickuhr & Smith, 2012). This is important as teenagers do appear to be less likely to understand the future ramifications of disclosing personal information, and the potential implications of their actions on their future careers or social lives (Yan, 2005).

Parents can protect their children online through direct intervention or active mediation (Livingstone, Haddon, Görzig, & Ólafsson, 2010). Direct intervention involves parents using the parental controls online and/or reading teenagers' browser history, whereas active mediation involves talking to teenagers about what they visit online. Direct intervention by itself has been found to have a suppressive effect on teenagers, reducing their exposure to online risk but also their ability to engage with others online and learn how to effectively cope with risks (Wisniewski, Jia, Xu, & Rosson, 2015). Clemons and Wilson (2015) investigated privacy concerns between teenagers and their parents and found parents' privacy concerns are very different to their children, and because of this parental monitoring may not be as effective as they could be missing key privacy issues. It may be better to combine active mediation with direct intervention so that parents can protect their teens from severe online risks while empowering teens to engage with others online and then learn to make safe online privacy choices. It is important for sexual health websites to encourage this, so teenagers and parents can feel comfortable accessing the information.

Online personal information can be accessed in a variety of different systems and users want the choice to be able to reveal or hide their information (Little & Briggs, 2006). Social media sites allow for this and in general, teens understand privacy and on social media, 60% keep their profiles private (Rainie & Madden, 2012). Teenagers also engage in several risk-reducing strategies such as falsifying information, providing incomplete information, or going to alternative websites that do not ask for personal information (Youn, 2005). A total 70% of teenagers (ages 13–17 years) reported they would ask a parent how to handle requests for personal information, and 64% reported they would read the privacy policy statement (Turow & Nir, 2000). Older teenagers are more likely to be competent in managing and understanding their online privacy settings (Youn 2005).

When accessing sensitive information online, physical privacy is also a concern. Little and Briggs (2009) found people show greater stress viewing information in a crowded versus isolated situation condition. Users are concerned that someone may see them accessing a sensitive website; for teenagers it is a particular worry that friends or parents may see them accessing a sexual health website (Bailey et al., 2015). Mobile phones can help ease this stress, and teenagers may prefer to use phones to search for sexual health information. Smaller screen sizes are perceived as more private than larger screens (Little, Briggs, & Coventry, 2005; Nilashi, Ibrahim, Mirabi, Ebrahimi & Zare, 2015). Therefore, teenagers may prefer to use their phones to search for and view sexual health information in comparison to a laptop or shared computer. In a design context, it has been found that teenagers prefer sexual health websites that warn them to use headphones before a sexual health video plays (Cranor, Durity, Marsh, & Ur, 2014). Sexual health websites that consider privacy concerns for teenagers, including discreet design features like warnings for headphones or allowing the website to be viewed on a mobile device, may help teenagers feel more comfortable using these websites (Table 3.6).

## Current Online Sexual Health Interventions

There are a wide range of current sexual health interventions available online. Four of the main ones that are discussed in this section are sexual health websites, social networking sites, text messaging (also known as short messaging service SMS), and mobile apps.

# TABLE 3.6
## Summary Points of Privacy Issues When Using the Internet for Sexual Health Information.

**Summary Points**

- Three types of privacy are important for teenagers and sexual health information: parental privacy concerns, user privacy concerns in the virtual world, and user privacy concerns in the physical world.
- Parents can protect their children online through direct intervention or active mediation.
- Teens want the choice to be able to reveal or hide their personal information online.
- Teens are concerned that parents or peers may see them accessing a sexual health website, therefore any interventions need to be discreetly designed.

## Sexual health websites

In recent years, sexual health websites have been used as part of interventions to increase sexual health knowledge, and research has found that websites can improve teenagers' sexual health knowledge (Simon & Daneback, 2013). Bailey et al. (2015) found that interactive sexual health websites that combine sexual health information with behavior change techniques can exert a positive influence on self-efficacy, intention to carry out health-promoting sexual behaviors, and sexual behavior itself. These sites typically provide interactive advice in accessible, nontechnical language allowing teenagers to freely express their health questions to sexual health professionals, as well as sharing their concerns with their peers. Therefore, these websites offer confidential advice and information that might be otherwise difficult to obtain (Borzekowski & Rickert, 2001; Suzuki & Calzo, 2004). Buzi, Smith, and Barrera (2015) investigated teenagers' interactions with sexual health websites, and found that on websites that included contact information teenagers regularly emailed the websites because of the privacy and anonymity it affords. Sexual health websites are effective because they provide teenagers with immediate advice without the embarrassment of discussing sexual health.

However, evaluations of current sexual health websites have found issues with the quality of the information they provide. In a review of 177 sexual health websites the information provided on more technically complex (e.g., contraception and STIs) and controversial topics (e.g., penis size, abortion, and emergency contraception) often contain inaccurate information (Buhi et al., 2010). In addition, there were no associations between quality scores and accurate information, therefore quality indicators were not related to accuracy of information. In a review of websites offering contraception advice, only 23% of 238 websites offered up-to-date information (Harris, Byrd, Engel, & Weeks, 2016).

Tietz, Davies, and Moran (2004) found that government-sponsored websites comprised more accurate and up-to-date information than university, nonprofit, or commercial websites. Keller et al. (2002) found that a number of important safe sex messages exist on the Internet, but such websites can be difficult to both locate and navigate for teenagers. Even though Internet-based interventions can increase teenagers' sexual health knowledge, only a few websites offer up-to-date and accurate information. Websites that do offer more reliable and updated information may be difficult for teenagers to locate and navigate, and therefore may be viewed as less credible. Rosen-Palmowki (2018) investigated what teenagers want from sexual health websites, and found that easy-comprehensive language and a clear layout were important.

An interactive sexual health website developed in the United Kingdom, *Sexunzipped*, aims to deliver reliable sexual health education to all young people in the United Kingdom. Development of the "Sexunzipped" website suggests that from a teenage user perspective, there is a preference for sexual health websites that present clear information, free from technical or complex language. Websites should cover a wide range of sexual health topics, including sexual pleasure, relationships, and STIs. Websites should also include videos that adolescents can relate to (McCarthy, Carswell, Murray, & Free, 2012). Teenagers also prefer resources that are accessible, trustworthy, private, and safe (Selkie & Benson, 2011). Using these recommendations, a pilot of a sexual health website used in a classroom setting improved self-efficacy for condom use and condom use intentions in 14–16 year olds. In addition, teenagers reported having high satisfaction with the website content and design (Willoughby, 2015). Another website (teenstalkhealth) that was designed to promote condom use and healthy decision-making in sexual and romantic relationships found that interactive message boards and videos allowed teens to feel high levels of comfort, perceived privacy, and credibility of health educators (Brady et al., 2015).

In summary, sexual health websites can be successful in increasing sexual health knowledge, intentions, and behaviors and teenagers are enthusiastic about using them. However, many websites comprise inaccurate information, which can make it difficult for teenagers to evaluate the most credible websites (Table 3.7).

### Social networking sites

Social networking sites are websites that enable people to form, use, and maintain their social networks (Boyd, 2007). The most popular global social networking sites for teens in 2017 were Instagram, Facebook, Snapchat, YouTube, and Twitter The growth of social networking sites are rapid, especially among teenagers (Antheunis & Schouten, 2016), in 2016 90% of teenagers were using social media, a 78% increase since 2005, and teenagers are among one of the heaviest users of social media (Perrin, 2016).

Most social networking sites are based on a Web 2.0 framework, which emphasizes collaboration and multilevel interaction between users (Thackeray, Neiger, Hanson, & Mckenzie, 2008). As discussed previously, most Web 2.0 platforms tend to focus on a single domain of media (for example, videos); however, social networking sites can support multiple media formats which allow for flexibility, creativity, collaboration, and user control (Byron, Albury, & Evers, 2013; Moreno & Kolb, 2012; Takhteyev, Gruzd, & Wellman, 2012). These unique properties make social networking sites potentially useful tools for conducting sexual health interventions. Most social networking sites also have direct messaging which allow for confidential one-on-one discussions. These sites can therefore provide a way of connecting teenagers with sexual health professionals (Ventola, 2014) and signposting to external sexual health services. Teenagers perceive social networking interventions as credible and essential methods of communication (Vyas, Landry, Schnider, Rojas, & Wood, 2012). Social networking sites are well placed to deliver health information because they are a cost-effective way to target sexual health information to a large number of teenagers in an interactive and confidential way.

Sexual health interventions on social networking sites have steadily increased over the past 5 years (Capurro et al., 2014; Lenhart, 2015). A systematic review of sexual health information on social networking sites found 71% of sexual health promotion was on Facebook (Gold & Pedrana, 2011). It was also found that social networking sites generally tend to be an addition to other sexual health websites or a way to advertise sexual health clinics rather than provide standalone information. Qualitative studies exploring teenagers' views of sexual health information on social networking sites have found that teenagers prefer positive messages that are peer-based and involve interaction (Veinot et al., 2011).

Researchers have also found that many teenagers are not comfortable accessing sexual health information on social networking sites (Lim, 2014), and this may be dependent on who moderates and shares the information. The moderator voice needs to be engaging and friendly so that teenagers feel they can engage with the sexual health information. Teenagers rated sexual health information as simplistic when the moderator was professional but unengaged (Nguyen, Gold, Pedrana, & Chang, 2013). Therefore, it is important that there is a moderator on social media who is an engaged and interactive presence designed to maintain users' interest, who can generate new material for discussion, and who is responsive to user requests (Syred, Naidoo, & Woodhall, 2014).

---

**TABLE 3.7**
**Summary Points of Sexual Health Websites.**

**Summary Points**

- Sexual health websites aim to act as interventions by providing sexual health information and increasing teenagers' sexual health knowledge.
- Sexual health websites aimed at teenagers typically provide interactive advice in accessible, nontechnical language.
- However, reviews have found that the majority of sexual health websites contain inaccurate or outdated information.
- Websites that aim to act as interventions with interactive, appropriate, and accurate sexual health information have been successful in improving teenagers' sexual health knowledge and attitudes.

Moretti, Cremaschini, Brembilla, and Fenili (2015) designed and evaluated a Facebook intervention for 15—18 year olds aimed at increasing STI knowledge. This Facebook intervention was tested in a classroom setting with half the students assigned to the intervention and half assigned acting as a control. The Facebook intervention involved sexual health information delivered on a closed group in Facebook, as well as a private chat. This encouraged the sharing of reliable sexual health information and provided a listening space for teenagers. After 1 month, there was a significant increase in knowledge in the intervention group, but no difference in behaviors.

A recent review of the literature of teenagers' use of social networking sites for sexual health information found both positive and negative implications. It was found that teenagers commonly use technology to access information about sexual health; however, most of the information they found on social networking sites were inaccurate or not age appropriate (Moreno, Standiford, & Cody 2018). (). On the other hand, they found that social media was effective in raising awareness and acceptance of sexual health, as it reduces the stigma of discussing sexual health.

Social networking sites are limited in terms of what content can be shown and promoted on the sites and may not be suitable for all sexual health concerns. Research has also found that in general teenagers are still wary of using social media sites for viewing health-related information (Watella, Rideout, Montague, Beaudoin-Ryan & Lauricella, 2016). Teenagers believe that the Internet is anonymous; however, they do not believe this is the case for social media, as their names can be associated with such information (Divecha, Divney, & Ickovics, 2012). This may indicate that social media may not be the best outlet for attempting to target teenagers with sensitive health information and instead may be better used as a signpost for reaching teenagers and directing them to reliable sexual health information (Table 3.8).

### Text messaging

A large percentage of teenagers use mobile media, with over 87% of youths aged 13—17 years owning a smartphone (Len-Ríos, Streit, & Killoren, 2016). In the United Kingdom 79% of 12—15 year olds owned a phone in 2016, which had gone up from 68% in 2014 (OfCom, 2016). Therefore, this shows that phone usage is rapidly expanding. On average, teenagers (aged 13—17 years) send more than 3300 texts a month; females send significantly more than males at an average of 4050 a month. As more teenagers have access to smartphone technology, the potential to reach this demographic through mobiles has grown.

There are many advantages of using text messaging services to receive sexual health information. Text messaging is fast, and transmitted messages are received almost immediately. It is convenient as text messages can be stored until the recipient is ready to read it, or until the phone is switched on (Lim, Hocking, Hellard, & Aitken, 2008). The cost of sending text messages is also relatively low and messages can be sent to multiple recipients simultaneously. In contrast to emails, text messages have not been extensively overused by spammers and marketing companies, making it a more respected mode of message sending (Muench, Weiss, & Kuerbis, 2013). Teenagers view text messages as more confidential for receiving sexual health information, especially given that mobile phones feel personal to them (Cole-Lewis & Kershaw, 2010). In a qualitative study, it was found that teenagers had not experienced sexual health information through text messaging but were enthusiastic about how this could work and liked the confidentiality of receiving information through text messaging (Selkie & Benson, 2011).

Willoughby and Jr (2013) investigated the types of text messages teenagers send about sexual health information. Questions were about sexual acts (33.9%), unplanned pregnancy (20.2%), contraception (13.7%), physical or sexual development (12.9%), and STIs (10.8%). Willoughby (2015) found that teenagers

---

**TABLE 3.8**
**Summary Points of Social Networking Sites.**

**Summary Points**

- Social networking sites allow for high collaboration and multilevel interaction between users and can be effective for sexual health promotion.

- However, they may not be appropriate for a standalone intervention and work better to signpost teenagers to appropriate information.

- Also, teenagers are wary of using social networking sites for health information as they may not be as anonymous as a website.

who have already had sex, been in a relationship, and low SES teenagers who are less connected to schools are more likely to use text messaging services.

Over the past 5 years there has been further development of sexual health text messaging interventions. In a text messaging intervention for adolescents and young adults (aged 16–29 years) it was found that text messaging was a feasible, popular, and effective way to promote sexual health information (Gold & Pedrana, 2011). Goodwin et al. (2011) evaluated a weekly text messaging intervention aimed at teenagers and young adults (aged 15–20 years) and found that participants enjoyed the informative content of the sexual health text messages. Participants also believed that the intervention was convenient and liked the low cost. Devine, Bull, Dreisbach, and Shlay (2014) evaluated a 4-week text messaging service for 14–18 year olds that covered all aspects of sexual health, and teenagers rated that they enjoyed receiving the messages. Teenagers received on average 11 text messages per week, which they rated as a sufficient amount. However, privacy was a concern with both interventions, and younger adolescents worried about the stigma from peers and worried that they may see the text messages. Teenagers perceive mobile phones as private but when they cannot control when a text message might pop up, for example, when their friends are looking at their phone, this causes anxiety that the sensitive messages may be viewed. Therefore, maintaining discretion is an important consideration in these types of interventions.

Interventions have also combined face-to-face sessions with text messaging. Cornelius and Appiah (2016) evaluated an intervention aimed at teenagers aged 15 years, promoting safe sex and preventing STIs. Participants received seven face-to-face sessions and then daily text messages for 3 months about STIs and contraception (text messages contained messages, pictures, and short videos). Participants believed they benefitted from the intervention and believed the texts were helpful. Buhi, Klinkenberger, and Hughes (2013) evaluated a text messaging intervention aimed at 13–19-year-old teenagers who visited a sexual health clinic. Teenagers preferred text messaging to social networking sites for sexual health information and believed that the text messages made them feel more comfortable attending the sexual health clinic. However, these evaluations are based on specific samples of teenagers who were already sexually active and attending sexual health clinics. This may not be generalizable to teenagers who are just seeking sexual health information before being sexually active.

France (2014) recruited teenagers from two secondary schools to evaluate a larger sample of teenagers who may not have sought sexual health information from external services; 202 teenagers between the ages of 11 and 16 years old were recruited. Teenagers were given a number to text the school nurse, and asked questions about sexual health and relationships (56%), emotional health (25%), physical health (7%), HPV (8%), and healthy eating (5%). This led to a rise of 83% of teenagers knowing about their school nurse, and 70.2% rated the service as a good way to seek help and access face-to-face methods. Teenagers also viewed the text messages as confidential. However, this intervention was time consuming for the school nurses running the program, as they had to respond to multiple text messages, therefore increasing administrative and potentially staff costs. However, it was a good starting point for advertising services and making teenagers feel more comfortable accessing sexual health information.

McGarthy et al. (2018) investigated the use of a text messaging intervention in lower income countries. This involved short daily text messages (on topics including contraception, attitudes to contraception, and reproductive health) delivered over 4 months. It was found that participants' sexual health knowledge and attitudes toward contraception significantly increased after the 4 months. This highlights that a text messaging intervention can be successfully used with low SES populations.

There have been successful sexual health text messaging interventions which have been developed for teenagers; however, there are limitations to these types of interventions. Text messages have a 160-character limit before expanding to an MMS which may not be received due to data limits; therefore, they are more suitable for directing teenagers to other information outlets. With a text message it is not possible to deliver complex or lengthy answers and having to collect phone numbers of teenagers compared to having information on a website is more time consuming. There are also potential privacy and safeguarding issues with collecting young teenagers' phone numbers, as they could be accessed by someone unauthorized to do so. In addition, if teenagers reply to messages, they may disclose sensitive or personal information. As digital technologies advance and grow and smartphones become more popular, it is important for health interventions to keep up-to-date in order to have real-time impact and feasibly target teenagers with the technology and applications that they are using (Table 3.9).

## TABLE 3.9
## Summary Points for Text Messaging Interventions.

**Summary Points**

- Text messaging is fast and received almost immediately, they are convenient as text messages can be stored until the recipient is ready to read it, or until the phone is switched on. It is also low cost and appropriate for low SES teenagers.
- However, there are limits on how much information can be received in a text message and they do not allow for interaction.
- Text messaging may work better alongside an external service or sexual health website, rather than a standalone intervention.

### Sexual health mobile apps

Even though text messaging has been identified as a successful way to target teenagers with sexual health information, it is important to keep up-to date with technology that the group are using in order to be able to reliably reach teenagers. There has been a decline in adolescents using text messaging as adolescents use mobile apps, for example, "WhatsApp," to send text messages instead (Holland, Sastry, Ping, & Knopp, 2014). There have also been apps aimed at teenagers for general health purposes (Buhi et al., 2010).

Mobile apps are different from text messaging and allow for more interaction, as they can constantly be accessed and updated (Apps & Krebs, 2016). While text messaging may be seen as indiscreet, well-designed apps could potentially solve this issue. In a privacy context, users want the ability to personalize settings, therefore apps may be viewed as a more private source (Little & Briggs, 2006). Apps also offer the potential for boosting peer-to-peer sharing of content, information, and interactivity (Levine, 2011). Apps offer a lot of potential because they offer a flexible way to reach a large audience at an affordable cost. This is especially important when working with hard-to-reach populations, such as low SES teenagers. Apps can provide individually tailored and interactive sexual health intervention and promotion that are constantly accessible and allow the user to seek information while maintaining anonymity. This is important as intervention customization and interactivity has been found to be important for effectiveness in behavior change interventions, including those that are technology based (Singh, Gibbs, Estcourt, & Sonnenberg, 2017).

However, there are limited reviews of sexual health apps, and there are no reviews of sexual health apps aimed at teenagers. In two reviews investigating STI prevention apps, Muessig, Pike, and LeGrand (2013) reviewed current sexual health apps aimed at all ages.

Among these apps, 71% provided information about STIs, 36% provided STI testing information or resources, 29% included information about condom use or assistance locating condoms, and 24% promoted information on safe sex. There were only six apps (11%) that covered all four of these prevention areas. In a more recent review, it was found that HIV and STI apps are not fit for purpose and tend to take a one-size-fits-all approach and do not support the breadth and complexity of sexual health (Singh et al., 2017). Therefore, current sexual health apps are lacking in detail and do not address all areas of sexual health.

Gibbs, Gkatzidou, and Tickle (2016) investigated sexual health apps on Google play and iTunes that covered all areas of sexual health for the purpose of seeking sexual health information for all ages. It was found that in general, sexual health apps are difficult to identify, and no apps documented where the information was sourced, so users have no way of assessing the reliability of the app. Only 1 app out of 87 comprised fully comprehensive and accurate information about chlamydia, the United Kingdom's most common STI. Over one-third of the apps comprised errors in more than one aspect of the information. These types of apps could potentially be undermining the benefits of ehealth.

There are also location-based sexual health apps that help teenagers find sexual health services. Steinberg and Griffin-Tomas (2018) reviewed a US-based mobile phone app that allowed users to search for sexual health service providers. Over 3 years it was found that the app was downloaded over 20,000 times, and helped teenagers discover and access a wide range of sexual health services. Therefore, while this study is limited in only investigating how many times the app was downloaded and used and does not provide information on teenagers' thoughts of this type of sexual health app, it does conclude that a location-based app could be useful

**CHAPTER 3** Sexual Health Education in and Outside of Schools **39**

---

**TABLE 3.10**
**Summary Points for Sexual Health Mobile Apps.**

**Summary Points**

- Mobile apps allow for more interaction, and teenagers are familiar with new technology.
- Currently the apps available are lacking reliable information and are difficult to identify
- It is unclear if teenagers would download a sexual health app and how they would determine the app's credibility.

---

in helping adolescents access and discover sexual health services.

More successful apps have concentrated on interactive games. An interactive game approach to RSE with traditional classroom delivery encouraged teenagers and teachers to engage in discussions during and after the game play (Arnab et al., 2013). Another sexual health game through the Facebook app found that teenagers believed the game to be interesting and interactive and close to reality. It was found that this game could significantly increase teenagers' sexual health knowledge (Kwan et al., 2015).

Wood, Wood, and Balaam (2017) designed and evaluated a "sex talk" multiplayer game that aimed to increase the likelihood of adolescents speaking about sex with each other. A total 58 adolescents (aged 13−19 years) took part in evaluating the game over a period of 18 months. The game was successful, and they found that particularly young adolescents (under 16 years) found the game lively, fun, and enjoyed speaking with their peers about sex. This shows that games can be effective in encouraging teenagers to discuss sex.

The evaluations of sexual health apps appear promising although it is not yet known whether teenagers would use these sexual health apps in their own time away from a study or school setting. Reviews of apps in general have found that sexual health apps are currently lacking detailed information, but there have been no reviews on apps specific to teenagers. Given that teenagers are comfortable with mobile apps, improving the currently available suite of sexual health apps to enhance the efficacy of this medium in teenage sexual health promotion seems sensible (Table 3.10).

## Chapter Summary

This chapter has reviewed the literature on UK school-based sexual health education programs, as well as sexual health interventions outside of schools, as school-based sexual health education in the United Kingdom is due to undergo extensive changes and it is not currently known what impact this will have on teenagers' understanding of sexual health. The chapter has also provided a summary on how teenagers use the Internet to search for sexual health information, including the issues and benefits of teenagers using the Internet to search for health information. In addition, it has provided an overview of current online sexual health interventions, including sexual health websites, social networking sites, text messaging, and mobile apps. More work is needed looking at teenagers' views of sexual health apps. Reviews evaluating existing sexual health apps aimed at all ages have found that they do not support the breadth and complexity of sexual health. Further, it is not clear how to assess the reliability of information on sexual health apps.

# CHAPTER 4

# Sexual Health Professional Views of Sexual Health Education

## CHAPTER OUTLINE

Introduction ...............................................................41
Methods .....................................................................42
   Approach.................................................................42
   Participants ............................................................42
   Materials and Procedure ....................................43
   Rank Order Task...................................................44
   Analysis Procedure..............................................44
   The Rank Order Task...........................................45
Results .......................................................................45
   Environment and Family......................................45

Society and Media.................................................46
Peer Influences .....................................................47
Self-esteem............................................................48
Moving Forward With Intervention Programs.....48
Rank Order Task....................................................50
Discussion ................................................................50
   Implications............................................................53
   Chapter Summary.................................................53

## ABSTRACT

This chapter aims to consider sexual health professionals' views of the ways that teenagers seek sexual health information. The chapter is divided into four sections. Section Introduction provides an overview of the literature on how teenagers search for sexual health information. Section Methods describes the method used in this current study, and subsequently Section Results discusses the main results of the interviews with sexual health professionals. The results and implications of the findings are then discussed in Discussion section.

## KEYWORDS

Interviews; Qualitative research; Sexual health; Sexual health education; Sexual health professionals; Teenagers.

## INTRODUCTION

Sexual health professionals are key stakeholders in implementing sexual health interventions (Department of Health, 2013, pp. 1−56). Yet, the perceptions and experiences of healthcare providers are largely absent from the literature. A large systematic review investigating 268 qualitative studies on sexual behavior of

teenagers and young people found most studies have focused on teenagers' views (55%) and parents' views (35%) with only a few studies incorporating sexual health professionals' views (10%) (Marston & King, 2006). There are few UK studies that have investigated healthcare professionals' views of sexual health, particularly around the predictors of risky sexual behaviors (for an exception see Jacobson et al., 2001). Most studies have focused on adolescents' or young parents' attitudes toward healthcare providers (Brown & Wissow., 2009; Freakem Barley & Kent, 2006; Norman, Moffatt & Rankin, 2016). The aim of this study, therefore, is to expand on the limited existing research to explore the views of professionals who specialize in adolescent sexual health issues, taking into account their experience and knowledge in the area.

As described previously in chapter 2, there are a number of predictors of teenagers' sexual risk-taking. Some of the key predictors found in previous research are socioeconomic status (SES), peers, personality traits, self-esteem, parental advice, support, and guidance (Buhi & Goodson, 2007). Most of these predictors have been elicited from research with teenagers themselves, or parents. However, the views of sexual health professionals are largely missing from the research. This is interesting as sexual health professionals are in

---

Teenagers, Sexual Health Information and the Digital Age. https://doi.org/10.1016/B978-0-12-816969-8.00004-7
Copyright © 2020 Elsevier Inc. All rights reserved.

a special and privileged position engaging with adolescents in an in-depth and confidential manner on the topic. GPs and nurses do not proactively address sexual health issues with patients (Gott, Galena, Hinchliff, & Elford, 2004), but sexual health professionals are uniquely able to identify issues around information seeking practices to highlight the barriers to female teenagers seeking sexual health information. Sexual health professionals are defined as professionals who work with any sexual heath or genitourinary medicine (GUM) advice or management (Department of Health, 2013, pp. 1–56). Sexual health professionals may be based in GP surgeries, family planning centers, GUM clinics, pharmacies, and smaller initiatives such as school nurse schemes. These professionals provide advice, knowledge, or treatment on all areas of sexual health, including contraception, relationships, pregnancy, and STIs. Sexual health professionals may also work with pregnant teenagers or teenage mothers. As they listen to the concerns and problems faced by teenagers during their discussions, their experience will provide insight into the factors that in their opinion lead to risky sexual behavior (Table 4.1).

The current study adopted a qualitative method to explore sexual health professionals' perspectives on sexual health information seeking. Furthermore, the study reexamined the predictors of risky sexual behaviors through the lens of the sexual health professionals. This enabled any overlap between the views of sexual

health professionals and those of parents and teenagers to be identified, particularly with respect to sexual health in female teenagers from low SES areas. If we can understand the perceived risk factors and the information seeking barriers from a key stakeholder perspective, then it would provide key information to feed into the development of an intervention program.

Therefore, in this current study we had two aims:

- Firstly, to explore the sexual health information seeking practices and barriers for teenagers from the point of view of sexual health professionals (through the use of semi-structured interviews)
- Secondly, to reexamine the sexual health predictors suggested by previous literature (through the use of a rank order task).

## METHODS
### Approach

A thematic approach was used to analyze the data in this study. The six-phase guide by Braun and Clarke (2006) for analyzing qualitative data was applied to strengthen the findings. This procedure provides researchers with a well-defined explanation of thematic analysis and how to effectively carry it out. Braun and Clarke highlight that it is a useful tool for allowing for social and psychological interpretations of the data.

Thematic analysis allows for theoretical flexibility regarding the level of depth and detail at which the data are analyzed. Thematic analysis allows for a position of essentialism or realism and constructionism, known as contextualist (Braun & Clarke, 2006). When adopting an essentialism or realism approach, motivations, experiences, and meanings can be theorized in a direct way (Braun & Clarke, 2006; Widdicombe & Wooffitt, 1995). This approach effectively allows the exploration of participants' individual experiences related to teenagers' sexual health issues and the meanings they attach to them, while also allowing investigation into the broader role of how societal factors influence sexual health issues.

### Participants

We recruited nine sexual health professionals across the North East of England, using a purposeful sampling method. Participants were from a range of health and associated professions from both the private and public sector which involve provision of sexual health advice, including working with pregnant teenagers and teenage mothers. All participants were required to have at least 1 years' experience working with teenagers. This ensured a sample of professionals who have expertise

| TABLE 4.1 Snapshot of Teenagers Existing Views of Sexual Health. | |
|---|---|
| What is the problem? | There are many predictors of teenage risk-taking and barriers to teenagers seeking sexual health information found in previous literature, yet the views of sexual health professionals are largely missing. |
| Why is this important? | Sexual health professionals are in a unique position to identify issues around information seeking practices to highlight the barriers to female teenagers seeking sexual health information. They regularly speak in a confidential manner about sexual health with a large number of teenagers. |

# CHAPTER 4 Sexual Health Professional Views of Sexual Health Education

in different sexual health issues with teenagers. See Table 4.2 for each participant's professional expertise.

## Materials and Procedure

The study received ethical approval from Northumbria University's Faculty of Health and Life Sciences Ethics Committee prior to the interviews taking place.

The study itself comprised two parts:

1. A semi-structured interview designed to explore the barriers to teenagers seeking sexual health information.
2. A rank order task designed to confirm the perceived predictors (from previous literature) of risky sexual health from a professional's perspective.

An interview schedule was formulated by creating open-ended and semi-structured questions grounded in current literature in order to keep on topic but allowing participants to provide further explanations and discuss their own experiences. A pilot interview with a teacher who works with teenagers was conducted to trial the interview schedule. All questions were deemed relevant to the research question and the timings were appropriate. Example questions on the interview schedule included: *"What are the main sexual health issues that teenagers want to discuss?" and "How do you reach teenage populations with your services?"*

Interviews took place over a 5-month period between December 2014 and April 2015. All of the interviews were carried out either at Northumbria University or a quiet location at the participants' workplace. Participants took part on a voluntary basis. Participants were informed about the confidentiality procedures in place, how their data were to be used, and that they were free to withdraw from the study at any time without explanation. All participants were provided with an information sheet, signed an informed consent form, and fully debriefed at the end of the session. See Fig. 4.1 for an overview of the procedure.

The length of the interviews ranged between 30 and 60 min. All interviews were digitally recorded using an

## TABLE 4.2
## Professional Expertise of Study Participants.

| Participant—Job Title | Years in Job Role | Sexual Health Issues Covered in Job |
|---|---|---|
| **1** - Health improvement specialist for the NHS | 11 years | Trains sexual health workers who work with adolescents. |
| **2** - Sex and relationship outreach worker for the NHS | 5 years | Works with individual and vulnerable teenagers in schools, youth groups, and shelters. |
| **3** - Midwife practitioner for a private pregnancy advisory clinic | 2 years | Deals with pregnancy, terminations, and postoperative care, for women of all ages starting at 13 years. |
| **4** - Client care coordinator for a private pregnancy advisory clinic | 6 years | Works with pregnant teenagers and offers advice and counseling. |
| **5** - Client care coordinator for a private pregnancy advisory clinic | 12 years | Works with pregnant teenagers and offers advice and counseling. |
| **6** - Project worker for an individual charity | 7.5 years | Works with teenagers and young adults aged 12–15 years; they have drop in sessions at their organization for individuals and groups. Covers all sexual health issues. |
| **7** - Volunteer and support worker for a teenage pregnancy team | 3 years | Volunteers with new teenager mothers, from the ages of 13 to 17 years and offers advice and guidance. |
| **8** - Teenage pregnancy and adolescent sexual health coordinator for the NHS | 10 years | Coordinates sexual health and pregnancy services across the North East of England. |
| **9** - Youth and school health worker for an individual charity | 7 years | Visits schools and youth groups offering sexual health services to groups of teenagers. Covers all sexual health issues. |

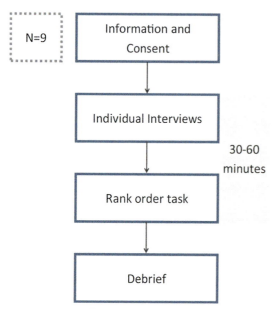

FIG. 4.1 Overview of procedure for study.

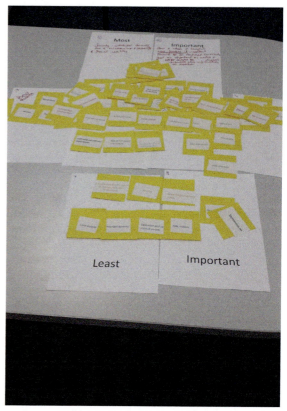

FIG. 4.2 Rank order task example.

Olympus Dictaphone. Questions were open-ended and semi-structured, allowing for flexibility and elaboration by the researcher or the participant. Closed questions were avoided and the researcher summarized back to the participant what had been said. This achieved a two-way dialogue allowing exploration of key themes.

## Rank Order Task

The rank order task comprised a list of 57 factors drawn from the current literature that have been found to predict risky sexual behaviors in teenagers (for example, parents, peers, and self-esteem). Each factor was typed on a small card. Participants were asked to arrange the cards in order from most important to least important in terms of the degree to which they believe that factor predicts risky sexual behaviors in teenagers. Participants were asked to "think aloud" as they completed this task and describe why they were putting the factor in that position. At the end of the task, participants were asked to summarize their choices and discuss whether any factors should be removed from or added to the list. The complete procedure lasted no longer than 90 min. See Fig. 4.2 for an example rank order task.

## Analysis Procedure

Thematic analysis was used to analyze the data. The data collected from all the interviews were transcribed verbatim and initial thoughts and ideas were noted down. The main researcher then familiarized herself with the data by "repeated reading" (Braun & Clarke, 2006). The transcribed data were read and reread several times and the recordings listened to in order to ensure accuracy of the transcription. The second stage was identifying initial codes within the data. These codes were generated by building on the notes and ideas generated through transcription, all of the codes identified features that were relevant to the research question. The third stage involved searching for themes; all initial codes were incorporated into a theme. Codes which were similar or explained the same aspect within the data were incorporated into a theme to explain a larger part of the data. However, to verify final themes, the full research team reviewed the data and by use of constant comparisons agreed on the initial themes. Analysis of the interviews at this stage suggested that no new themes around professionals' perceptions of teenagers' sexual health information seeking practises were emerging. A thematic map was created to visualize the links between the themes and to ensure each theme had enough data to support it (Braun & Clarke, 2006). Coding was repeated to ensure no important codes or information had been missed out at earlier stages. Finally, stage five then involved naming and defining the themes. It was important to have appropriate names for each theme. The final stage of producing the report involved choosing examples of quotes from the transcript to illustrate each theme and to give a good explanation of the point being made.

## The Rank Order Task

We took photos of each of the rank order tasks on the interview day; this allowed us to have a record of each participant's rank order. Using the photos and the think aloud data in the transcripts, each factor was grouped into one of three categories; low importance, medium importance, and high importance. These categories were based on the rating of each factor provided by most participants. To verify final categories the full research team reviewed the data, and by use of constant comparisons, agreed on the ranking of importance.

## RESULTS

The themes are described below, followed by a summary snapshot of each theme. We found five key themes: *"environment and family"*; *"society and media"*; *"peer influences"*; *"Self-esteem"*; and *"moving forward with intervention programs"*. These were viewed as essential to understanding the participant's knowledge and attitudes toward information seeking practices and barriers.

## Environment and Family

Participants discussed that there is a societal perception that low SES female teenagers want to become pregnant before age 16 years. This is not because they do not have sexual health education but because pregnancy is associated with perceived benefits such as social housing. This becomes a barrier to teenagers seeking sexual health information, as this stigma makes teenagers feel that they may be judged if they seek sexual health advice.

*Teenagers, particularly, feel really vulnerable coming in here. Because they don't know whether they are going to be judged and things.*

### (SEX AND RELATIONSHIP OUTREACH WORKER)

The professionals in this study believed teenagers feel that seeking advice will result in being labeled as "wanting to get pregnant". In addition, there are fewer opportunities in lower SES areas, less access to information and intervention programs, and less access to abortion clinics. In some particularly low SES areas teenagers do not have much access to sexual health services, and so they are not sure where to seek information from.

*It's likely they don't have access to, to services, like abortion clinics, sexual health advice because of the area they live in.*

### (MIDWIFE PRACTITIONER)

Family can reinforce this barrier to seeking sexual health information, especially if parents see teenage pregnancies as a norm. Mothers can be excited about their daughters becoming pregnant at a young age, due to norms surrounding teenage pregnancy in some low SES communities. This can lead to an inherent self-fulfilling cycle of teenage mothers that because of family influences can be difficult to break away from.

*Some of the mums bringing along their daughters who were pregnant the mums were delighted. For 16 year olds or younger, they are saying it is marvellous, they are so excited to be a grandma.*

### (TEENAGE PREGNANCY COORDINATOR)

Participants discussed that there can be an expectation and even pressure from some families for their teenagers to have a baby. This is because in some areas it is the norm to have a teenage pregnancy, especially if teenagers do not have the support to aspire and achieve in their own lives. If teenagers do not have any role models that motivate them to have higher aspirations and future plans, then they do not see any benefits or rewards of achieving in their own lives.

*That's environment with little chance of social and economic advancement, poverty and lower socio-economic status. I am going to put it slightly higher, because, we do know that, that does have an impact*

### (SEX AND RELATIONSHIP OUTREACH WORKER)

Participants believe that teens' parents' attitude toward sexual health is important, especially in an environment that has a norm of young pregnancies. Family and environment are therefore interactive; if parents' attitudes are positive, then this can overcome the environment they live in. If they can talk to their parents openly about safe sex, then this can have a big impact on their own attitudes.

*you can come from a very, very poor environment but you can still have very positive messages from your parents or carers, so it kind of links in with these again, if you are getting negative messages it doesn't matter what your address is*

### (PROJECT WORKER)

Thus, parental attitudes can protect against the environment they live in because living in a lower SES area can increase the prevalence of other factors such as negative parenting, norm of young pregnancies, and reduced access to services. However, if these other factors are not present and parental influences and attitudes are positive, then environment on its own does not have a major effect on sexual health decisions. In the same way, teenagers that do not speak openly to their parents about sexual health decisions may be influenced more by their environment. Participants mentioned that many teenagers would not discuss sexual health issues with their parents.

*A lot of the teenagers that come here come without their parent's knowledge, they don't have to have their parents but they do have to have an adult with them, when they come for treatment but that adult doesn't have to be a parent. And we don't have to inform the parents.*

(MIDWIFE PRACTITIONER)

Therefore, sexual health information seeking practices can be affected by environment and family support as the stigma in the environment can lead to teenagers having lower aspirations and motivation to seek sexual health information and advice. Parents can reinforce this stigma or have positive attitudes that can protect against the environment. This theme links onto the next theme of peer influences, as parents can shape teenagers' initial understandings and attitudes of sexual health but if teenagers choose not to talk to parents, then peers can be highly influential (Table 4.3).

## Society and Media

This theme is described by the way that there is a taboo around openly discussing sexual health information, and this causes problems for sexual health workers. Society and the media can heavily impact on adolescents' understanding of sex and relationships. It is difficult for sexual health workers to get access to teenagers because of the taboo in society. This also results in difficulty discussing sexual health information openly and becomes a barrier for teenagers seeking advice, making this group vulnerable and often confused.

*Teenagers think it's a big deal coming here, and that they are not allowed to discuss sex, we have to let them know it's a safe environment*

(VOLUNTEER AND SUPPORT WORKER FOR A TEENAGE PREGNANCY TEAM)

*Sometimes we will go into school once, and do five of the same session that day, maybe like, twice a year or something like that. But we always prefer ones were we can build a relationship and go into the same ones again because society has made teenagers think they can't discuss sex, so we have to build that relationship with the teens first.*

(YOUTH AND SCHOOL HEALTH WORKER FOR AN INDIVIDUAL CHARITY)

Society also views sex differently for males and females, and this double standard can be a confusing concept for teenagers. Participants discussed how this issue could stop teenagers feeling comfortable accessing sexual health information or discussing what a healthy relationship is as there are a lot of unrealistic images and information readily available to teenagers which causes pressure for males and females. There is also still a societal stigma that is reinforced in the media that while pornography is easily available, females will be shamed if they have too many sexual partners, and so they do not want to be seen as seeking sexual health information.

*I think there are equal amounts of pressure on boys and girls about how they look as well. That has a lot of input. There are certain TV shows out there, and of course they can access porn a lot easier these days. We do cover sessions on that as well. So I think there are a lot of unrealistic, images and information, out there to what sex is meant to be and what it is all about. But there is still the double standard of whether a girl actually does anything or not, she is called a slag and then that is it, but it is still ok to have as many partners as they want.*

(HEALTH IMPROVEMENT SPECIALIST)

Yet, even though it is not acceptable to speak openly about sexual health, sex is portrayed widely and negatively in the media. It was clear during the interviews that participants had negative views of the media. Participants became angry and defensive when discussing how sexual health is often portrayed. Participants believe the media normalizes risky sex and objectifies women, which can be confusing for teenagers and ignores information on safe sex. This becomes an issue as teenagers do not have the resources to understand that pornography is fake.

---

**TABLE 4.3**
**Snapshot of Environment and Family Theme.**

**Environment and Family**

- There is a stigma that teenagers from a low SES area have no aspirations and "want" to become pregnant before age 16 years and this stops teens from seeking sexual health advice.
- Positive parental attitudes can be protective against this societal stigma.

# CHAPTER 4 Sexual Health Professional Views of Sexual Health Education 47

*Interestingly I never have to explain that lord of the rings is fake or whatever is playing at the cinema, I never have to explain that is fake, but I am forever explaining that pornography isn't real, and that kind of behaviour is sex for film, it isn't generally an accurate reflection*

**(PROJECT WORKER)**

*it's that whole thing about consent and that, they are not like, the girls might look like they are not agreeing and then they might come around to liking it in porn, so it's kind of like aggressive but then they start enjoying it. That's quite a confusing image for a teenage boy, and I think that causes problems in relationships*

**(CLIENT CARE CO-ORDINATOR)**

Therefore, pornography is easily accessible and can portray negative views of consent and contraception. Teenagers are not equipped to understand that pornography is fake, and consent can be a confusing issue for teenagers to begin with. Pornography violates consent and there is usually not any contraception involved, which can cause confusing images for teenagers. It is worrying that this is easily accessible and more accessed than speaking about safe sexual health because of the taboo in society (Table 4.4).

## Peer Influences

Sexual health professionals discussed that teenagers are most likely to talk to their peers about sex. Because of this, peers become a major influence on teenagers' understandings of sexual health. Participants felt that teenagers are less likely to talk to adults (e.g., parents or teachers) about sex and relationships.

*Your peers, have a massive effect I think. Quite a big influence, especially at that age*

**(SEX AND RELATIONSHIP OUTREACH WORKER)**

Teenagers feel more comfortable talking to their peers about sex and relationships, and seek sexual health advice from their peers. This can be positive as friendships are important to developing teenagers, especially if they need someone to talk to. However, peers are not going to be the most reliable sources of information about sex.

*from peers and stuff like that so, where, where adults might go to more reliable sources of information, children because they don't have that experience to source where is reliable or not are going to maybe the loudest or most popular voice.*

**(PROJECT WORKER)**

This can become an issue if peers provide one another with misinformation. Participants discussed a time that teenagers were scared to have the contraception injection because they believed that it would affect their fertility long-term. Participants discussed that this happens often, where misinformation will be passed around friends, and very quickly it can spread to the whole school, so it is really important that teenagers have access to reliable information sources as well.

*And I said no it's not true, but where they have got that from is the injection is the only contraception which actually delays your fertility, so it doesn't mean that it doesn't come back it just means that it delays it for a bit. So if you want to have a family, it may take you 6 months or a year for your fertility to come back because it is still in their system, So you can see where the kids have got that from can't you, and they think or god I'm not having the injection because that means I can't have a child in the future when I want one.*

**(SEXUAL HEALTH NURSE)**

Peer pressure also led to other risky behaviors, having a bigger peer group may lead to greater peer pressure. This peer pressure may be more influential if having sex at a younger age is seen as normal and expected within the individual's peer and sociocultural group. Therefore, peers can become a barrier to teenagers seeking sexual health advice, as if they believe all their friends are having sex, then this puts pressure on them and makes them feel like they should also be having sex to fit in with their peer group (Table 4.5).

*yeah believing peers have had sex, because that puts pressure on them, more and more.*

**(SEX AND RELATIONSHIP OUTREACH WORKER)**

*I am going to put the believing peers have had sex next to the social norms because it comes up so much*

**(PROJECT WORKER)**

---

**TABLE 4.4**
**Snapshot of Society and Media Theme.**

**Society and Media**

- There is a double standard in society that it is a taboo to discuss safe sex, yet risky sex is widely displayed in the mass media and through pornography.
- This double standard causes confusion for teenagers as they do not want to be seen as seeking sexual health information.

**48**    Teenagers, Sexual Health Information and the Digital Age

---

**TABLE 4.5**
**Snapshot of Peer Influences Theme.**

**Peer Influences**

- Teenagers are more likely to talk to their friends about sex than anyone else.
- This can be a problem as teenagers often get their sexual health information from unreliable sources.
- Peer pressure is a huge issue, as teenagers want to fit in with their peer group and often believe all their friends are having sex.

---

## Self-esteem

Self-esteem is defined by the way participants expressed that seeking sexual health information is dependent on the individual person, including their self-esteem, self-standards, personality, self-resilience, self-regulation, attitudes, beliefs, and self-efficacy. The influence of the other themes is all dependent on these aspects of the self. If a person's self-esteem is low, then they may look to heighten their self-esteem in other ways, which often involves risky sex.

*For girls who have low self-esteem, I think they look to heighten their self-esteem in so many different ways, and it can just lead to like, not good judgements really, you can end up doing things that are not, I just think it is such a shame*

**(SUPPORT WORKER FOR TEENAGE PREGNANCY)**

Participants believe that self-esteem is highly important; low self-esteem will influence aspirations leading to more risky sexual behaviors. In addition, a person with higher self-esteem will be more likely to seek sexual health information and have the confidence to use the information.

*It's all due to self-esteem. Sometimes it works like that, sometimes it does give them the push*

**(SUPPORT WORKER)**

This links in with friends as participants mentioned that teenagers who do not have many friends to talk to can become isolated and this becomes a barrier to them seeking sexual health advice. Participants mentioned that a lot of pregnant teenagers feel they do not have anyone to speak to and this stopped them seeking sexual health advice before they became pregnant.

*we get a lot of pregnant girls who have been in who have felt that they do not have any friends and they are being bullied, stuff like that*

**(CLIENT CARE CO-ORDINATOR)**

Thus, self-esteem and personality traits are very important to risky sexual behaviors. Sexual health professionals believe that it is important that teenagers have strong self-esteem to be able to make their own informed decisions. For example, if a teenage girl has higher self-esteem she may feel more confident in seeking sexual health advice, and speaking to adults about sex. Therefore, while all the themes are important, participants believed that it all comes back to a person's individual self-esteem (Table 4.6).

## Moving Forward With Intervention Programs

Professionals highlighted the idea that sexual health education needs to focus on a more holistic view of sexual health. Professionals believe that the majority of sexual health education focuses on pregnancy and STI prevention and does not provide an overview of the other parts of sexual health, such as relationships. There is still a stigma around sexual health and in particular unplanned pregnancies and STIs, and because of this, it is this information that is targeted at teenagers.

*They get so much information about, well don't get pregnant, don't get an STI, but they don't get a lot about what actually, you know having a good relationship with somebody*

**(SEX AND RELATIONSHIP OUTREACH WORKER)**

---

**TABLE 4.6**
**Snapshot of Self-esteem Theme.**

**Self-esteem**

- Seeking sexual health information is dependent on the individual person.
- It is important to build teenagers' self-esteem so that they feel confident in seeking sexual health information and making their own informed decisions.

*I mean pregnancy is obviously a big thing, because it can cause at that age, it's not ideal for them or, and in some cases, obviously everyone is different but I think STI's is really, really, not talked about enough, because I don't think they have the education to know what it involves. Cause I think it is just, you know, the fact that there are life treating ones they are just brushed over, or they think it will never happen to me. I think there needs to be a lot more, maybe even in schools, just talking about it.*

**(PROJECT WORKER)**

This need for a more holistic view of sexual health was further emphasized by the current inconsistencies in sexual health education. Professionals explained that some schools do currently offer an extensive holistic sexual health service to teenagers; however, not all schools currently do this, and may only provide a brief talk on pregnancy and STIs. While school sexual health education programs are so varied, it is impossible to ensure that all teenagers have access to vital sexual health information.

*and relationship education is very variable and patchy, some schools deliver it brilliantly and it's part of the time table on a regular basis all young people through the school there is a whole, kind of, it's not just taught in year 9 for an hour on a Wednesday afternoon, once. And that's it. There is a more holistic approach, where sexual health is looked at holistically, they look at relationships, they look at consent, they look at pornography, values, whereas some schools might just have a brief talk on STI's and pregnancy and contraception or condoms, and that's it. And if you weren't in that week it's too bad. Or they will get a school nurse in to do some. So that's very variable and that is a massive issue.*

**(CLIENT CARE CO-ORDINATOR)**

Also, professionals highlighted that a lot of sexual health education programs are outdated, and do not focus on issues in the modern world. The ease of access of the Internet and pornography are important and teenagers need education on digital sexual health issues. A lot of schools are not having conversations about pornography.

*I think there is a massive lack of interventions, that cover these factors, and I don't think schools are talking about thinks like porn and consent, and understanding consent.*

**(SUPPORT WORKER)**

These interventions also need to be age appropriate, and the timing of the information is important. Teenagers need to start learning about sexual health before they start becoming sexually active, but this information needs to be age appropriate. For example, teenagers could start learning about relationships, including friendships and then romantic relationships. This could then move onto more sexual health issues; this could break down any stigma and negativity around what sexual health issues are appropriate to discuss.

*think as soon as they start having sexual, you know the sexual talks at the school talking about sex, I think it should definitely be involved straight away, as it is a big deal you know.*

**(PROJECT WORKER)**

*well it all has to be age appropriate, obviously, and we do know that there are a lot of young people having sex, very young, so I think well gosh, I think the parents should be taught about it just as much as the young people, so we can hopefully break the cycle of any negativity and attitudes and beliefs around it. I would say from 12 up over, easily. But then again it would have to be very much age appropriate, because you could have a mixture of young people in that class, you could have some very mature 12 year olds and some very immature 12 year olds. And I think it's just changing attitudes towards sexual health, and if the government just put it on the national curriculum, and they actually taught it and felt it was just as important as maths and English then we would get somewhere.*

**(SEX AND RELATIONSHIP OUTREACH WORKER)**

However, as well as having age-appropriate programs, sexual health professionals highlight that because there is already this negative family cycle that exists, it is important that parents are included in sexual health programs as well. The cycle of parents not speaking about sexual health and having negative attitudes and beliefs toward young people having sex will not change unless parents are also included in sexual health education (Table 4.7).

*and we do know that there are a lot of young people having sex, very young, so I think well gosh, I think the parents should be taught about it just as much as the young people, so we can hopefully break the cycle of any negativity and attitudes and beliefs around it*

**(HEALTH IMPROVEMENT SPECIALIST)**

---

**TABLE 4.7**
**Snapshot of Moving Forward With Intervention Program Theme.**

**Moving Forward with Intervention Programs**

- Sexual health education should provide a comprehensive and holistic view.
- This information should be taught at a younger age when teenagers are starting to think about sex, but should be age appropriate.

## Rank Order Task

Fifty-seven predictors that were drawn from the literature were rated during the rank order task. Professionals did not remove any of the factors but did add two extra predictors to the list: consent and pornography. The factors were split into three categories: high importance factors, medium importance factors, and low importance factors. Table 4.8 shows that 32 predictors out of the original 57 were perceived as highly important.

As shown in Tables 4.9 and 4.10 participants ranked 32 of the 57 factors as highly important in predicting risky sexual behaviors for female teenagers. These core findings are important, as most of these factors have previously been found in teenager and parent studies; however, it is important to know that sexual health professionals who are implementing interventions also perceive these factors as important. Therefore, this confirmation of factors endorses the fact that these high importance factors should be taken into consideration during intervention programs. This rank order task also highlights the importance of self-esteem.

Sexual health professionals believed that self-esteem is one of the most important factors that can predict risky sexual behaviors.

As shown in Table 4.9, 30 factors were rated as medium important and 6 factors were rated as low importance. These are still seen as important in predicting risky sexual behaviors as professionals noted that they could not disregard any of these factors. However, while they have some degree of importance in predicting risky sexual behaviors in terms of implementing these factors in intervention programs, they are not perceived as important as the higher rated factors.

## DISCUSSION

This study explored sexual health professionals' perceptions of the factors they believe predict risky sexual behaviors for teenagers and barriers to teenagers' sexual health information seeking. Professionals believed that teenagers are not being targeted with reliable sexual health information that covers everything that teenagers need and want to know. Sexual health intervention

### TABLE 4.8
### Factors Rated as High Importance.

| High Importance Factors | Previous Literature | Behavior |
| --- | --- | --- |
| Self-esteem | (Buhi & Goodson, 2007) | Systematic reviews have found mixed findings of self-esteem and sexual behavior/ attitudes and intentions. |
| Belief in the future | (Gavin, Catalano, David-Ferdon, Gloppen, and Markham (2010) | Females who have no aspirations have earlier sexual initiation. |
| Pornography | (Owens, Behun, Manning, & Reid, 2012) | Higher permissive sexual attitudes, more casual sex, and greater occurrence of sexual intercourse. |
| Media | (Brown, L'Engle, Pardun, & Guo, 2006) | Females who see more sex in the media have more permissive sexual attitudes. |
| Consent | (Hlavka, 2014) | Females who do not understand consent have earlier sexual initiation. |
| Alcohol | (Hipwell, Keenan, Loeber, & Battista, 2010) | Alcohol use is significantly related to a higher number of partners and higher incidents of unprotected sex. |
| Drug use | (Hipwell et al., 2010) | Drug use is significantly correlated with a higher number of partners and higher incidents of unprotected sex. |
| Conforming to peer norms | (Skinner, Smith, Fenwick, Fyfe, & Hendriks, 2008) | Significantly higher intention to have sex. |
| Self-efficacy | (Sionéan et al., 2002) | Significantly earlier sexual initiation. |
| Knowledge | (Wight & Fullerton, 2013) | Earlier sexual initiation. |
| Age of partner | (Vanoss Marín et al., 2000) | Having an older partner leads to significantly earlier sexual initiation. |

# CHAPTER 4 Sexual Health Professional Views of Sexual Health Education

**TABLE 4.8**
**Factors Rated as High Importance.—cont'd**

| High Importance Factors | Previous Literature | Behavior |
|---|---|---|
| Low aspirations | (Pearson, Child, & Carmon, 2011) | Earlier sexual behavior. |
| Body image | (Valle et al., 2009) | Inconsistent condom use. |
| Social norms | (Skinner et al., 2009) | Intention to have sex. |
| Not seeing the long-term implications | (Rothspan & Read, 1996) | Systematic reviews have found not seeing the long-term implications is related to higher accounts of teen pregnancy and STIs. |
| No direction | (Buhi & Goodson, 2007) | Teen pregnancy and higher amounts of STIs. |
| Self-standards | (Dilorio, Dudley, Soet, Watkins, & Maibach, 2000) | Teen pregnancy and higher amounts of STIs. |
| Believing peers have had sex | (Gillmore et al., 2002) | Earlier sexual initiation and higher number of sexual partners. |
| Depression | (Skinner, Robinson, Smith, Chenoa, & Robbins, 2015) | Higher frequency of having sex, higher number of partners, and more alcohol and drug use. |
| Peers' approval of sex | (Santelli, Abma, et al., 2004) | Earlier sexual initiation and higher number of sexual partners. |
| Coercion from sexual partners | (Skinner et al., 2008) | Intention to have sex. |
| Connectedness | (Markham et al., 2010) | Protective against sexual risk-taking. |
| Beliefs and attitudes toward sex | (Sieverding, Adler, Witt, & Ellen, 2005) | Positive beliefs related with less sexual initiation. |
| Personality | (Hoyle, Fejfar, & Miller, 2000) | Big five related to higher number of sexual partners and more unprotected sex. |
| Low school aspirations and performance | (Pearson et al., 2011) | Earlier sexual initiation. |
| Peers | (Hlavka, 2014) | Earlier sexual initiation. |
| Peer pressure | (Hlavka, 2014) | Earlier sexual initiation. |
| Spontaneous sex | (Buhi & Goodson, 2007a) | Inconsistent condom use. |
| Peer communication | (Busse, Fishbein, Bleakley, & Hennessy, 2010) | Higher intention to have sex. |
| Social support | (Valle et al., 2009) | Lower social support correlated with higher likelihood of STIs. |
| Self-determination | (Gavin et al., 2010) | High self-determination correlated with less teen pregnancy and STIs. |
| More egocentric thinking | (Catania et al., 1989) | Earlier sexual initiation. |

programs should include information on digital world issues such as pornography and sexting, so that teens are able to discuss these topics with reliable sources in an open manner. A double standard in society was also highlighted; safe sexual health is not discussed, yet risky sexual health widely displayed in the mass media prevents teenagers seeking safe sexual health information. Pornography is easily accessible (Owens et al., 2012; Ybarra & Mitchell, 2005), and presents a very unrealistic and potentially harmful resource regarding sexual health information (Martellozzo, Monaghan, Adler, Davids & Horvath, 2016). It is

## TABLE 4.9
## Factors Rated as Medium Importance.

| Medium Importance Factors | Previous Literature | Behavior |
|---|---|---|
| Sexual abuse | (Valle et al., 2009) | Earlier sexual behavior. |
| Role models | (Guilamo-Ramos et al., 2012a, 2012b) | Negative role models correlated with age at first intercourse. |
| Fatalism | (Rothspan & Read, 1996) | Intention to have sex. |
| Poor self-regulating | (Raffaelli & Crockett, 2003) | Greater number of sexual partners. |
| Lack of awareness | (Buhi & Goodson, 2007) | Earlier sexual behaviors and inconsistent condom use. |
| Family support | (Wight & Fullerton, 2013) | Earlier sexual intercourse. |
| Parental influences and monitoring | (Skinner et al., 2008) | Knowledge and behavior improved after parental interventions. |
| Negative parenting | (Guilamo-Ramos, Bouris, Lee, McCarthy, Michael,, Pitt-Barnes, & Dittus, 2012) | Age at first intercourse. |
| Boredom | (Buhi & Goodson, 2007) | Earlier sexual behaviors. |
| Poverty | (Catania et al., 1989) | Earlier sexual behaviors. |
| Age of first sexual intercourse | (Manning, Longmore, & Giordano, 1995) | Higher number of partners and STIs. |
| Lower socioeconomic status | (Catania et al., 1989) | Earlier intercourse. |
| Time spent alone at home | (Resnicow et al., 2001) | Earlier sexual behaviors. |
| Intention or motivation to have sex | (Gillmore et al., 2002) | Earlier sexual behaviors. |
| Early physical intimacy experiences | (Pearson et al., 2011) | Higher number of teen pregnancy and STIs. |
| Age of puberty | (De Genna et al., 2011) | Earlier sexual behavior and unplanned pregnancies. |
| Education and social class of parent | (Manning et al., 1995) | Age at first intercourse and higher number of partners. |
| Environment with no chance of social and economic advancement | (Duncan, Duncan, Biglan, & Ary, 1998) | Age at first intercourse and higher number of partners. |

## TABLE 4.10
## Factors Rated as Low Importance.

| Low Importance Factors | Supported by Previous Literature | Behavior |
|---|---|---|
| Low awareness of contraception | (Lader, 2009) | Higher number of STIs. |
| Parental attitudes toward sex | (Dittus & Jaccard, 2000) | Negative attitudes correlated with earlier sexual intercourse and inconsistent condom use. |
| Younger parents | (Manning et al., 1995) | Higher number of sexual partners. |
| Love of babies | (Fedorowicz, Hellerstedt, Schreiner, & Bolland, 2014) | Teen pregnancy and earlier sexual intercourse. |
| Lone parents | (Guilamo-Ramos et al., 2012a, 2012b) | Earlier age at first intercourse. |

# CHAPTER 4 Sexual Health Professional Views of Sexual Health Education

known that large numbers of young people are accessing pornography (Adler & Livingstone, 2015, pp. 1–34); however, it is less clear as to whether teenagers are regularly accessing safe and reliable sexual health information. The participants in this study do not believe that teenagers are being targeted with the information that they need to know.

Peers, environment, and family were also discussed as barriers to teenagers seeking sexual health information. Family influences are well established in the literature; female teenagers from low SES areas are more likely to become pregnant during their teenage years, especially those with a sister or mother who became parents during their teens (East, Reyes, & Horn, 2007; Karakiewicz et al., 2008). This current study has added that teenagers can feel stigmatized and are reluctant to seek sexual health information, in case they are seen as "wanting" to become pregnant. This becomes an issue for both male and female teenagers, as all teenagers need to be able to access reliable sexual health information. Interestingly, professionals highlighted that a teenage pregnancy can be normal and expected, and in some cases even encouraged. This presents a potential conflict for teenagers and can make it difficult for them to seek alternative, safe sex information. It is important that sexual health intervention programs also include information for parents. If parents have negative attitudes toward sexual health, then this will influence teenagers' sexual health views. Peers are also a huge influence on teen's views of sexual health; in early adolescence, individuals start to emotionally separate from their parents and form strong peer identification (Viner & Macfarlane, 2005). Peer-to-peer resources are seen as an increasingly important aspect of health information and communication (Ziebland & Wyke, 2012). Thus, incorporating accurate, credible peer-to-peer resources into intervention programs could thus provide a powerful tool for increasing safe sex knowledge and intention.

One of the most important barriers to teenagers seeking sexual health information was self-esteem. Teenagers need to have high self-esteem and confidence to seek reliable sexual health advice. Low self-esteem was identified in the rank order task as a strong perceived risk factor for risky sexual behaviors. Self-esteem has provided a mixed picture in previous research; systematic reviews have found no evidence for self-esteem as a statistical predictor of sexual behaviors, attitudes, or intentions (Goodson, Buhi, & Dunsmore, 2006). Whereas, in longitudinal research, it has been found that self-esteem predicts risky behavior (Donnellan & Trzesniewski, 2005). However, this may reflect the complex nature of self-esteem development, which is known to interact with SES background, family, and individual characteristics (Boden & Horwood, 2006). In early adolescence self-esteem is still developing, peer interest is strong, and health risk behaviors such as sexual risk-taking and alcohol use behaviors begin to emerge (Viner & Macfarlane, 2005). As previously mentioned, self-esteem development in adolescents occurs among a myriad of other intrapersonal characteristics, which can make its detection as a risk factor in quantitative studies difficult. This current study indicates the importance that sexual health professionals place on this key risk factor, which suggests that future intervention programs would benefit from focusing on improving self-esteem, despite a lack of quantitative evidence to support self-esteem as a significant predictor of sexual behaviors. We know that knowledge-based interventions on their own are not effective (Campbell et al., 2000), but there is scope for combined self-esteem and knowledge interventions. Teenagers may know about the importance of condom use; however, they also need the confidence to insist their partner actually uses a condom.

## Implications

Peers were a main influence on adolescent sexual health information seeking decisions; therefore, sexual health intervention strategies should try to incorporate accurate, reliable information delivered via a peer channel (for example, videos in which teenagers discuss safe sexual health practices). In addition, intervention programs that aim to develop teen's sexual health knowledge should also aim to build self-esteem so adolescents feel confident to make their own informed sexual health decisions. Teenagers need intervention programs that provide a combination of self-esteem and sexual health information.

## Chapter Summary

This chapter described a qualitative study designed to explore sexual health information seeking practices and barriers for female teenagers from the point of view of sexual health professionals and to reexamine the sexual health predictors suggested by previous literature. The focus on sexual health professionals was deemed relevant given their position as key stakeholders in implementing sexual health interventions, yet their views are largely absent from the literature. The barriers identified were "society and media", "environment and family", "peer influences", and "the self". In terms of the sexual health predictors, sexual health professionals ranked 33 of the 57 identified predictors as highly important, agreeing with previous research. Some of the barriers identified were consistent with previous research while others were particularly novel. Interestingly, sexual health professionals identify self-esteem as a highly important factor influencing teenagers' likelihood to seek sexual health information, while also being an important predictor of risky sexual behaviors. Yet, limited evidence for self-esteem has been found in previous quantitative studies. This suggests that going forward sexual health interventions that build self-esteem and address socioeconomic stigma may encourage adolescents to feel confident to make their own informed sexual health decisions.

In the next chapter, we provide an overview of the ethical considerations when conducting sexual health research with teenagers. We explore existing ethical guidelines and how these can be applied to teenage populations, and reflect on some of the ethical issues we encountered in our own studies. The ethical considerations that we discuss in this chapter are what we used as ethical guidelines in our studies with teenagers discussed in Chapters 6,7, 8, and 10.

# CHAPTER 5

# Ethical Issues When Researching Sexual Health With Teenagers

## CHAPTER OUTLINE

A Brief Background to the Importance of
Ethics..................................................................55
Existing Ethical Guidelines ...................................56
   Ethical Guidelines for Child Research...............56
   General Data Protection Regulation ..................63
   Guidance on Teenagers and GDPR...................63
Lessons from Our Own Research Projects.........64
   Seeking Legal Guidance....................................64
   Gaining Consent ................................................65

   *Offline consent* .......................................65
   *Online consent*.......................................66
Reflections and Guidance ....................................67
   Recruiting Teenagers.........................................67
   Explaining Ethics and Gaining Consent..............67
   Parental Consent ..............................................67
   Chapter Summary..............................................68

## ABSTRACT

This chapter aims to consider the importance of ethical issues when conducting sexual health research with teenagers. The chapter is divided into four sections. Section A Brief Background to the Importance of Ethics discusses the importance and background of ethics. Section Existing Ethical Guidelines considers existing ethical guidelines, and Section Lessons from Our Own Research Projects provides a consideration of our own personal experiences of the ethical issues encountered in sexual health research. Section Reflections and Guidance draws the key issues together and provides guidance on how to implement ethical procedures when researching sexual health with teenagers.

## KEYWORDS

Digital health interventions; Ethical issues; Ethics; Ethics in research; Online sexual health interventions; School-based sexual health education; Sexual health; Sexual health education; Sexual health interventions; Teenagers.

## A BRIEF BACKGROUND TO THE IMPORTANCE OF ETHICS

Why are ethical standards important in research? Research ethics provide guidelines for the responsible conduct of research to ensure all research is conducted at a high ethical standard. This is especially important in relation to research with teenagers as those under

the age of 18 years are deemed as vulnerable members of society, and special considerations of consent, understanding of the research, and anonymity are often legal, as well as moral, requirements.

> *… Our primary obligation is always to the people we study, not to our project or to a larger discipline. The lives and stories that we hear and study are given to us under a promise, that promise being that we protect those who have shared them with us.*
>
> (DENZIN, 1989:83)

As Denzin (1989) suggests, any researcher's obligation is to their participants, and ensuring that they do not suffer any psychological harm or discomfort. A consideration of ethical standards should always be a critical part of the planning, design, and conduct of the research process. This consideration will help the researcher to fully understand what moral principles guide the research, the researcher's responsibility to the participants, and how the research will benefit those who participated in their study. Research should be conducted safely and meet agreed principles, standards, and codes of practice. Research should also produce knowledge, which benefits participants and society and deepens academic understanding of the subject area. Consequently, ethics should be fully considered from the planning stages to ensure moral, strong, and ethically sound research is being conducted.

Up-to-date research ethics began with a desire to protect human subjects involved in research projects.

Teenagers, Sexual Health Information and the Digital Age. https://doi.org/10.1016/B978-0-12-816969-8.00005-9
Copyright © 2020 Elsevier Inc. All rights reserved.

There is a set of laws for defining good medical practice and morals, the Hippocratic oath; however, there is currently no such oath for scientists. One of the first guidelines for good ethical practice began during the doctors' trial of 1946–47. The doctor' trials were a segment of the Nuremberg trials for Nazi war criminals. In the trial, 23 German Nazi physicians were accused of torturous experiments, including exposing participants to extreme temperatures and altitudes. As a result, the "Nuremberg code" was created consisting of 10 guidelines (Nuremberg code, 1949):

1. Participants must give their voluntary consent for research participation.
2. The aims of the research study should benefit society.
3. Research studies must be based on prior animal testing and sound theory.
4. Researchers must avoid all unnecessary physical and mental suffering.
5. If serious injury and/or death to human participants are potential outcomes, then the research project cannot go forward.
6. The degree of risk to research participants cannot exceed predicted benefits of results.
7. Appropriate environment and protection for research participants is necessary.
8. Experiments must only be conducted by a qualified person.
9. Human subjects have the right to withdraw from their participation at any time.
10. If there is cause to believe that the research project will be harmful or result in injury or death, the project must be terminated.

This code led to the Helsinki declaration. The Declaration of Helsinki was adopted in 1964 by the World Medical Association, an asset of ethical principles covering human experimentation. The key ethical articles are (Goodyear, Krleza-Jeric & Lemmens, 2007) as follows (Table 5.1):

- Respect for the individual (Article 8)
- The right to self-determination and the right to make informed decisions (Articles 20–22).
- The duty of the researcher is toward the patient or the volunteer (Articles 2, 3, 10, 16, 18).
- The welfare of the participant must always take precedence over the research (Article 9).
- Individuals or groups who are deemed to be "vulnerable" require special vigilance (Article 8).
- Even if consent is granted by someone else legally permitted to give it, the individual must still give their assent (Article 25).

These ethical guidelines were the first set of guidelines put in place specifically to protect research participants. These provide the basis for leading to current ethical guidelines that are used by researchers. An overview of two existing guidelines that we have used in our research is discussed in the following section.

## EXISTING ETHICAL GUIDELINES

As Psychologists working in the United Kingdom, we follow the British Psychological Society's (BPS) ethical principles. These are strict codes of ethics practice, and the BPS is regarded as a prominent authority on ethical guidelines involving human participants for the social and behavioral sciences. These ethical principles cover four main areas: respect, competence, responsibility, and integrity. The BPS Code of Conduct (2018) provides guidelines, and therefore the language used is "should" rather than "must" and suggests that researchers reinforce the advisory nature of the code as a framework in support of professional judgment. The code has been written to guide researchers and not to punish. The four principles are set out in Table 5.2. We have taken the principles and detailed below how they can be applied to research involving teenagers. This is also shown in Table 5.2.

### Ethical Guidelines for Child Research

Another useful set of guidelines for research with teenagers is the Society for Research in Child Development, which has outlined 16 principles of ethical standards in research (SRCD Governing council, 2007). In these principles, children are defined as anyone under the age of 18 years, and therefore, covers research with teenagers. These are similar to the BPS Code of Ethics and Conduct and are summarized in Table 5.3. Once again,

| TABLE 5.1 Snapshot of Why Ethics are Important. | |
| --- | --- |
| | **Ethical Considerations** |
| What are ethics? | Research ethics provides guidelines for the responsible conduct of research to ensure all research is conducted at a high ethical standard. |
| Importance to teenagers? | Ethics are there to protect research participants, those under the age of 18 years are deemed as vulnerable members of society and special considerations of consent, understanding of the research, and anonymity are often legal, if not moral, requirements. |

**CHAPTER 5** Ethical Issues When Researching Sexual Health With Teenagers

**TABLE 5.2**
**BPS Codes of Conduct Guidelines and How These Can Be Applied to Teenagers.**

| | Definition | Main Principles | Applying to Teens |
|---|---|---|---|
| Respect | "Respect for the dignity of persons and peoples is one of the most fundamental and universal ethical principles across geographical and cultural boundaries, and across professional disciplines. It provides the philosophical foundation for many of the other ethical Principles. Respect for dignity recognises the inherent worth of all human beings, regardless of perceived or real differences in social status, ethnic origin, gender, capacities, or any other such group-based characteristics. This inherent worth means that all human beings are worthy of equal moral consideration." (BPS Codes of Ethics and Conduct, 2018: p5). | Researchers must think about participants' privacy and confidentiality and value the dignity and worth of all persons. | • Researchers need to ensure teens, parents, and teachers are given sufficient information and time to understand their research participation. All information must be kept securely and confidentially.<br>• Researchers must comply with the requests of participants who are withdrawing from research. If a teenager withdraws from the research, it must be managed carefully. If the research is taking place at an organization (for example, a school), the researcher should arrange with the teachers for a space to be provided for any teenagers who decide to withdraw during the study and an alternative activity should be arranged for teenagers, until the other participants have completed their participation. |
| Competence | "Psychologists, whether academic, practitioner or in training, may offer a range of services that usually require specialist knowledge, training, skill and experience. Competence refers to their ability to provide those specific services to a requisite professional standard. A psychologist should not provide professional services that are outside their areas of knowledge, skill, training and experience." (BPS Codes of Ethics and Conduct, 2018: p6). | Researchers value the continuing development and maintenance of high standards of competence in their own work and understand their own limits of their knowledge, skill, training, education, and experience. | • Researchers should recognize that ethical dilemmas will inevitably arise in the course of professional practice and attempt to resolve such dilemmas with the appropriate combination of reflection, supervision, and consultation.<br>• In order to do this researchers should be committed to the requirements of the code of practise they are following, and check they are up-to-date with the current versions. Once researchers have reflected on any ethical dilemmas (preferably as part of a research team), they should seek peer review to ensure they have fully considered the ethical dilemmas and attempted to resolve them. Researchers should be able to justify any action on ethical ground while meeting ethical principles and legal requirements (for example, safeguarding). Safeguarding is a term that is broader than "child protection" and relates to the action of promoting welfare of children and teenagers and protecting them from harm. |

*Continued*

## TABLE 5.2
### BPS Codes of Conduct Guidelines and How These Can Be Applied to Teenagers.—cont'd

| | Definition | Main Principles | Applying to Teens |
|---|---|---|---|
| Responsibility | *"Because of their acknowledged expertise, Psychologists enjoy professional autonomy; responsibility is an essential element of autonomy. Psychologists must accept appropriate responsibility for what is within their power, control or management. Awareness of responsibility ensures that the trust of others is not abused, the power of influence is properly managed and that duty towards others is always paramount."* (BPS Codes of Ethics and Conduct, 2018: p6). | Psychologists value their responsibilities to people, and to their profession, including the avoidance of harm and the prevention of misuse or abuse of their contribution to society. | • Researchers should consider all research from the standpoint of the research participants, for the purpose of eliminating potential risks to psychological well-being, physical health, personal values, or dignity. All procedures should be risk assessed and health and safety checked. However, an issue that is not immediately obvious is psychological well-being of the participant. For example, teenagers' well-being may be affected by becoming embarrassing or feeling "uncool" in front of their peers. This is an issue which is not often considered or noticed by adults, yet it may be extremely important to participants.<br>• Participants should be debriefed at the conclusion of their participation; this should include informing them of the outcomes and nature of the research and identifying any unforeseen harm, discomfort, or misconceptions. Researchers should take particular care when discussing outcomes with research participants, as seemingly evaluative statements may carry unintended weight. They also need to phrase the debrief in a teen-centric way, making sure all specialist language is adequately explained. |
| Integrity | *"Acting with integrity includes being honest, truthful, accurate and consistent in one's actions, words, decisions, methods and outcomes. It requires setting self-interest to one side and being objective and open to challenge in one's behaviour in a professional context."* (BPS Codes of Ethics and Conduct, 2018: p7). | Researchers value honesty, probity, accuracy, clarity, and fairness in their interactions with all people, and seek to promote integrity in all facets of their scientific and professional actions. | • Researchers must be honest and accurate in representing their professional affiliations and qualifications, including knowledge, skill, training, education, and experience. For example, if a researcher is developing an app for forum support for teenage pregnancy, participants should be informed right at the beginning of the research within both the written information and verbally if the researcher is not an expert in pregnancy so that participants do not gain unrealistic expectations or ask questions that the researcher could not answer. |

TABLE 5.3

**The 16 Principles of Ethical Standards in Research and How They can be Applied to Teenagers.**

| Principle | Main Principles | How It Can be Achieved |
|---|---|---|
| 1. Nonharmful procedures | The child should not be harmed psychologically or physically by the research procedure. | • All procedures should be piloted with participants who are knowledgeable of teenagers' capabilities (e.g., teachers) and risk assessed.<br>• Consultations should be sought from others who have knowledge of the procedures. |
| 2. Informed consent | The child should show some form of agreement to participate in the research. | • Teenagers should be informed in simplistic language of all tasks and requirements of the research, before the research begins.<br>• Teenagers should have the chance to ask questions and questions should be appropriately answered.<br>• Teenagers should have freedom to take part and to withdraw at any point during the research without prejudice or reason.<br>• If consent cannot be sought, because it would make the research impossible to carry out, then the research should be ethically suitable and participant's anonymity protected. Judgments on this should be made with an institutional review board. |
| 3. Parental consent | The informed consent of parents, legal guardians, or those who act in loco parentis (e.g., teachers, superintendents of institutions) should be obtained, if possible in writing. | • Parents or caregivers should be fully informed of the research and given the chance to ask the researcher questions.<br>• If parents/carers refuse to consent, then their decision should be respected. Parents and carers should be reminded that they can withdraw at any time without any penalty to them or their child.<br>• Two methods of parental consent are usually sought, either opt-in, where parents give permission for their child to take part in the research, or opt-out, where parents inform the researcher if they do not want their child to take part in the research. Opt-out consent is suitable when working with an organization that can give consent for the opt-out procedure (for example, a school). Whereas, opt-in consent is most suitable for sensitive research topics or tasks and when recruiting participants from the general population or recruiting through parents. |
| 4. Additional consent | The informed consent of any persons, (e.g., teachers) whose interaction with the child is the subject of the study should also be obtained. | • Any teachers who will be involved in the research should be fully informed of all features of the research and have the chance to ask questions.<br>• Teachers should be reminded that they are free to withdraw themselves or their pupils from the research at any time without giving a reason.<br>• Written permission should be gained from the school if recruiting teenagers from a school, normally from the head teacher. |
| 5. Incentives | Incentives to participate in a research project must be fair and must not exceed the range of incentives that a child normally experiences. | • Incentives must be considered early in the research stage, be age appropriate, and separate from parental incentives. If there are any invasive or additional burdens on the child, then the incentive should be increased but incentives should not be coercive (Rice & Broome, 2004). Incentives could be considered coercive as they are influencing the participant to take part in the research.<br>• No persuasion or pressure of any kinds should be put on participants; any participants from financially disadvantaged groups should be carefully considered when offering incentives (Alderson & Morrow, 2004). |

Continued

TABLE 5.3

| Principle | Main Principles | How It Can be Achieved |
|---|---|---|
| | | • All incentives should be discussed with the researcher's institutional review board.<br>• Participants should know before they start the research that they can withdraw from the study at any time without losing their payment. |
| 6. Deception | Although full disclosure of information during the procedure of obtaining consent is ethically ideal, a particular study may need to withhold certain information. | • If deception is necessary, employ methods that will have no known effects on the teenagers or their family.<br>• All procedures must have scientific validity, avoid and minimize harm, have full parental permission with the parents informed of the deception (Fisher, 2005). |
| 7. Anonymity | Anonymity of any information should be preserved and not used other than for that which permission was obtained. | • Anonymity should be explained to teenagers in a way that they can understand. For example, it should be fully explained that names and other identifying information will be removed. It should also be made clear who will have access to the data and what will happen to the data once the research is complete.<br>• All participants have the right to anonymity. Except where they disclose a risk of harm; for example, child protection and safeguarding laws would be more important than anonymity, and this should be explained to teenagers and parents in the information sheets.<br>• The teenager needs to know what action may be taken in the event that they disclose that they are at risk of harm, or where the researcher observes or receives information that is likely to cause harm, arrangements need to be made in advance, following professional advice, on agreed procedures and support for the child. The researcher needs to know where their duty of care ends. The researcher should set up a process with the school for how any disclosures of harm will be managed. For example, researchers may report this to a designated teacher or safeguarding officer, who will then deal with the matter further. |
| 8. Mutual responsibilities | There should be a clear agreement between the investigator and the parents, guardians, or those who act in loco parentis, and the child, when appropriate, that defines the responsibilities of each. | • Responsibilities should be clearly defined at the start of the research project in writing. Researchers must honor all promises and commitments made in this agreement. |
| 9. Jeopardy | If any information comes to the investigator's attention that may jeopardize the child's well-being, the investigator has a responsibility to discuss the information with the parents or guardians and with those expert in the field in order that they may arrange the necessary assistance for the child. | • Researchers should ensure they have necessary assistance for all participants if there is a chance they will be in jeopardy. For example, if a researcher is evaluating the usability of a health app and the teenager discloses information that the researcher believes them to need assistance, there should be a process in place for who the researcher reports this to, so the teenager can receive the necessary assistance. |

| | | |
|---|---|---|
| 10. Unforeseen consequences | When research procedures result in undesirable consequences for the participant that were previously unforeseen, the investigator should immediately employ appropriate measures to correct these consequences. | • Any procedure that has led to harm or undesirable consequences for participants should be amended before further studies. The new procedure may need to be checked again by the institution's ethics committee. |
| 11. Confidentiality | The investigator should keep in confidence all information obtained about research participants. The participants' identity should be concealed in written and verbal reports of the results, as well as in informal discussion with students and colleagues. When a possibility exists that others may gain access to such information, this possibility, together with the plans for protecting confidentiality, should be explained to the participants as part of the procedure of obtaining informed consent. | • Confidentiality procedures, for example, removing names and anonymizing data, storage of data, and who will have access to the data, should be considered at the very early stages of the research project.<br>• The researcher may need to report incidents to a teacher or a safeguarding officer if they believe that the teenager is in jeopardy or at a risk of harm. Therefore, this should be explained to teenagers, and how this will affect their confidentiality if information is disclosed |
| 12. Informing participants | Immediately after the data are collected, the investigator should clarify for the research participant any misconceptions that may have arisen. | • The researcher should fully debrief teenagers once their research participation is completed. The researcher should clearly and in simplistic terms explain the aims of the study and provide time to answer any questions that teenagers might have. Teenagers should also be aware that they will be provided with a summary of the full results and when this summary will be available. If any information had to be withheld at the start of the research project, then this should be explained. |
| 13. Reporting results | A researcher's words may carry unintended weight with parents and children; caution should be exercised in reporting results, making evaluative statements, or giving advice. | • The researcher should report the general findings to all participants in terms appropriate to their understanding. For example, using words that are within teenagers' comprehension level and checking the wording with teachers to ensure teenagers in that age group will understand.<br>• Special concern should be for the psychological and physical well-being of the children and teenagers in the research; researchers should be careful of failure to report and overreporting suspected problems (Scott-Jones, 2010). |
| 14. Implications of findings | Researchers should be mindful of the social, political, and human implications of their research and should be especially careful in the presentation of findings from the research. | • Researchers should be careful in the way they report the implications of their findings and discuss with their research team, before reporting to teenagers or parents. The report must be suitable for the audience, and the wording and phrasing used must be carefully considered in case the language could be misinterpreted. The implications should only be reported factually and no judgments should be made.<br>• Different versions of the report should be created, for example, reporting the implications to an academic audience should be different to reporting to teenagers or parents. For younger teenagers (aged 13–15 years), it might be more appropriate to |

Continued

**TABLE 5.3**
**The 16 Principles of Ethical Standards in Research and How They can be Applied to Teenagers.—cont'd**

| Principle | Main Principles | How It Can be Achieved |
|---|---|---|
| | | use images and present in simplistic language. Whereas, it might be more appropriate to report the implication in a more formal style to older teenagers (aged 16—19 years). However, the wording and style should be checked with a professional (e.g., teacher). |
| 15. Scientific misconduct | Misconduct is defined as the fabrication or falsification of data, plagiarism, misrepresentation, or other practices that seriously deviate from those that are commonly accepted within the scientific community for proposing, conducting, analyzing, or reporting research. It does not include unintentional errors or honest differences in interpretation of data. | • Researchers should ensure they do not fabricate or falsify data. Incomplete data need consideration about what led to this and whether it can be used. <br> • Any data that cannot be interpreted with accuracy should be discussed with the research team and peer-reviewed before reporting. |
| 16. Personal misconduct | Personal misconduct that results in a criminal conviction of a felony may be sufficient grounds for a member's expulsion from their ethical society. | • Researchers should avoid any misconduct and ensure if they are working with an external organization (e.g., school or youth group), they receive a copy of their safeguarding and health and safety policies in order to familiarize themselves with the guidelines before the research study begins. |

## CHAPTER 5 Ethical Issues When Researching Sexual Health With Teenagers

we have also shown how these principles can be applied to research with teenagers. These guidelines are useful combined with the BPS guidelines, as there are specific ethical issues to consider when recruiting teenagers for research, for example, parental consent.

### General Data Protection Regulation

There have been recent changes in the European Union with regards to the holding of personal data. The introduction of the General Data Protection Regulation (GDPR) now governs the processing of personal data in the United Kingdom. This was not designed specifically for research; however, it is important that researchers who collect personal data are complying with GDPR. Personal data are any data that relate to a living person or persons from which they could be directly or indirectly identified. GDPR was not designed to impede research and allows research certain privileges, by recognizing that any data can be useful for research, and that research can be longitudinal. The Information Control Officer allows research data to be stored indefinitely, if the data controller has set out a legitimate justification for an indefinite retention. Therefore, research can be exempt from the purpose and storage limitations as long as the other data protection principles and specific safeguards are met; in particular the new law states that data processing is lawful, fair, and transparent.

Research must meet new transparency requirements and necessary safeguards. In psychological research, for example, the safeguard requirements can largely be demonstrated by reference to existing university ethical standards. Being fair with research participants includes respecting their rights and ensuring that personal data are used in line with their expectations, transparency is therefore linked to fairness. The fairness and transparency requirements give control to participants: they have greater awareness of how their data are being used and can object if they wish. The new legislation sets out the transparency information that should be provided to participants. Information must be concise, easy to understand, and easy to find. It is recommended that researchers work with their Data Protection Officer to ensure that the information provided to participants is coordinated, relevant, and understandable, and explains how data are used to support research. Privacy information should be appropriate for the study population, for example, appropriately explained on participant information sheets.

### Guidance on Teenagers and GDPR

The information commissioner's office (ICO) defines anyone under the age of 18 years as a child, and children may be less aware of the associated risks, consequences, and rights in relation to the processing of their personal data. One of the legal bases of GDPR with teenagers is consent; there are strict rules to ensure that consent is valid, specific, informed, and must be freely given. Consent must be opt-in consent, and individuals should be able to withdraw their consent at any time. However, it is still good practise to gain parental consent if the child is not competent enough to consent for themselves, and to involve their family as part of the decision-making process unless the child specifically asks the researcher not to do so. Consent as a legal basis for processing personal data is different from consent to agreeing to participate in research. Consent to participate in the research still needs to be sought.

Information needs to be provided to children before their data are processed in order for the processing of personal data to be fair and lawful under data protection legislation, individuals (whether they are children or adults) must be provided with particular information for the processing to be carried out. The information should include what the data will be used for, with whom it will be shared with, and how long it will be kept for. If you seek consent to process personal data for research purposes, you should be as specific as possible when informing the relevant children or adults how their data will be used, at least identifying the general areas of research. Where possible, individuals should be given options to consent only to certain areas of research or parts of research projects. Transparency is key in this context, and it is good practice to explain the risks inherent in the processing and the safeguards you have put in place. When providing information notices to children, you should write in a concise, clear, and easy-to-read style. This should be age appropriate and presented in a way that appeals to a young audience. To ensure that children will be able to understand this information, it is good practice to pilot the information with a professional, for example, a school teacher. This will ensure that the information is targeting the relevant age group. For example, you should make a distinction between addressing a 13-year-old and addressing a 16-year-old child. If your target audience covers a wide age range, consider providing different versions of your notice. Graphics and videos that will attract and interest children may be appropriate. If you are relying upon parental consent as your lawful basis for processing, it is good practice to provide separate privacy notices aimed at both the child and the responsible adult. In order to comply with the new accountability requirement under the GDPR, data controllers must be able to demonstrate compliance with data protection

# 64    Teenagers, Sexual Health Information and the Digital Age

legislation. In practice, this means that in addition to establishing a legal basis for processing, the selected basis must be documented. Evidence of the fair processing information provided to data subjects must also be kept, along with evidence of how the other data protection principles have been complied with as part of the research project (Table 5.4).

## LESSONS FROM OUR OWN RESEARCH PROJECTS

This next section contains details from our own research studies conducted with teenagers (each of the studies are described in more detail in other chapters). The studies were all on the topic of sexual health and used both face-to-face and online research methods. We discuss some of the main ethical issues we encountered.

### TABLE 5.4
### Snapshot of GDPR Guidance and Teenagers.

| | The General Data Protection Regulation |
|---|---|
| What is the General Data Protection Regulation (GDPR) | The GDPR governs the processing of personal data in the United Kingdom. This was not designed specifically for research, but it is important that researchers who collect personal data are complying with GDPR. |
| What are the main implications for research? | GDPR has principles for storage of data protection and storage, in particular the new law states that data processing is lawful, fair, and transparent. Participants should be aware of how their data are being used. |
| How does it affect research with teenagers? | One of the main guidance for teenagers is consent; there are strict rules to ensure that consent for processing personal data is valid; it must be freely given, specific, and informed. Consent must be opt-in consent, and individuals should be able to withdraw their consent at any time. |

## Seeking Legal Guidance

We begin by discussing our small qualitative sexual health study with teenagers (see Chapter 6 for full details). This study aimed to explore teenagers' awareness of sexual health information and assess whether they had access to sufficient sexual health intervention programs targeting these issues. Teenagers from low socioeconomic status (SES) backgrounds, aged 13 and 14 years, were recruited and asked to keep a paper-based sexual health diary for 4 weeks. In the diaries, teenagers were asked to record any thoughts to do with sexual health they had on that day and any sexual health information they had encountered on that day. The diaries were written confidentially each day, folded and placed into a locked box at their schools' reception, a participant code (composed only of numbers) was the only identifying information on the diaries.

Before the research began, several ethical issues were taken into account. As the research was collecting teenagers' thoughts on sexual health, it was vital to ensure participants' data would be kept confidential and that anonymity was maintained throughout. However, due to the sensitive nature of the research topic, we had to consider that participants could disclose in the diaries information relating to their own or another person's risk of harm. Therefore, while confidentiality was important, there needed to be a way to identify a participant if they disclosed information that suggested they were at risk of harm.

In order to achieve this, the lead researcher contacted the University's law team and met with them to discuss the legal obligations and the duty of care of researchers have to report any concerns regarding safeguarding issues. It is important that researchers seek help when working with teenagers and sexual health, to ensure that they are adhering to legal as well as moral standards. After consideration by the law team they concluded there were no legal obligations to report. However, child protection and safeguarding legislation states that if a known (not anonymous) young person aged under 18 years discloses any sexual abuse or any information that suggests that they or someone else is at risk of harm, there is a duty of care to report. This should be reported to a relevant safeguarding officer, but not to the child's parents or to the police. Therefore, a structure of safeguarding and reporting was put in place in case any safeguarding issues were to arise. This meant making safeguarding officers at each school aware of the research and contacting them if any information arose, and the safeguarding officers would identify and contact that child. It is important to note that

## CHAPTER 5 Ethical Issues When Researching Sexual Health With Teenagers

laws change over time and vary between countries and therefore it is essential that each piece of research is considered independently.

The lead researcher made contact with each school and asked for the name and contact details of their school safeguarding officer. A face-to-face or telephone meeting was arranged to discuss each school's safeguarding policies and the procedure if they believe a child is at risk of harm. A mutual responsibility of the safeguarding issues that may be encountered in the research was determined between the lead researcher and the safeguarding officers. The safeguarding policies were then forwarded to the lead researcher and she made herself familiar with each school's safeguarding policies and highlighted the key information around risk of harm. The information, consent, and debrief forms for teenagers and parents were updated, explaining that participants' data will remain confidential; however, if any information was disclosed indicating that they or someone else was at risk of harm, then this information would be disclosed to their school's safeguarding officer. The safeguarding officer would then take this matter further, and identify and contact the child(ren) involved. This was a beneficial structure, so that the research participants were protected, and the researcher knew where their duty of care ended.

The lead researcher also met with participants twice before the study began, to fully explain the study and safeguarding procedures. The content was delivered through a discussion with a group of 10 participants at a time, and typically lasted 30–40 min. The study was explained using terms teenagers could understand, and participants had sufficient time to ask questions. It was emphasized that participants could take a break at any time and if they were not comfortable answering a question they could leave it blank. Participants were reminded they could withdraw from the study at any time, without having to give a reason why. It was important that a support structure was in place to ensure any issues arising through participation in the study could be dealt with by appropriate experts. To do this the lead researcher worked closely with each school to confirm there was a school sexual health nurse or counselor available, in case participants had questions or were affected in any way by the research. Sexual health practices in the area were also contacted and asked if they were happy to be contacted by participants and the name and contact details of the practice were added to the debrief forms. Therefore, assistance was available for participants in and outside of the school.

## Gaining Consent
### Offline consent
During the same research project (see Chapter 6 for full details) we also used online data collection techniques. This involved a web-based questionnaire via Qualtrics. The questionnaire was used to determine age, SES background determined by parental education, and previous sexual behaviors. This was an important aspect of the research to be able to link participants' demographic background and previous sexual behaviors to their diary entries. Given that data collection would take place online we first explored the possibility of gaining parental consent online. However, during the course of discussions with the participating schools, it was decided consent from parents would be sought offline. The researcher discussed opt-in and opt-out options with the head teachers of each school and because they had previously used opt-out consent it was decided that an opt-out method would be the most appropriate. The head teacher believed the teachers and parents were familiar with this method because it was a standard practice within the school. An opt-out sample consists of the children whose parents *have not* indicated that they do not want their child to take part in the research.

The opt-out method utilized included head teachers granting the school's permission to use an opt-out method and signing a consent form. The parental opt-out form was then mailed to parents directly from the school rather than given to the teenagers themselves to ensure parents received them. Letters given to teenagers to take home does not guarantee that parents see the letters, and this is a particularly important issue when using an opt-out method. The parents were given a 2-week period to reply if they did not want their child to take part. The letters included the lead researcher's contact details and affiliations, so parents were able to contact the researcher with questions. After the 2-week period, teenagers could not take part in the research if their parents had contacted the school or the lead researcher to opt out of the study.

Before the study began, participants themselves gave their informed consent to take part online. This included an online information sheet and a consent question online; participants agreed to the consent online or closed the browser if they did not want to take part. The participants were given full information about the study and asked if they were happy to take part before the opt-out consent forms were sent to parents. This was to ensure that teenagers did not feel pressured by their teachers or parents to take part as research participation had to be voluntary. There were no incentives for taking part in this study; due to teenagers being low SES, it was important to make sure that teenagers did not feel coerced into taking part due to receiving incentives. Participants had a half-an-hour session explaining how they could withdraw from the questionnaire by closing the browser and their partial data would not be used.

Using the opt-out method, the study achieved adequate participation rates. During the debrief session, teenagers commented that they enjoyed the online questionnaire as it felt more confidential than completing it in front of people in a classroom, especially as the questions were of a sensitive nature. However, they enjoyed completing the diary in paper format as they could take the diary home and personalize it (by drawing pictures) and writing on it, which was different to the questionnaire which was completed at school. Teenagers believed it was easy to complete the questionnaire at school as they are used to working on computers and liked the opportunity to complete the questionnaire in this way. Participants commented that they enjoyed the combination of offline and online methods, as it avoids boredom. Consequently, as the ethical issues were considered at the start of the research project it allowed to gain rich, meaningful data, and the participants were protected and enjoyed taking part in the research. At the end of the study, a general summary of findings was provided to the schools, to publish in their monthly newsletters. A general summary was going to be provided to ensure individual participants were kept anonymous, and outlined the type of sexual health questions teenagers wanted to know and the current information that is available for them. This summary would allow schools to evaluate whether their current sexual health intervention programs were useful for students. However, because we found a real lack of sexual health knowledge displayed in the diaries, we decided that a more detailed summary should be provided to schools. This was a moral and an ethical consideration, as there was a duty of care to pass on the finding concerning the serious lack of sexual health knowledge to the schools so that they could address this issue. However, we ensured that even though we were providing a more detailed summary, we still kept each of the participants' identities confidential. Therefore, even though it is important to consider ethics right from the start of a study, ethics needs to be continually discussed throughout the project if any unforeseen matters like this arise.

### Online consent

Following on from this study, we conducted a large online questionnaire study (see Chapter 7 for more detail). This study was conducted online as in our previous studies teenagers had enjoyed completing sexual health questions online, as they perceived it to be more confidential. Therefore, we explored how to gain consent from participants and parents using an online method. We consulted the BPS Ethical Guidelines for Internet-Mediated Research (IMR) (2013) which provided guidance on ethical issues when implementing IMR. When conducting IMR studies there are some ethical issues that require special consideration as the complexities with IMR are not always obvious. Therefore, it was essential that we considered ethics at the planning stages of the project.

One key aspect to consider was the process of obtaining informed consent from parents and/or carers using an online method. In this study, this was discussed in depth by the research team. We came up with the following possible options to ensure that we had valid consent from parents/carers:

1. Parents to sign an online consent form and then provide a phone number online; the researcher would then ring the parent/carer to allow parental consent to be verified verbally.
2. Parents to sign an online consent form and then provide a postal address to post parents a paper consent form for parental consent to be verified.
3. Developing a process by which an email address is provided to which a password is sent, in order to access the consent form.
4. To recruit parents/guardians rather than teenagers, and parents/guardians would subsequently ask their child(ren) to participate in the research.

Following careful consideration by the research team, the first two options were chosen, and we gave parents/carers the choice of being contacted by phone or post. These options were chosen and allowed for some flexibility on the part of parents and guardians and allowed us to recruit teenagers directly rather than recruiting parents/guardians. We hoped this would avoid any potential bias in terms of the sample and avoid teenagers feeling any pressure to take part in the study.

Teenagers were recruited and asked to provide their informed consent online. Parents were then asked to provide their online consent and provide their telephone number or postal address to verify their consent. Teenagers then accessed and completed the online questionnaire. If a parent/carer did not enter their telephone number or postal address, or did not answer the phone or return the paper-based consent form, then their child's data were immediately deleted. Overall, this method was successful, and we felt confident that we did have appropriate parental consent for their child to take part in the online questionnaire. However, this was a lengthy process, and we also recruited teenagers through schools, where we gained parental consent offline—again using the opt-out method. The offline recruitment proved vital to reaching the target data collection figure needed within our time frame. However, recruiting participants online and offline allowed us to recruit an appropriate number of participants.

## REFLECTIONS AND GUIDANCE
### Recruiting Teenagers
Though recruiting teenagers can be a lengthy process, it is vital that the appropriate number of participants is recruited (in order to ensure studies have sufficient power). One of the main problems we encountered regarding recruitment and participation was teenagers worrying about the perceived implications of their taking part in a sexual health study. Teenagers were concerned that peers would assume they were sexually active and so were reluctant to volunteer to take part in the study in front of their peers. Thinking through the ways in which a study is advertised to teenagers is therefore really important. To begin with we advertised the study to teenagers during an assembly or class and then left the information sheets at the front of the room for teenagers to collect. This proved unsuccessful as teenagers did not want to take the information sheet as they felt embarrassed taking one in front of their friends. We got around this by leaving the written information sheets with their teachers or at the back of the classroom for participants to get in their own time. Teenagers then had a week to let their teacher know discreetly if they would like to take part. While this method took longer, it was valuable to do this, as we knew teenagers had the correct information about the study and did not feel embarrassed.

### Explaining Ethics and Gaining Consent
We found it important to make sure teenagers fully understood the research and the ethical considerations (for example, confidentiality and anonymity) before they consented to taking part. Especially when dealing with a sensitive research topic such as sexual health, it is key that teenagers understand what types of questions they will be asked and if it could potentially cause them embarrassment. It is likely teenagers will understand more than children, however, it needs to be explained to them in a way they can comprehend. Teenagers cannot give their voluntary informed consent if they do not fully understand the research and the ethical

considerations. We piloted our ethical forms with teachers, to ask for their opinions on the kinds of words teenagers would understand. They recommended that the forms should not be too long, should be bullet pointed, and the key information should be highlighted. Also, researchers recruiting through schools had the opportunity to visit the teenagers beforehand and explain the study procedure and ethical procedures face to face and give participants the opportunity to ask questions. Copies of paper forms were also available for teenagers, in case they needed to check the information at a later date. By fully considering these issues, there was a better chance teens had understood the information and were able to give their informed consent. Teenagers also need to know how the data that they provide will be kept confidential, as sexual health is a sensitive topic. If participants do not believe that the research is anonymous and confidential, then they may not give honest answers. However, at the same time, safeguarding needs to be explained, if teenagers disclose that they or someone else is at a risk of harm, then this information may have to be passed on to a relevant safeguarding person. If this is the case, then this should be clearly explained verbally and in the written information to teenagers.

Finally, as a researcher, it is important that you explain your own qualifications and knowledge to teenagers (and to any organizations that you are working with). For example, if you are not an expert in sexual health and unable to answer teenagers' sexual health questions, then this should be explained to the teenagers at the start of the project. Otherwise, teenagers (or teachers) may ask you sexual health questions that you are unable to answer. If teenagers do have sexual health questions, then they should be signposted to an appropriate information source, for example, a sexual health website or a sexual health nurse/professional.

### Parental Consent
One of the main ethical decisions we made was whether an opt-in or opt-out consent method would be most appropriate. We found that each project required different methods, and every project needs to be considered on a case-by-case basis. As discussed earlier in the chapter, opt-in methods are achieved by parents providing their informed consent for their child to take part in the research. This can be a favorable method as the researcher knows they have consent from parents and that parents have read information about the study. However, in opt-out consent methods, the parent only contacts the researcher if they do not want their child to take part in the research; therefore it is not always guaranteed the parent has received information about

the study. This is particularly an issue if information sheets are given to teenagers to give to their parents. An issue we encountered with opt-in consent was very low recruitment numbers. We found parents would not return the forms, or teenagers would lose or forget the forms. It was very difficult to recruit large numbers of teenagers using this consent method. Whereas, a larger number of teenagers could be recruited using an opt-out method. We found that parents were more likely to respond to letters if they had an objection to the research, than if they were happy for their child to take part. However, making sure that parents have seen the letter needs to be carefully considered. We mailed the letters to parents, rather than let teenagers take the letter home; this provided a better chance of the parent seeing the letter. Some schools have electronic mailing lists for parents, and this can be a useful means of directly contacting parents to ensure they have read the information sheets. We also found that it is worthwhile checking with schools, as some schools are familiar with an opt-out procedure and have their own guidelines on how the letters are sent out. For example, sending text messages to parents or including a summary of the research in their monthly newsletters, so parents know to look out for the letter. There is scope for using a combination of both opt-in and opt-out consent methods. For example, if a researcher needs to recruit a large number of teenagers, they may consider recruiting through schools and recruiting teenagers using posters and web adverts. Therefore, opt-out consent may be most appropriate for the teenagers recruited through schools, and opt-in consent may be most appropriate for teenagers recruited outside of

schools. This may maximize research participation, by recruiting a larger number of participants.

It is also important when gaining parental consent that it is explained to parents that their child has not been targeted to take part in the research. For example, it should be explained that research projects require a number of teenagers for different reasons, and the inclusion and exclusion criteria should be fully explained so that parents do not think their child has been targeted to take part in a sexual health study. The benefits and any potential downsides of their child taking part should also be fully explained. This is important as previous research has shown that parents do not like speaking to their child about sexual health because they worry that it may encourage sexual behaviors (Turnbull, van Wersch, & van Schaik, 2011).

## Chapter Summary

This chapter has described the ethical considerations when conducting sexual health research with teenagers. It has provided an overview of some existing ethical guidelines and how to apply these to research with teenagers. As well as reflecting on some of our own personal experiences with ethical considerations in our studies. Overall, ethics needs to be considered at the start of a research project as recruiting teenagers and gaining parental consent can be a lengthy process. The next chapter moves onto one of our own sexual health research projects with teenagers. Described briefly in this chapter, it is a qualitative study in which teenagers were asked to provide their thoughts about sexual health and sexual health intervention programs.

# CHAPTER 6

# Teenagers' Views of Sexual Health Education

## CHAPTER OUTLINE

Introduction .................................................. 69
Methods ........................................................ 70
    Participants .................................................. 70
    Socioeconomic Status Background .................. 70
    Materials......................................................... 71
        *Demographic form* ................................. **71**
        *Diary* ......................................................... **71**
        *Procedure* ............................................... **72**
        *Analysis procedure* .............................. **73**

Results .......................................................... 73
    Can I Ask You a Question? ............................. 74
    The Social Consequences of Sex ..................... 75
    Information Sources ....................................... 75
Discussion .................................................... 76
    Future Directions ........................................... 77
    Implications.................................................... 77
    Chapter Summary........................................... 77

## ABSTRACT

This chapter aims to consider teenagers' existing thoughts about sexual health and views of sexual health education. The chapter is divided into four sections. Section Introduction provides an overview of the literature around teenager's knowledge and sexual health education. Section Methods describes a diary method used to collect data from teenagers, and Section Results presents the qualitative results from the diary study. The results are then discussed and reflected on in Section Discussion.

## KEYWORDS

Diary methods; Digital health interventions; Online sexual health interventions; Qualitative research; School-based sexual health education; Sexual health; Sexual health education; Sexual health interventions; Teenagers.

## INTRODUCTION

It is important to understand what existing sexual health knowledge teenagers have and what sexual health issues are important to teenagers. Teenagers cannot be targeted with relevant and useful sexual health information, without understanding teenager's current sexual health knowledge and information sources. A better understanding of these issues will aid the

development of intervention programs to target teenagers with key and up-to-date sexual health information.

Currently, as discussed in Chapter 3, Sex and Relationship Education (SRE) in the United Kingdom is a nonassessed subject within schools and as such remains inconsistent (UK Department of Education and Employment, 2000, pp. 1–34). It is only compulsory for local authority maintained schools to teach basic biology and reproduction (Schulkind, Hurst, Biggart, & Bowsher, 2015). Furthermore, academies and free schools do not have to teach this, and sex education in these schools varies from extensive sex education to no sex education (Long, 2017). In a 2002 review it was found that over a third of schools' SRE was outdated and needed improving (OfSTED, 2002). Teenagers need to have access to up-to-date and relevant sexual health information. Female teenagers with increased sexual health knowledge are more likely to delay first sexual initiation and have greater confidence in using condoms (McElderry & Omar, 2003; Weinstein, Walsh, & Ward, 2008).

SRE in schools is provided primarily by teachers (Walker, 2001), although teachers are concerned about insufficient knowledge of STIs and emergency contraception to deliver the subject effectively (Westwood & Mullan, 2007). It is not clear where else teenagers may go to seek their sexual health information. Research conducted in the United Kingdom has found that

---

Teenagers, Sexual Health Information and the Digital Age. https://doi.org/10.1016/B978-0-12-816969-8.00006-0
Copyright © 2020 Elsevier Inc. All rights reserved.

parents do not often talk to their children about sexual health because they feel embarrassed (Turnbull, van Wersch, & van Schaik, 2011) or worry that speaking about sex may encourage sexual activity (Hyde et al., 2013). Teenagers often regard the media as a more useful source for learning about sex and relationships (Buckingham & Bragg, 2004) with teenagers from low socioeconomic status (SES) backgrounds most likely to search for sexual health information online (Zhao, 2009). Sexual health professionals are ideally placed to provide SRE but are not teenagers' preferred source of information (Westwood & Mullan, 2009). Therefore, it remains unclear as to the extent to which teenagers come into contact with sexual health information during the course of their everyday lives.

If current SRE programs are outdated, then it is unlikely teenagers are accessing vital sexual health information (OFSTED, 2013, pp. 1−34) but the fact that teenagers do not like talking about sexual health (Buzi, Smith, & Barrera, 2015) means it can be difficult to assess teenagers' understanding or identify gaps in their knowledge (Table 6.1).

In this study, qualitative diaries are used to address this problem. Diary studies are appropriate for teenagers, as they are familiar with diary keeping and diaries provide a more confidential way of recording sexual health information than face-to-face methods. Previous diary studies have provided rich and valuable sexual health data (Hoffman, Sullivan, Harrison, Dolezal, & Monroe-Wise, 2006; Kiene, Barta, Tennen, & Armeli, 2009). Daily written diaries provide as rich and detailed data as telephone interviews (Morrison et al., 2009). Also, as diaries allow teenagers to note sexual health information each day, they provide a more accurate

record of the day relative to retrospective self-report. Therefore, using this qualitative approach this research aimed to:

(1) Identify gaps in knowledge regarding sexual health information and to identify what sexual health issues are important for teenagers
(2) Understand to what extent teenagers come into contact with sexual health information over a 4-week period

## METHODS

Female teenagers were recruited for this study and asked to keep a diary for 4 weeks detailing their sexual health knowledge and information sources. The full details of the study are explained in the following sections.

### Participants

Thirty female pupils were recruited to take part in this study. Participants were all aged 13 and 14 years old (Mean = 13.6, SD = 0.48) and were from two schools in the North East of England. Eleven of the participants reported that they were in heterosexual romantic relationships, with a single partner and had been with their partners between 1 and 12 months. For all participants who reported that they were in a relationship, their partners were the same age or no more than 2 years older than the participants. Six participants reported previously having sex with condom and three participants reported having sex without a condom. The sample was representative of both teenagers who were sexually active and nonsexually active; 24% of the sample were sexually active, which is representative of sexually active teenagers in England; in the latest NATSAL survey, 25% of teenagers had their first sexual experience before the age of 16 years (Mercer, 2016). See Table 6.2 for full overview of previous sexual behaviors.

### Socioeconomic Status Background

This research was investigating the sexual health knowledge and information available to teenagers from low SES backgrounds. Six questions were asked in order to assess SES status measured by parental income and parent's educational background. Questions included *(1) are you on full price or reduced school meals, (2) do you live with both parents, (3) what is the highest educational attainment your parents have received, (4) mother's job, (5) father's job, (6) (or) carer's job.* Participants were categorized as low SES if they were on free or reduced price school meals (parent's/carer's yearly gross income was below £16,190), or if parent's highest educational attainment was primary or secondary school or if their

| TABLE 6.1 Snapshot of Teenagers Existing Views of Sexual Health. | |
|---|---|
| | **Teenagers Views of Sexual Health** |
| What is the problem? | UK schools currently provide an inconsistent and outdated approach to sexual health education. |
| Why is this important? | It is unclear what knowledge teenagers have of sexual health and whether the sexual health information they want is accessible for them. |

# CHAPTER 6  Teenagers' Views of Sexual Health Education

**TABLE 6.2**
**Overview of Participants' Previous Sexual Behaviors.**

| Age | Haven't Yet *n* (%) | Under 13 years *n* (%) | 13 years *n* (%) | 14 years *n* (%) |
| --- | --- | --- | --- | --- |
| Kissing | 2 (7.4%) | 16 (59.3%) | 8 (29.6) | 0 |
| Touching a partner's genitals | 14 (53.8%) | 3 (11.5%) | 9 (34.6%) | 0 |
| Being touched on genitals | 15 (57.7%) | 1 (3.8%) | 9 (34.6) | 1 (3.8%) |
| Giving oral sex | 16 (61.5%) | 2 (7.7%) | 7 (26.9%) | 1 (3.8%) |
| Receiving oral sex | 20 (76.9%) | 0 | 4 (15.4%) | 2 (7.7%) |
| Sex with a condom | 20 (76.9%) | 1 (3.8%) | 3 (11.5%) | 2 (7.7%) |
| Sex without a condom | 23 (88.5%) | 0 | 1(3.8%) | 2(7.7%) |

parents were either unemployed or had working-class jobs (for example, builder or factory worker). If all of these questions were left blank or participants selected *"don't know"* to all questions, then their data were removed from further analysis. These categories for SES background were consistent with previous studies measuring the socioeconomic background of children and teenagers (Santelli, Lowry, & Brener, 2000).

From these categories, 29 participants were categorized as low SES and 1 participant was categorized as high SES and was excluded from further analyses. Of these 29 participants, 26 participants completed the full 4-week diaries. See Table 6.3 for an overview of participants' demographic background.

## Materials
### Demographic form
*Demographic* information was measured using a self-developed online questionnaire. The questionnaire consisted of seven items aimed to measure age, ethnicity, SES status, and parental background. *Previous sexual behaviors* were measured using the Raine previous sexual behaviors scale (Skinner, Robinson, Smith, Chenoa, & Robbins, 2015). Participants were asked what age measured from *"Haven't yet"* to *"16 years"* they had engaged in kissing to vaginal sex without a condom (See Table 4.1 for full list of behaviors). Four questions measured relationship status, partner gender, age, and length of relationship.

### Diary
Participants kept a 4-week paper-based diary; the diary asked participants to discuss *"Any thoughts and feelings of anything to do with sexual health, you have had today. This could be anything to do with sexual health or sexual health intervention programs."* The second part of the

diary asked teenagers to write *"Any information you have had about sexual health or sexual health intervention programs. This could be anything to do with someone talking about sexual health or sexual health intervention programs.*

**TABLE 6.3**
**Demographic Background Information for Participants.**

| | | N (%) |
| --- | --- | --- |
| | Free or reduced price lunches | 5 (19.2%) |
| *Ethnicity* | White British | 23 (57.7%) |
| | Black or black British African | 1 (3.6%) |
| | Other mixed background | 2 (7.7%) |
| *Living with parents* | Living with mum | 8 (28.6%) |
| | Live with both parents | 15 (53.6%) |
| | Living in care | 1 (3.6%) |
| | Other | 2 (7.1%) |
| *Parents' education background* | Primary school | 2 (7.7%) |
| | Secondary school | 13 (46.4%) |
| | Sixth form or college | 10 (35.7%) |
| | University (undergraduate) | 1 (43.6%) |

**72** Teenagers, Sexual Health Information and the Digital Age

Participant number: _____
Date: _____

*Any thoughts and feelings of anything to do with sexual health, you have had today.* This could be anything to do with sexual health or sexual health intervention programs.

> Is it okay if I have sex & do things with my boyfriend after a 2 year relationship?
>
> If your pregnant how do you know

*Any information you have had about sexual health or sexual health intervention programs.* This could be anything to do with someone talking about sexual health or sexual health intervention programs. Or any information you have heard or seen about sexual health or sexual health intervention programs.

> I saw a poster in the chemist about STIs

FIG. 6.1 Example of a diary entry.

Or any information you have heard or seen about sexual health or sexual health intervention programs." See Fig. 6.1 for an example of one of the diary entries.

### Procedure

Testing took place in a school setting. Parental consent was sought using an opt-out procedure (See Chapter 5 for more detail). The schools sent home parental letters explaining the study, and parents informed the schools within 2 weeks if they did not want their daughters taking part in the research. Participants gave their consent to take part in the diaries on the testing day. Participants were allocated an anonymous participant number on a small card and were asked to keep this number safe throughout the study.

Firstly, participants completed the online demographic questionnaire at school; to access the questionnaire, participants entered their anonymous participant number. This asked participants about their previous sexual behavior, parental education background, age, and school year. The researcher then introduced and explained the diary to the participants and asked them to complete diaries at home over a 4-week period. It was explained to participants that they needed to write their participant number and the date at the top of the page each day. A locked box was placed in the schools' reception area and participants ripped out the page of the diary, folded it, and placed it in the locked box every day. Throughout the 4 weeks, teachers reminded the pupils to complete the diaries. At the end of the 4 weeks, the diaries were collected and participants were thanked for their time and fully debriefed. For an overview of the procedure see Fig. 6.2.

### Analysis procedure

Thematic analysis was used to analyze the diaries, in order to find similar themes across all of the diaries (Braun & Clarke, 2006). See Chapter 4, second section for an overview of thematic analysis. In total 234 diary pages were collected. The diaries were read and reread and any initial ideas related to the research questions were noted down. The diaries were categorized into topic areas and a count of each topic area was made. This then allowed us to explore inductively the nature of participants' concerns. Initial codes in each of the topic areas were then identified. During the next stage, each code was incorporated into a theme, and the themes were able to explain a larger part of the data. These themes were aided by a thematic map, which allowed us to visualize the links between the themes, and to ensure that each theme had enough data to support it. Coding was then repeated to ensure no important codes or information had been left out at earlier stages. Each of the three themes were then named and defined. Finally, the report was produced which involved choosing example extracts from the diaries to illustrate each theme and to provide a clear example of the point being made. See Fig. 6.1 for an example diary.

### RESULTS

The full results of the diary study are displayed in the following section, and then each theme is summarized in a snapshot box. In explaining their sexual health knowledge and access to information, data presented around three themes: (1) *Can I ask you a question?*; (2) *The social consequences of sex*; (3) *Information sources*. The first two themes relate to the first research question and explore gaps in teenagers' sexual health knowledge and the sexual health issues that they believe are important. The final theme explores the extent and type of the sexual health information that teenagers experienced over a 4-week period. The themes are illustrated with verbatim quotes from the diaries.

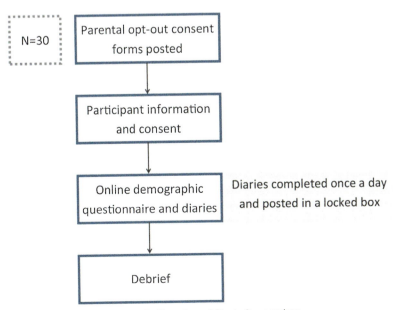

FIG. 6.2 Overview of Study 2 procedure.

## Can I Ask You a Question?

Teenagers displayed their lack of knowledge and misunderstandings around sexual health in eight main categories: naivety, pregnancy, STIs, contraception, oral and anal sex, legal issues, and slang term clarification. In each category, participants expressed their lack of knowledge by writing questions in the diaries. These questions showed that teenagers lacked knowledge in these subjects but also that they wanted to know more about them. Teenagers asked how to have sex and how long to have sex, showing a general naivety around sexual intercourse. These general sexual health questions showed that teenagers are thinking about sex but at the same time have gaps in their knowledge and show misunderstandings about the topic.

*Why do people have sex?*

*Can you have sex while you are on your period?*

*How long does it take to have sex?*

This naivety of sexual health knowledge was also apparent in relation to pregnancy. Questions about pregnancy centered on participants worrying that they could be pregnant and how they could become pregnant. As well as showing a general confusion about the ways to become pregnant, the questions show that pregnancy is one of the main sexual health concerns for female teenagers. The diaries also showed a clear lack of reproductive knowledge surrounding the ways in which you could become pregnant.

*How do you know if you are pregnant?*

*If you toss someone off and they cum on their hands then poke you, can you get pregnant?*

*If you never wear a condom, will you get pregnant?*

In addition, teenagers worried that they may become pregnant from having oral or anal sex. The questions around anal and oral sex showed again a severe lack of knowledge around the biological aspects of sex and pregnancy. This again highlights how much pregnancy is a concern for young female teenagers, and that anal and oral sex is something that they want more information on.

*If someone cums [sic] inside my bum can I get pregnant?*

*If you have oral sex with a boy and swallow their sperm can you become pregnant?*

Both oral and anal sex was discussed throughout the diaries. It was clear from the diary entries that participants had some understanding of oral and anal sex and although some participants were sexually active, there are still misunderstandings around this topic. It was a topic that was frequently discussed.

*Can you have sex and anal sex at the same time?*

*Is using your mouth on a penis sex?*

Teenagers had some basic knowledge around contraception methods such as condoms and the oral pill; however, it was clear from the diary entries that they wanted more information on this topic. However, teenagers still wanted to know more about these methods and participants were not sure which methods would be the best for them. The questions showed that while teenagers had heard of some contraception methods, they were unsure of the positives and negatives of each type of contraception. Many of the diaries mentioned condoms splitting and teenagers believed that condoms were not fully effective; teenagers believed that they were likely to become pregnant even if they used a condom. There was a general agreement in the diaries that teenagers did not believe that condoms were the best method of contraceptive, but were not sure what alternative would be suitable.

*Why isn't there anything better than condoms because most of the time they split whilst having sex so basically they aren't preventing young teenagers get pregnant*

Teenagers have some basic STI knowledge; however, they showed misunderstandings about how they might contract an STI and how to protect themselves from an STI. Participants wanted more information on how you contract an STI and about the different types of STIs. However, interestingly, despite a lot of diary entries mentioning STIs, there were no questions surrounding how to get treatment for an STI, only how they might contract one. Therefore, participants were worried about how they might get an STI or what the symptoms might be but were not thinking about how they might treat it if they did get an STI. Also, even though participants were aware of condoms, none of the diaries mentioned that condoms could be used to prevent STIs. Therefore, participants showed a lack of understanding around the ways you can contract an STI, treatments, and prevention of STIs.

*How do you get an STI?*

*Can you get STIs all over your body?*

Teenagers also showed a lack of knowledge around the legal issues of sex. Teenagers asked questions around what the legal age of consent was. This has also been found in previous literature, that teenagers are unaware what consent means, and what age they can legally give sexual consent. Teenagers also worried about where it was legal to have sex and showed misunderstandings around whether it was legal to have sex outside. It was clear from their diary entries that legal issues were something that they wanted to know more about.

*What age can you legally have sex?*

*Is it illegal to have sex outside?*

Lastly, teenagers had misunderstandings around appropriate terminology; they had heard various slang words, but they were not sure what the words meant. If there are inconsistencies in formal sexual health education, then it is not surprising that teenagers are unsure of appropriate terminology and even slang words for this terminology. This can lead to confusion for teenagers (Table 6.4).

*My boyfriend asked to "lick my muff" what does that mean?*

*What is a "sucky"?*

## The Social Consequences of Sex

Teenagers also reported misunderstandings and anxiety around the social consequences of sex. It was clear from the diary entries that teenagers often spoke about sex with their friends; in fact, the only communication teenagers reported about sexual health was with their friends. However, these exchanges did not comprise reliable sexual health information per se but rather focused on a broader discussion of the social implications of having sex. Despite their naivety around sex, it was clear that teenagers were sexually active; however, they only discussed sexual activity when speaking about it with their friends.

*Me and my friends always talk about sex*

*One of my friends were wondering can you get pregnant while on your period*

*My friend said she couldn't walk after having sex*

Throughout the diaries when discussing the sexual experiences of their friends the participants often used shaming words. It was commonplace for participants to name and "shame" their friends who had had sex with someone. Yet, participants worried themselves, that they might be shamed if they then had sex with someone. It was clear that participants were aware that females were often shamed for having sex, and this led to confusion about what is and is not acceptable.

*If I have sex with two people will that make me a slut?*

*A lot of the girls in my year get called slags, they think it looks good that they have had sex, but it really isn't.*

The diary entries showed that while participants have a lack of understanding around the basic biological aspects of sex, teenagers also worry about the social context and wider issue of relationships in general. Teenagers worried that having sex would be considered "wrong". Teenagers also worried about the social consequences of having sex (Table 6.5).

## Information Sources

These misunderstandings around biological and social aspects of sex tied in with teenagers' information sources on the topic. In the majority of the diaries, teenagers indicated that they had not seen any sexual health information over the full 4-week period of the study. Teenagers acknowledged their lack of formal sexual health education and stated that they would like more sexual health sessions. Teenagers were aware that they do not know a lot about sexual health or their own bodies but they do want more information on this topic, and know that it is an important topic to understand.

---

**TABLE 6.4**
**Snapshot of Can I Ask You a Question.**

**Can I Ask You a Question?**

- The teenagers in this sample have a severe lack of knowledge around the biological aspects of sex.
- Used the diaries as a way of asking sexual health questions.
- In particular teenagers asked about pregnancy, STIs, contraception, oral and anal sex, legal issues, and slang term clarification.

---

**TABLE 6.5**
**Snapshot of the Social Consequences of Sex.**

**The Social Consequences of Sex**

- Teenagers speak regularly to their friends about sex.
- Teenagers would name and "shame" their friends if they had sex with someone—a process that appeared to be commonplace
- This naming and shaming was a source of anxiety for participants and they were worried they might be shamed themselves
- Teenagers were unsure as to whether they should be having sex at their age and wondered whether it would be considered "wrong"

*I need more sexual health lessons in school I don't hardly know out [anything]*

*Me and my friends talk about sex as a joke a lot, but really we don't even know the different parts of a vagina.*

Yet, teenagers are passive receivers of information; despite stating a desire for more sexual health information, they did not actively search for this information at any point over the 4-week period. The sexual health information that teenagers did come across was almost coincidental to their daily lives. For example, teenagers had read a poster about sexual health or they had seen a television show that featured some sexual health information. Teenagers also stated that they had come across some sexual health information through advertisements on social media. None of the teenagers in this study had actively searched for sexual health information.

*I saw some posters about*

*Not seen anything*

There was not a lot of discussion about the types of sexual health information that participants preferred because the sources of information within the diaries were very limited. However, a few of the diaries mentioned that participants were aware of a confidential text messaging service for sexual health advice; this had previously been advertised to teenagers. Teenagers commented that they liked the sound of this because it was confidential. It is known that teenagers are less likely to speak to someone reliable; for example, a teacher or sexual health nurse directly but they are happier to access this information in a confidential way. It was not clear if teenagers had accessed this service previously, but they were all aware of it (Table 6.6).

*I understand that you can get chlamidia [sic] test in {town name} centre they then send you a text conferming [sic] if you have or haven't got an STI/STD.*

---

**TABLE 6.6**
**Snapshot of Information Sources.**

**Information Sources**

- Over a 4-week period teenagers in this study were not directly targeted with any sexual health information.
- Participants passively saw sexual health information via posters.
- Teenagers liked the idea of a confidential text messaging service for STI tests.

---

## DISCUSSION

The findings of this study highlight a juxtaposition between the lack of understanding about the biological and social aspects of sex and at the same time the curiosity and thirst for knowledge about sexual health. Teenagers have numerous misunderstandings about the biological and reproductive aspects of sex, particularly with respect to pregnancy, STIs, contraception, slang terminology, oral and anal sex. This is surprising given the age of participants, as is expected that 13 and 14 year olds would have some sexual health knowledge from SRE taught in British schools (Long, 2017). However, teenagers demonstrated a clear desire to know more about sexual health and their own bodies through the questions they asked in the diaries. Teenagers taking part in the study used the diaries as a tool to ask questions about the topics and issues that concerned them. The confidentiality afforded by the diary encouraged participants to be open in expressing their questions. We know that teens, particularly those of low SES, are more likely to use confidential sources of sexual health information, such as the Internet (Zhao, 2009; McKellar, Sillence & Smith, 2017). This emphasizes the need for private and confidential ways of asking sexual health questions.

This juxtaposition was situated within a context that emphasizes perceived social norms, as teenagers worried about the social consequences of having sex before the age of 16 years. This is a confusing concept for teenagers as they openly talk to their friends about sex, yet they worry about the shaming that could come from engaging in the activity. We know that peer communication and popularity are huge influences on sexual health (Allen, Porter, & McFarland, 2006; Bobakova, Geckova, Klein, van Dijk, & Reijneveld, 2013; Neppl, Dhalewadikar, & Lohman, 2015; Prinstein, Meade, & Cohen, 2003), but the double standards between peers speaking openly about sex and also shaming peers who have had sex causes confusion for teenagers. There was a disconnect in the diaries between sex and relationships. Teenagers worried about becoming attached to their sexual partners. Some participants expressed that they wanted to wait to have sex, in case they became attached to their partner. This indicates that female teenagers may be seeking more short-term relationships, which is already known from existing literature (Manlove, Welti, Wildsmith, & Barry, 2014). In the United Kingdom, SRE is to become a compulsory subject by 2019 (Sellgren, 2017). This research has highlighted a need for comprehensive knowledge of sex and relationships. It is important that SRE programs are designed to help teenagers fully

## CHAPTER 6 Teenagers' Views of Sexual Health Education

understand the emotional and social aspects of sexual health. In addition, due to the anxiety around the stigma and shaming of females who do engage in sexual intercourse, it is important that any misinformation or double standards provided by peers is incorporated into sexual health education programs.

This study suggests that current sexual health interventions are not meeting teenagers' sexual health needs. Over a 4-week period teenagers had very limited exposure to sexual health information. Certainly, the teenagers in this sample had no direct sexual health interventions targeted at them and teenagers did not actively seek sexual health information themselves. Instead they discovered this information coincidentally via posters, TV, and social media adverts (Table 6.7).

### Future Directions

The diary method has allowed participants to disclose their sexual health thoughts in an anonymous way. Because of this, participants were very honest and open with respect to the information that they disclosed. The material derived may not have been as rich had an alternative methodology been used, such as a face-to-face interview. However, the method did not allow to compare sexually active and nonsexually active teenagers, in regards to their knowledge and sexual health information seeking practices. This was because participants were required to write their own participant number on the top of each diary, and the majority of diaries were missing the participant number. In this sample, 24% of the participants reported having sex with a condom and 12% reported having

sex without a condom. As previous research has identified that sexually active teenagers are more likely to seek sexual health information than nonsexually active teenagers (Jones & Biddlecom, 2011), it would be interesting for future research to compare the information seeking practices of sexually active and nonsexually active teenagers. This information would provide insight into the most effective time and ways to target teenagers with sexual health information. This could have been achieved in the current study, if participant numbers were typed on the diaries before they were given to participants. However, if this was the case, participants may not have perceived the diaries as confidential and anonymous, and participants may not have been as open and honest with the information that they disclosed. Future research could seek to employ methods that allow to link diaries with the questionnaire data, yet are still perceived as anonymous to teenagers. One way this could be achieved is through the use of online diaries. With the constraints of a school-based study, and the number of websites that are blocked on school computers, this was not possible to trial in this study, but would be interesting for future research to address.

### Implications

Female teenagers from low SES areas lack key and basic knowledge around the biological and emotional aspects of sexual health. Over a 4-week period, teenagers were not targeted with comprehensive sexual health information. Even though teenagers want sexual health information, they do not actively seek information. The sexual health information that teenagers do encounter is through posters, the Internet, and television. Peers are a huge influence on sexual health decisions, as teenagers do not want to be judged or shamed. Teenagers worry that there might be negative social implications from having sex. The findings of this study indicate that teenagers from low SES areas need to be able to access reliable sexual health information in a convenient and confidential way, as teenagers will not actively seek out information. In addition, incorporating peer stigma and social norms into sexual health interventions could minimize worry about social implications and promote positive peer influence. The findings from this study highlight important implications for the way sexual health education programs are advertised and delivered to female teenagers.

### Chapter Summary

This chapter described a qualitative study designed to explore low SES female teenagers' existing sexual health

---

**TABLE 6.7**
**Snapshot of Discussion Points.**

**Discussion Points**

- Female teenagers from low SES areas lack key and basic knowledge around the biological and emotional aspects of sexual health. Over a 4-week period, teenagers were not targeted with comprehensive sexual health information.
- Peers are a huge influence on sexual health decisions, as teenagers do not want to be judged or shamed. Teenagers worry that there might be negative social implications from having sex.
- The findings of this study indicate that teenagers from low SES areas need to be able to access reliable sexual health information in a convenient and confidential way, as teenagers will not actively seek out information.

knowledge and information sources. The study utilized a 4-week diary approach due to the difficulties examining teenagers' sexual health knowledge and information, as they do not like talking about sexual health. Using thematic analysis data presented around three themes: (1) *Can I ask you a question?*; (2) *The social consequences of sex*; (3) *Information sources*. The first two themes explored teenagers' lack of knowledge and misunderstandings around the biological and social experiences of sexual health. The final theme explored the limited ways in which teenagers come into contact with sexual health information currently despite their desire to understand more. The findings of this study highlight the juxtaposition between teenagers' lack of understanding about the biological and social aspects of sex and at the same time their curiosity and thirst for knowledge. This point was emphasized in the teenagers' use of the diaries as a confidential way of seeking sexual health information. This emphasizes that teenagers do not have access to reliable sexual health information, have very limited sexual health knowledge, but are thinking about sex.

In the next chapter, another of our studies is reported, a quantitative study, in which a large number of low SES female teenagers were recruited. As we know that female teenagers have limited access to reliable information and limited sexual health knowledge, the focus moved to the predictors of risky sexual behaviors.

# CHAPTER 7

# Predictors of Risky Behaviors for Female Teenagers

## CHAPTER OUTLINE

Introduction ....................................................... 79
Method: Initial Phase: Pilot of Questionnaire ...... 81
  Approach............................................................ 81
  Participants ....................................................... 81
    *Stage 1: review* ........................................... 81
    *Stage 2: testing* .......................................... 81
  Materials............................................................ 81
  Construction of Questionnaire .......................... 86
    *Stage 1: review* ........................................... 86
  What Were Professionals, Parents, and
  Teenagers Asked to do as Part of the
  Review?............................................................. 86
  Results .............................................................. 88
    *Pilot findings* ............................................... 88
    *Revised findings* ......................................... 88
    *Findings from pilot stage 2 (testing)* ...... 89
  Method: Main Study .......................................... 89
    *Design* ......................................................... 89

*Participants* ..................................................... 89
*Materials* ......................................................... 90
*Self-measures* ................................................. 90
*Personality measures* ..................................... 90
*Peers and parents* .......................................... 91
*Sexual health* .................................................. 91
*School performance* ....................................... 91
*Overview of questionnaire* ............................. 92
Procedure.......................................................... 92
Results .............................................................. 92
  *Treatment of data* ........................................ 92
  *Early sex* ...................................................... 92
Intention to Have Sex ........................................ 92
Discussion.......................................................... 95
Limitations and Strengths ................................. 96
Implications ....................................................... 97

## ABSTRACT

This chapter aims to consider the predictors of risky sexual behaviors for female teenagers. The chapter is divided into five sections. Section 1 provides an overview of the predictors identified in current literature and our previous studies described in this book. Section 2 describes a pilot study to develop a questionnaire to measure the predictors with a sample of low socioeconomic status female teenagers, and Section 3 discusses the main deployment of the questionnaire. The results of the questionnaire and discussion of the findings are then presented in sections 4 and 5.

## KEYWORDS

Digital health interventions; Online sexual health interventions; Questionnaire study; School-based sexual health education; Sexual health; Sexual health education; Sexual health interventions; Sexual health survey; Survey; Teenagers.

## INTRODUCTION

An extensive list of predictors of risky sexual behaviors has been identified in sexual health literature and from our own research. In our research (described in chapter 4) sexual health professionals identified that self-esteem, peer pressure, parental influences, and the presence of pornography and safe sex in the media are highly important predictors of risky sexual behaviors for female teenagers. In the previous chapter (Chapter 6), female teenagers demonstrated, through their diary entries, a chronic lack of sexual health knowledge and difficulties accessing reliable sexual health information sources. However, previous quantitative evidence is mixed and there remains a lack of consensus regarding

*Teenagers, Sexual Health Information and the Digital Age.* https://doi.org/10.1016/B978-0-12-816969-8.00007-2
Copyright © 2020 Elsevier Inc. All rights reserved.

the factors that predict sexual risk-taking in female teenagers from low SES areas.

Self-esteem has been identified as highly important by sexual health professionals, yet it remains uncertain (Goodson, Buhi, & Dunsmore, 2006) the extent to which this factor plays a role in teenage sexual risk-taking. Longitudinal research has found statistically significant links between self-esteem and sexual behaviors (Jackman & MacPhee, 2017), whereas, no statistically significant links have been found in cross-sectional studies (Salazar & Crosby, 2005). School performance, body image, and depression are three important factors that have been identified which all relate to self-esteem. Self-esteem, school performance, and lower school grades have been associated with earlier sexual initiation (Perry, Braun, & Cantu, 2014) and greater sexual activity (Wheeler, 2010). Females who feel more confident and higher in self-esteem evaluate their body image more positively and are less likely to report risky sexual behavior (Gillen, Lefkowitz, & Shearer, 2006). Depression and low self-esteem have been linked with adolescents reporting being more sexually active, having a greater number of sexual partners, and not using condoms (Brawner, 2012; Brawner, Gomes, Jemmott, & Deatrick, 2012; Mazzaferro, Murray, Ness, & Bass, 2006). Our research findings have been consistent with previous literature identifying self-efficacy, peer pressure, and parents as important predictors to risky sexual behaviors (Dilorio, Dudley, Soet, Watkins, & Maibach, 2000; Sionéan et al., 2002; Velez, 2016; Wight & Fullerton, 2013).

In Chapter 6, we saw that female teenagers lacked often basic sexual health knowledge and had limited access to reliable sexual health information. Access to sexual health information is especially important for female teenagers, as females with increased sexual health knowledge are more likely to delay first sexual initiation and have greater confidence in using condoms (McElderry & Omar, 2003; Weinstein, Walsh, & Ward, 2008). It is also important that teenagers are accessing reliable sexual health information to counteract any misinformation in pornography (for example, issues around consent) because pornography is easily available. It has been reported in the United Kingdom that approximately 53% of 11−16 years olds have seen pornography online, and 94% of those has seen it before age 14 years (Martellozzo, Monaghan, Adler, Davids & Horvath, 2016). A review of the literature found that adolescent males are more likely to use pornography than females; however, sensation seekers with weak or troubled family relationships are most likely to access pornography. Accessing pornography

in teenagers is associated with higher permissive sexual attitudes, more casual sex, and greater occurrence of sexual intercourse (Peter & Valkenburg, 2016). Therefore, it is clear that pornography is having a significant influence on teenagers' sexual behavior and attitudes. However, it is less clear whether pornography use is a predictor of earlier sexual intercourse and whether exposure to safe sex in the media affects teenagers' earlier sexual initiation.

The link between individual personality traits and sexual risk-taking is well documented in previous literature. High sensation seeking and impulsivity can predict earlier sexual initiation, a greater number of partners, and unprotected sex in adolescents (Hoyle, Fejfar, & Miller, 2000). Conscientiousness, which shares features with impulsivity and sensation seeking, has been negatively associated with unprotected sex, and neuroticism is weakly associated with number of partners and unprotected sex (Hoyle et al., 2000). Miller et al. (2003) found that low agreeableness, low openness to experience, and high extraversion were significantly related to multiple high-risk sexual behaviors. Delayed gratification can enhance mechanisms of self-control and reduce unprotected sex in relation to peer pressure (Reyna & Wilhelms, 2016) (Table 7.1).

In summary, there is an extensive list of risky sexual behavior predictors identified as being important both in the literature and in our own studies. These predictors, however, are typically examined in isolation and until now have been examined across both male and female teenagers across a range of SES backgrounds. Furthermore, the definitions used for risky sexual behaviors have varied considerably in the previous

| TABLE 7.1 Snapshot of Important Predictors. | |
|---|---|
| | Predictors of risky sexual behaviors for female teenagers |
| Our previous studies | Self-esteem, peer pressure, peer conformity, peer/parental support, sexual health information, pornography, and safe sex in media. |
| Literature | Big five personality traits, self-efficacy, sensation seeking, body image, delayed gratification, peer conformity, peer/parental support, communication, sexual attitudes, depression, school performance, sexual health knowledge. |

# CHAPTER 7  Predictors of Risky Behaviors for Female Teenagers

literature. For example, some studies have used early sexual initiation as a risky behavior (Perry et al., 2014), whereas other studies have identified multiple sexual partners and condom misuse as a risky behavior (Brawner, Davis, & Fannin, 2012; Mazzaferro et al., 2006). The aim of our study was to explore which predictors are important in predicting early sexual initiation in female teenagers from low SES backgrounds, given that these individuals have been identified as a high-risk group for early sexual initiation and sexual risk-taking more generally. Drawing on the definition proposed in chapter 2, risky sexual behavior is defined as early sexual initiation before age 16 years because of its link with other risk-taking behaviors (Zimmer-Gembeck & Helfand, 2007). Therefore, the most important predictors identified from the literature and our own previous two studies were combined into a survey for use with female teenagers. The predictors were *self-esteem, big five personality traits, self-efficacy, sensation seeking, body image, delayed gratification, peer pressure, peer conformity, peer/parental support, communication, sexual attitudes, depression, school performance, sexual health knowledge, sexual health information, pornography, and safe sex in media.*

This research was conducted in two parts both of which are reported in the following section. The first part consisted of the development and piloting of the survey to assess its appropriateness for female teenagers. The second part involved the deployment of the survey and the collection of data from a large number of low SES female teenagers from the North East of England.

## METHOD: INITIAL PHASE: PILOT OF QUESTIONNAIRE

### Approach

Questionnaires suitable for teenagers that measured the identified predictors were chosen. Following its initial development, the questionnaire was piloted using a two-stage process; stage 1: reviewed by professionals, parents, and teenagers and stage 2: tested by teenagers. The importance of piloting a questionnaire is highlighted by previous literature (Oppenheim, 1992; Rattray & Jones, 2007) and is particularly important with questionnaires with children and teenagers (Bell, 2007; Presser et al., 2004).

### Participants
#### *Stage 1: review*

Fifteen female participants took part (five professionals, five parents, and five teenagers). Professionals were recruited due to their expertise in working with teenagers. Two sexual health professionals were recruited due to their understanding and knowledge of the area and familiarity of working with teenagers (job experience ranged from 2 to 5 years). Three teachers were recruited and asked to evaluate, from their experience, the suitability of the questions and the length of the questionnaire overall (job experience ranged from 1 to 12 years). Five parents of female teenagers (aged 13–16 years) were recruited due to their understanding of whether teenagers would find the questionnaire appropriate, and if they would be happy with their daughters completing the questionnaire. Five female teenagers aged 13–15 years were recruited (Mean age = 13.5 SD = 0.53), in order to evaluate if they understood the questionnaire. Participants were recruited using personal networks and via advertisements in the University.

#### *Stage 2: testing*

An opportunity sample of 10 female teenagers was recruited for the stage 2 pilot. Participants were recruited through parents; parents were recruited on social media platforms, for example Facebook and Twitter. Parents asked their daughters if they would be interested in taking part in the online pilot study. Participants were from the North East of England, aged 13–14 years old (Mean = 14.2, SD = 0.84). Participants were all White British, six participants were from a low SES background measured by parental education (highest education was secondary school), and four participants were from a high SES background measured by parental education (highest education was University Postgraduate).

### Materials

The survey was conducted online and contained 11 standardized questionnaires and 13 self-developed questionnaires. The questionnaires covered five different areas: self, personality, peers and parents, sexual health, and school performance, which covered the previously identified high-risk predictors.

## Self-measures

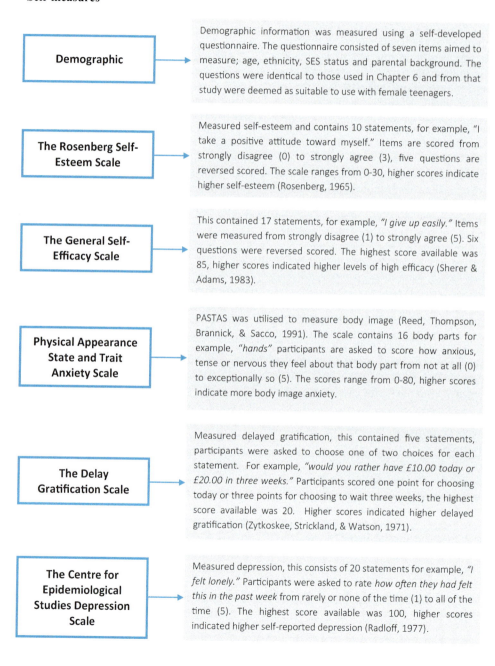

## Personality measures

**The Big 5 Mini-Markers**

Measured personality traits, this contains 40 adjectives for example, *"kind"* participants were asked to score how much the adjective applies to them from extremely not accurate (1) to extremely accurate (9). The questionnaire has five sub-scales; extraversion, agreeable, conscientious, neurotic and openness. Each sub-scale has a possible score of 72. Higher scores indicate that the participant identifies more with that personality trait (Saucier, 1994).

**The Child Sensation Seeking Scale**

Consisted of 26 statements, participants were asked to choose one out of two choices for each statement for example, *"I like to do 'wheelies' on my bike.* (1) Or *Kids who do "wheelies" on their bikes will probably get hurt sometime* (0)." Each sensation seeking statement chosen was scored with a 1, the highest score was 26. Higher scores indicated higher levels of sensation seeking (Russo, Stokes, Lahey, & Christ, 1993).

## Peers and parents' measures

**Peer Pressure, Popularity and Conformity**

All three scales were measured on a scale of strongly disagree (1) to strongly agree (5). Eleven items were utilised to measure peer pressure, for example *"I've felt pressured to get drunk at parties."* The highest score was 55, higher scores indicated more peer pressure. Twelve items were utilised to measure popularity for example *"I've neglected some friends because of what other people might think."* The highest score available was 60, higher scores indicated more popularity. Conformity was measured using seven items for example *"I Rarely follow the rules."* The highest score available was 40, higher scores indicated higher conformity levels (Santor, Messervey, & Kusumakar, 2000).

**Peer and Parental Support, Sex Communication and Sexual Attitudes**

Were measured using self-developed questionnaires due to there being no suitable questionnaires available. Each scale had 15 items, five items measuring parental support for example, *"I receive a good deal of attention from my parents/carers."* Five items measuring parental sex attitudes *"My parents/carers believe teenagers should be encouraged to stay virgins."* Five items measuring sex communication *"I feel I can talk to my parents/carers about STIs."* The questionnaire was then repeated with *parents/carers* changed to *friends*. The scale was scored on a 5-point Likert scale from strongly disagree (1) to strongly agree (5). Two questions were reversed scored; the highest score available was 25 for each sub-scale. A higher score in the parental/peer support scale indicated teenagers had higher support from their parents/carers or peers. A higher score in the parental/peers sex attitudes scale indicated their parents/carers or peers had more open sexual attitudes and a higher score in sex communication indicated teenagers felt they could talk more openly to their parents/carers or peers about sex. The scoring system was developed based on the previous peer pressure scale, to keep all scales similar and easier for teenagers to navigate.

## Sexual health

**The SKAT-A**

This contains 43 statements scored on a *Strongly Disagree* (1) to *Strongly Agree* (5) scale. The statements included question such as *"Masturbation is unhealthy."* The scale has four sub-scales Sexual myths, responsibility, sex and its consequences and sexual coercion. Each sub-scale is scored out of 55, with higher scores indicating a more liberal attitude (Lief, Fullard, & Devlin, 1990).

**A Sexual Health Knowledge**

Questionnaire was utilised developed from the NHS website, this contained 14 statements about sexual health for example *"16 is the age of sexual consent in England."* Items were scored with a Yes (1), No (0) or Don't Know (0) response. Two items were utilised that allowed participants to free type responses to the questions *"Please write the contraception methods you have heard of"* and *"Please write the sexually transmitted infections (STIs) you have heard of."* Participants gained one point for every correct STI (for example, chlamydia) or contraception method (For example, condom), using NHS guidelines there was a maximum of 8 points for the STI question and 10 points for the contraception question. Overall, the maximum score was 32, with higher scores indicating higher sexual health knowledge.

**Sexual Health Information**

Measured on a self-developed question. Participants were asked to type any sexual health information they had encountered over the past month. This was scored from (0) no information, (1) low quality information and (2) high quality information. Low quality information included speaking to friends and seeing sexual health information on social media. High quality information included attending a sexual health talk or speaking to a sexual health professional or teacher about sexual health.

**Safe Sex in the Media and Pornography**

Measured using self-developed questions. For example, *"How often have you seen safe sex portrayed in magazines or comics in the last six months?"* These were scored from never (0) to about once a week or more (3), the highest score available was nine. Higher scores indicated participants had seen more safe sex in the media or pornography. The questions and scoring system were adapted and modified to suit a female UK sample from the *'Exposure to Pornography in Traditional media'* scale (Lo & Wei, 2005) which has found to be reliable with Taiwanese teenagers.

**Previous Sexual Behaviours**

Measured using the Raine previous sexual behaviours scale (Skinner et al., 2015). Four questions measured relationship status, partner gender, age and length of relationship. Early sex before 16 was measured using two questions, participants were asked what age measured from *Haven't yet* to *16 years* they had vaginal sex with and without a condom.

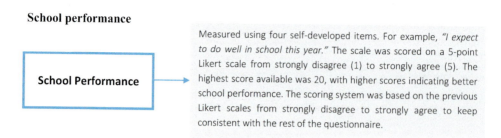

## Construction of Questionnaire

Barker and Weller (2009) identified that it is important to ensure questionnaires are fun for children and teenagers in order to keep them engaged and interested. Reliable data cannot be collected if participants become bored with the questionnaire. Therefore, after each questionnaire, interesting facts and pictures were added to keep the questionnaire exciting and interesting. The facts included items such as *"Did you know? Deer can't eat hay!"* A bold and bright color scheme was used throughout the questionnaire, with animal pictures added; see Fig. 7.1.

FIG. 7.1 Pictures and facts used to keep teenagers' attention throughout the questionnaire.

## Stage 1: review

After ethical approval, professionals, parents, and teenagers reviewed the questionnaire in paper format. This builds upon Bell's (2007) recommendation to use a review panel to pilot a questionnaire designed for teenagers. Professionals and parents were asked to review the questionnaire as they were likely to know whether teenagers would find the questionnaire interesting and whether they believed the questionnaires were appropriate for teenagers. This was particularly important as the questionnaire was targeting sexual health, a highly sensitive topic. Teenagers were asked to review the questionnaire in order to fully identify any questions or words that teenagers found ambiguous or could not understand (Table 7.2).

### What Were Professionals, Parents, and Teenagers Asked to do as Part of the Review?

Professionals and parents were asked to individually review the questionnaire in paper format. Participants were asked to read and annotate the questionnaire with any comments, amendments, or suggestions. Participants were asked to think about whether questions were suitable for female teenagers, aged 13–16 years and whether the wording was appropriate and within teenagers' comprehension level. Participants also commented on the overall questionnaire, wrote down overall strengths and weaknesses, and whether they believed teenagers would find the task engaging. Teenage participants were asked to read the questionnaire in paper format and highlight any words that they did not understand. Teenagers were asked to write a few comments about the overall questionnaire and whether they found it interesting. Following the study all participants were fully debriefed and thanked for their time.

**CHAPTER 7** Predictors of Risky Behaviors for Female Teenagers **87**

**TABLE 7.2**
**Gaining Consent From Teenagers.**

| | Gaining Consent From Teenagers |
|---|---|
| Pilot study | Opt-in consent—parents gave their informed consent for their child to take part in the study. Teenagers provided their informed consent offline to take part. |
| Main study (schools) | Opt-out consent, parents informed the school if they did not want their child to take part in the study. Teenagers gave their informed consent online. |
| Main study (external) | Opt-in consent, parents provided their written informed consent or verbal consent (telephone) for their child to take part in the study. Teenagers gave their informed consent online. |
| | See chapter 5 for full details on gaining consent from teenagers in sexual health studies |

Stage 2: Pilot testing with teenagers

Parents were recruited on social media and gave their opt-in consent for their child to take part in the study (see Table 7.2). Ten female teenagers completed the online questionnaire, with any amendments made from the Stage-1 pilot (see Table 7.3 below). Participants worked through the online questionnaire and were timed to evaluate how long the questionnaire took to complete. At the end of the questionnaire participants were asked to write down how they found the questionnaire overall, and write any strengths and/or limitations with the questionnaire.

**TABLE 7.3**
**Overview of Suggested Amendments to the Questionnaire, by Professionals, Parents, Teachers, and Teenagers.**

| Scale | Comments Professionals | Comments Teenagers | Amendments |
|---|---|---|---|
| Demographic questionnaire | Like the picture (n = 7) Change parents/guardians to parents/carers (n = 4) | Like the picture (n = 2) | Slight wording changes |
| Mini-markers | Teenagers will struggle with these words (n = 8) | Words highlighted that they did not understand (e.g., complex) (n = 5) | Scale removed |
| Self-esteem | Questions could be worded better (n = 8) | Issues with wording (n = 5) | Scale reworded for example, satisfied changed to happy |
| Self-efficacy | Questions not aimed at teenagers (n = 6) | Questions seem childish (n = 3) | Replaced with 8-item self-efficacy scale (Muris, 2001) suitable For teenagers |
| Sensation seeking | Too long (n = 7) Some choices not relevant to teenagers (n = 3) | Too long (n = 3) | Replaced with the brief sensation seeking scale (Hoyle, Stephenson, & Palmgreen, 2002) |
| PASTAS | Not suitable for teens (n = 4) | This is embarrassing (n = 2) | Scale removed |
| Delayed gratification | Enjoy this task because different to other scales (n = 3) | No comments | No amendments |
| Peer pressure | Slight wording changes | No comments | Slight wording changes, for example, "urged" changed to "made" |

*Continued*

## TABLE 7.3
Overview of Suggested Amendments to the Questionnaire, by Professionals, Parents, Teachers, and Teenagers.—cont'd

| Scale | Comments Professionals | Comments Teenagers | Amendments |
|---|---|---|---|
| Popularity | No comments | No comments | Scale removed |
| Peer conformity | No comments | No comments | Scale removed |
| Peer support, communication, and sexual attitudes | No comments | No comments | No amendments |
| Parental/carer support, communication, and sexual attitudes | No comments | Like picture (n = 2) | No amendments |
| Depression | Words not suitable (n = 4) Scale not appropriate for young people (n = 7) | Issues with wording | Scale removed |
| School performance | No comments | Like picture (n = 4) | No amendments |
| Sexual health knowledge | Slight wording changes | No comments | Slight wording changes for example, "obtain" to "get" |
| Sexual health information | No comments | No comments | No amendments |
| SKAT-A | Teenagers will struggle with a lot of these words and feel awkward—will not take scale seriously (n = 3) | Questionnaire is embarrassing (n = 2) | Scale removed |
| Safe sex in media | No comments | No comments | No amendments |
| Pornography in media | No comments | No comments | No amendments |
| Sexual behaviors | "Relationship" should be defined (n = 1) | No comments | Definition added in for "relationship" |

## Results
### Pilot findings
Professionals and parents annotated the questionnaire with suggestions and amendments, commenting on the overall questionnaire and any questions they believed were not suitable for teenagers. Teenagers highlighted any words that they did not understand and provided comments on the overall questionnaire. See Table 7.3 for overview of changes.

### Revised findings
Professionals, parents, and teenagers provided comments on what they thought about the overall questionnaire. All participants agreed that the questionnaire was too long. Professionals commented that *"Students can only concentrate for 20 minutes; this is twice as long"* (Teacher). Teenage participants mentioned that they would become *"bored"* and stop the questionnaire because it was too long. In terms of strengths of the questionnaire, professionals and parents believed that the interesting facts and pictures would keep teenagers engaged. Professionals also believed that the scales were in-depth and liked the easy-to-use Likert scales. Teenagers thought that the online questionnaire was appealing as they could complete it on their phones and laptops. Teenagers also liked the pictures and facts used throughout, especially the animal pictures.

Following this first stage of the pilot study the survey was amended, five questionnaires were removed, and two questionnaires were replaced. This was due to participants commenting that the overall survey was too long, therefore, questionnaires measuring factors that were not deemed highly important from professionals in our previous study (popularity and peer conformity) or questionnaires that participants in this pilot study deemed as not appropriate for teenagers were removed from the survey (PASTAS, depression, and SKAT-A). Therefore, the big 5 mini-markers (Saucier, 1999),

PASTAS (Reed, Thompson, Brannick, & Sacco, 1991), conformity questionnaire (self-developed), Center for Epidemiological studies depression scale (Radloff, 1977), and the SKAT-A scale (Lief, Fullard, & Devlin, 1990) were removed from the survey. Two questionnaires were removed and the self-efficacy scale was replaced with a shorter 8-item self-efficacy scale (Muris, 2001). The sensation-seeking scale was replaced with the brief sensation seeking scale (Hoyle et al., 2002). Therefore, the 240-item questionnaire was reduced to 118 items.

### Findings from pilot stage 2 (testing)

Teenagers were able to complete the full questionnaire. They took between 20 and 35 minutes to complete the questionnaire with an average time of 23 minutes. Teenagers commented that they *"enjoyed the facts"* and *"pictures"* throughout the survey and felt that it was *"not too long."* The pilot results showed that all the teenagers selected *"haven't yet"* to the previous sexual behaviors questionnaire. Therefore, two questionnaires were added measuring intention to have sex in the next year and intention to have safe sex in the next year.

Having reviewed, amended, and then tested the questionnaire the final version was then deployed.

## Method: Main Study

### Design

The final list of predictor variables was self-esteem, self-efficacy, sensation seeking, delayed gratification, peer pressure, peer support, peer sex communication, peer sex attitudes, parental support, parental sex communication, parental sex attitudes, sexual health knowledge, safe sex in media, pornography, sexual health information, and school performance. The criterion variables were early sex before 16 years and no early sex before 16 years. In addition, criterion variables included intention to have sex in the next year and intention to have safe sex in the next year. Age was included as a control variable. For an overview, see Fig. 7.2.

### Participants

A total 360 female teenagers were recruited from the North East of England. Teenagers were aged between 13 and 16 years old (Mean = 14.2 SD = 0.87). Teenagers were recruited using an opportunity sample from schools (320) and the wider population. The survey link was advertised on social media, through youth group organizations' Twitter and Facebook accounts. SES status was determined using parental education background and parental income, using the same

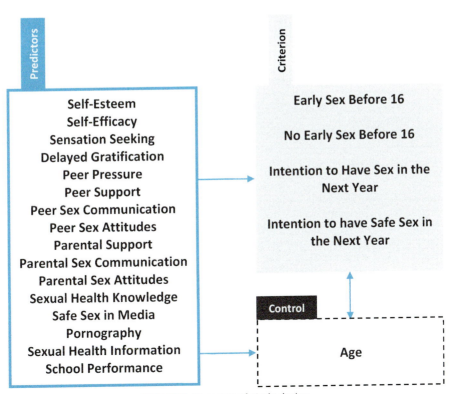

FIG. 7.2 Overview of study design.

## TABLE 7.4
### Overview of Participant Demographic Information, Including Free School Lunches, Ethnicity, and Parental Educational Background.

| | | N (%) |
|---|---|---|
| Age | 13 | 59 (18.9%) |
| | 14 | 149 (46.9%) |
| | 15 | 80 (25.2%) |
| | 16 | 30 (9.4%) |
| School lunches | Free or reduced price lunches | 92 (28.7%) |
| Ethnicity | White British | 275 (85.9%) |
| | Black or black British Caribbean | 3 (0.9%) |
| | Other mixed background | 3 (9%) |
| | Other white background | 18 (4.4%) |
| | Asian or Asian British | 15 (3.7%) |
| | White Irish | 6 (1.5%) |
| Living with parents | Live with mother | 120 (29.4%) |
| | Live with father | 33 (8.1%) |
| | Live with both parents | 104 (25.5%) |
| | Living in care | 34 (8.3%) |
| | Other | 20 (4.9%) |
| | Live with another relative | 9 (2.2%) |
| Parents' education background | Primary school | 5 (1.6%) |
| | Secondary school | 98 (30.6%) |
| | Sixth form or college | 47 (14.8%) |
| | University (undergraduate) | 34 (10.6%) |
| | Don't know | 134 (41.9%) |

criterion as discussed in Chapter 6 (see Table 7.4 for full demographic background). Participants were categorized as low SES if they were on free or reduced price meals (parents/carers yearly gross income was below £16,190), or if parent's highest educational attainment was primary or secondary school or if their parents were either unemployed or had working-class jobs (for example, builder or factory worker). If all of these questions were left blank or participants selected *"don't know"* to all questions, then their data were removed from further analysis. A total 12 participants were categorized as high SES and 30 participants failed to complete the full survey and were excluded from the analysis. Complete data were available from N = 318 participants.

Participants were split into early sex before 16 years (n = 39) and no early sex before 16 years (n = 279). The age range in the early sex group was 13–16 years (Mean = 14.6, SD = 0.74). Six of the *"early sex"* participants (15%) reported being in a heterosexual relationship and reported being with their partners between less than 3 months to 3 years. All partners were the same age or 1 year older than the participants were. In the no early sex group the age range was 13–16 years (Mean = 14.2, SD = 0.87). Seventy (24%) participants reported being in a heterosexual relationship and reported being with their partners less than 3 months to over 3 years. All partners were the same age or 2 years older than the participants were. See Table 7.5 for full overview of previous sexual behaviors for all participants.

### Materials
The final amended survey consisted of 16 questionnaires: 11 self-developed questionnaires and 5 standardized questionnaires. The survey was hosted on Qualtrics and all amendments from the pilot study were incorporated.

### Self-measures
*Demographic* information was measured using a self-developed questionnaire. The questionnaire consisted of seven items aimed to measure age, ethnicity, SES status, and parental background. *Self-esteem* was measured with the amended Rosenberg Self-esteem Scale (Rosenberg, 1965). The original scale consisted of 10 items ($\alpha = 0.83$); in this sample the scale was found to be highly reliable ($\alpha = 0.883$). *Self-efficacy* was measured with the 8-item self-efficacy scale (Muris, 2001). An example item was *"How well can you give yourself a peptalk when you feel low?"* Items were scored from *Not at all* (1) to *Pretty well* (5), the highest score available was 40. A higher score indicated higher levels of self-efficacy. The original scale consisted of eight items ($\alpha = 0.94$); in this sample the scale was also found to be highly reliable ($\alpha = 0.844$).

### Personality measures
*Delayed gratification* was measured with the modified Delay Gratification Scale (Zytkoskee, Strickland, & Watson, 1971). The Delayed Gratification Scale was deemed reliable four items ($\alpha = 0.656$). *Sensation seeking* was measured using the Brief Sensation Seeking Scale (Hoyle et al., 2002). The questionnaire has eight items, for example, *"I like to do frightening things."* Items

## CHAPTER 7 Predictors of Risky Behaviors for Female Teenagers

**TABLE 7.5**
**Overview of Previous Sexual Behaviors for the age in Which Participants Reported Having First Experience With Each Behavior. Frequencies and (Percentages) are Reported for Each Behavior the Percentages Add up to 100% for Each Behavior (e.g., Kissing).**

| Age | Haven't yet n (%) | Under 13 years n (%) | 13 years n (%) | 14 years n (%) | 15 years n (%) | 16 years n (%) |
|---|---|---|---|---|---|---|
| Kissing | 71 (22.3%) | 114 (35.7%) | 86 (27.0%) | 42 (13.2%) | 5 (1.6%) | 1 (0.2%) |
| Touching a partner's genitals | 221(69.3%) | 11 (3.4%) | 39 (12.2%) | 24 (7.5%) | 15 (4.7%) | 9 (2.8%) |
| Being touched on genitals | 237 (74.8%) | 9 (2.8%) | 23 (7.3%) | 20 (6.3%) | 19 (6.0%) | 9 (2.8%) |
| Giving oral sex | 249 (78.1%) | 6 (1.9%) | 21 (6.6%) | 14 (4.4%) | 18 (5.6%) | 11 (3.5%) |
| Receiving oral sex | 257 (60.6%) | 4 (1.3%) | 15 (4.7%) | 16 (5.0%) | 15 (4.7%) | 12 (3.8%) |
| Sex with a condom | 269 (84.6%) | 1 (0.3%) | 9 (2.8%) | 15 (4.7%) | 13 (2.8%) | 11 (3.5%) |
| Sex without a condom | 269 (84.6%) | 1 (0.3%) | 9 (2.8%) | 14 (4.4%) | 15 (4.7%) | 10 (3.1%) |

are scored from Strongly Disagree (0) to Strongly Agree (7). The scale ranges from 0 to 56; higher scores indicate higher levels of sensation seeking. The original item scale had a Cronbach's α coefficient of α = 0.81; it was also deemed reliable in this current sample (α = 0.763).

### Peers and parents

*Peer pressure* was measured with the peer pressure scale (Santor, Messervey, & Kusumakar, 2000). The original scale Cronbach's α coefficient was 0.69; in this current sample it was 11 items (α = 0.896). *Peer and parental/carers support, sex communication, and sex attitudes* scales were utilized from the pilot study with no amendments. All scales in this current sample were reliable; Peer Support five items (α = 0.910), Peer Sex Communication five items (α = 0.893), Peer Sex Attitudes five items (α = 0.745), Parental Support five items (α = 0.934), Parental Sex Communication five items (α = 0.930), and Parental Sex Attitudes five items (α = 0.673).

### Sexual health

*Sexual health knowledge, Sexual health information, safe sex in the media,* and *pornography* were measured with the self-developed questionnaires in the pilot study. No amendments were made to these scales. All scales in this current sample were reliable; Sexual Health Knowledge 12 items (α = 0.810), Safe Sex in the Media three items (α = 0.692), and Pornography three items (α = 0.692).

*Previous sexual behaviors* were measured using the Raine previous sexual behaviors scale (Skinner,

Robinson, Smith, Chenoa, & Robbins, 2015). Four questions measured relationship status, partner gender, age, and length of relationship. Early sex before 16 years was measured using two self-developed questions. Following from the pilot study a definition was added for relationship status:

> *A relationship is an emotional connection with another person. You may have relationships with your friends and family. For this relationship, we mean a romantic relationship with another person. This may also include a sexual relationship. You may have multiple romantic or sexual relationships, but for this question just think about if you are in a romantic relationship with ONE other person.*
>
> **NHS CHOICES, 2016.**

Participants were asked at what age they had vaginal sex with and without a condom; this was measured from *"Haven't yet"* to *"16 years"*. *Intentions to have sex* was measured using three questions. For example, *"During the next year I expect to have sex."* Intentions to have safe sex was measured using three questions. For example, *"During the next year if I have sex it is likely I will use contraception."* Items are scored from *Strongly Disagree* (0) to *Strongly Agree* (7). The scale ranges from 0 to 21; higher scores indicate higher intentions to have sex and higher intentions to have safe sex. The intentions questions and scoring system were developed from Godin, Bélanger-Gravel, and Vézina-Im (2012) recommendations for developing intention questionnaires.

### School performance

*School performance* was measured using the previously described self-developed scale. No amendments were

## 92 Teenagers, Sexual Health Information and the Digital Age

made to this scale. The final scale for this current sample was deemed reliable four items ($\alpha = 0.738$).

### Overview of questionnaire

The majority of questionnaires demonstrated an acceptable level of $\alpha$ normally deemed to be 0.70 and above (Hinkin, 1998; Kline, 1999). However, a few self-developed or modified questionnaires fell short of this 0.70 level (e.g., delayed gratification, parental sex attitudes, and safe sex in the media); however, they were still above 0.65 level considered to be at the lower end of the acceptable level for new scales (Hair, Anderson, Tatham, & Black, 2006). Therefore, all questionnaires were deemed as reliable for the study.

### Procedure

Participants were recruited from schools and the wider population (see Fig. 7.3 for overview of study procedure). An opt-out parental consent procedure was utilized with participants who were recruited from schools. Parents were posted parental consent letters and informed the school within 2 weeks if they did not want their daughter to take part. For participants recruited externally, parental consent was sought online. Parents/carers were asked to review and sign an online consent form and supply a phone number or postal address and convenient times to be contacted. The researcher then contacted parents/carers and asked if they were happy for their consent to be used. All participants gave their informed consent online.

In schools, the participants completed the survey in a class room setting with a teacher and the researcher present, in case any issues arose. Participants recruited externally completed the survey on their own. Participants completed the questionnaires online via Qualtrics online instructions provided so that participants could work through the survey on their own. The survey took approximately 25 minutes to complete. At the end of the survey, participants were fully debriefed online and directed to a sexual health website if they had any further sexual health questions. The researcher's email address was online in case participants had any questions about the research. Parental debrief forms were posted home to parents by schools. For participants who were recruited eternally parents were emailed electronic debrief forms.

### Results
### Treatment of data

All questionnaires were scored and the data entered into SPSS for analysis. Descriptive statistics including frequencies, means, and standard deviations were calculated for each scale and age group. Due to there being an uneven split of ages (see Table 7.4) with 46.9% of participants being aged 14 years, age was added in the analysis as a control variable. A logistic regression was conducted to assess the likelihood of the predictors predicting early sex before age 16 years. Two multiple regressions were conducted to assess the likelihood of the predictors predicting intention to have sex and intention to have safe sex. The full statistics are discussed below followed by a summary table of results (Table 7.8).

### Early sex

Logistic regression analysis was conducted to predict likelihood of early sex before age 16 years using self-esteem, self-efficacy, sensation seeking, delayed gratification, peer pressure, peer support, peer sex communication, peer sex attitudes, parental support, parental sex communication, parental sex attitudes, sexual health knowledge, safe sex in media, pornography, sexual information, and school performance. Age was included as a control variable.

A test of the full model against a constant only model was statistically significant, indicating that the predictors as a set reliably distinguished between early sex and no early sex ($\chi^2(17) = 59.015$, $p < .001$). Hosmer and Lemeshow tests nonsignificant value indicates a good fitting model. See Table 7.6 for overview of predictors.

The odds ratio shows that likelihood of early sex before age 16 years significantly increases with higher sensation seeking ($P = 0.008$) and higher high quality sexual health information ($P = 0.039$). Early sex decreases with higher self-esteem ($P = 0.022$), higher delayed gratification ($P = 0.037$), and higher sex knowledge ($P = 0.044$). The other predictors were nonsignificant.

### Intention to Have Sex

A multiple regression was carried out for intention to have sex in the next year with the predictors *self-esteem, self-efficacy, sensation seeking, delayed gratification, peer pressure, peer support, peer sex communication, peer sex attitudes, parental support, parental sex communication, parental sex attitudes, sexual health knowledge, safe sex in media, pornography, sexual information,* and *school performance. Age* was included as a control variable (see Table 7.7).

Using the enter method it was found that the predictors could explain a significant amount of the variance in intention to have sex in the next year $F(17, 300) = 2.956$, $P < 0.001$ ($R^2 = 0.14$, $R^2_{Adjusted} = 0.09$).

### CHAPTER 7 Predictors of Risky Behaviors for Female Teenagers

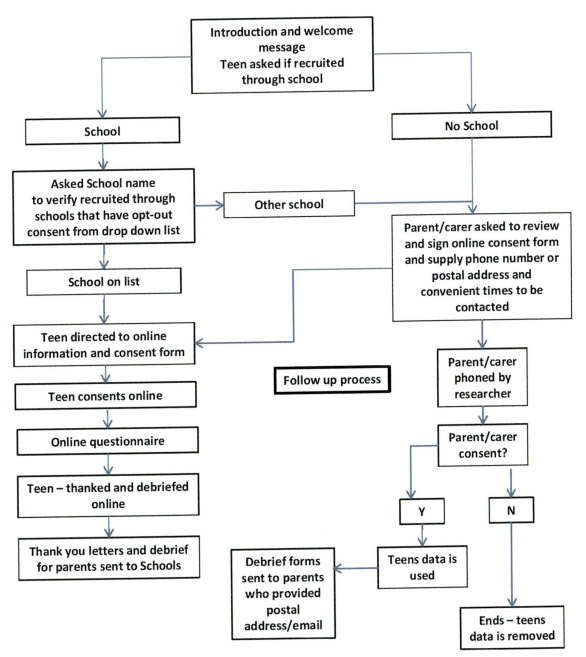

FIG. 7.3 Overview of study procedure for participants recruiting through schools and externally.

The analysis shows that higher *peer pressure* ($\beta = 0.26$, $t(17) = 4.46$, $P < 0.001$) and higher *pornography* ($\beta = 0.15$, $t(17) = 2.26$, $P = 0.024$) significantly predicts intention to have sex in the next year. The other predictors were nonsignificant.

A second multiple regression was conducted on intention to have safe sex in the next year with the predictors *self-esteem, self-efficacy, sensation seeking, delayed gratification, peer pressure, peer support, peer sex communication, peer sex attitudes, parental support, parental sex*

# 94 Teenagers, Sexual Health Information and the Digital Age

**TABLE 7.6**
**Logistic Regression Model Assessing Independent Predictors of Early Sex Before age 16 years.**

| Variable | B(SE) | Odds Ratio | 95% CI FOR THE ODDS RATIO | | p- value |
|---|---|---|---|---|---|
| | | | Lower | Upper | |
| Constant | −10.580 (4.334) | | | | |
| Age | | | | | |
| Self-esteem | −0.108 (0.047)[a] | 0.898 | 0.819 | 0.984 | $P = 0.022$ |
| Self-efficacy | −0.037 (0.038) | 0.965 | 0.895 | 1.038 | $P = 0.328$ |
| Sensation seeking | 0.116 (0.044)[a] | 1.123 | 1.031 | 1.223 | $P = 0.008$ |
| Delayed gratification | −0.078 (0.038)[a] | 0.925 | 0.859 | 0.995 | $P = 0.037$ |
| Peer pressure | −0.010 (0.023) | 0.990 | 0.947 | 1.035 | $P = 0.671$ |
| Peer support | −0.077 (0.052) | 0.926 | 0.836 | 1.026 | $P = 0.140$ |
| Peer sex communication | 0.084 (0.055) | 1.088 | 0.977 | 1.211 | $P = 0.126$ |
| Peer sex attitudes | 0.063 (0.071) | 1.065 | 0.927 | 1.225 | $P = 0.372$ |
| Parental support | −0.056 (0.059) | 0.946 | 0.842 | 1.062 | $P = 0.347$ |
| Parental sex communication | −032 (0.049) | 1.033 | 0.939 | 1.136 | $P = 0.504$ |
| Parental sex attitudes | 0.109 (0.071) | 1.115 | 0.969 | 1.282 | $P = 0.128$ |
| Sex knowledge | −0.075 (0.037)[a] | 0.928 | 0.863 | 0.998 | $P = 0.044$ |
| Safe sex in media | −0.116 (0.194) | 0.890 | 0.608 | 1.302 | $P = 0.549$ |
| Pornography | −2.68 (0.245) | 0.765 | 0.474 | 1.236 | $P = 0.274$ |
| Low quality sex information | 0.596 (0.711) | 1.814 | 0.451 | 7.306 | $P = 0.402$ |
| High quality sex information | 1.556 (0.753)[a] | 4.738 | 1.082 | 20.741 | $P = 0.039$ |
| School performance | 0.073 (0.085) | 1.076 | 0.910 | 1.272 | $P = 0.389$ |

$R^2 = 0.195$ (Cox & Snell), 0.371 (Nagelkerke), 0.051 (Hosmer & Lemeshow) Model $\chi^2(17) = 59.015$, $P < 0.001$.
[a] $P < .05$.

**TABLE 7.7**
**Multiple Regression Analysis of the Individual Predictors Related to Intention to Have Sex in the Next Year.**

| | B | SE B | B | P |
|---|---|---|---|---|
| **STEP 1** | | | | |
| Constant | 1.61 (−9.27, 12.50) | 5.53 | | $P = 0.771$ |
| Age | 0.51 (−0.26, 1.26) | 0.38 | 0.07 | $P = 0.197$ |
| **STEP 2** | | | | |
| Constant | −5.60 (−17.64, 6.43) | 6.11 | | $P = 0.360$ |
| Age | 0.46 (−0.39, 1.33) | 0.43 | 0.06 | $P = 0.291$ |
| Self-esteem | 0.12 (−0.02, 0.26) | 0.07 | 0.11 | $P = 0.100$ |
| Self-efficacy | −0.10 (−0.21, 0.02) | 0.06 | -0.11 | $P = 0.106$ |
| Sensation seeking | −0.30 (−0.15, 0.09) | 0.06 | -0.03 | $P = 0.619$ |
| Delayed gratification | 0.01 (−0.10, 0.16) | 0.06 | 0.01 | $P = 0.923$ |
| Peer pressure | 0.16 (0.11, 0.22) | 0.03 | 0.26 | $P < 0.001$[b] |

*(continued)*

**CHAPTER 7** Predictors of Risky Behaviors for Female Teenagers    **95**

**TABLE 7.7**
**Multiple Regression Analysis of the Individual Predictors Related to Intention to Have Sex in the Next Year.—cont'd**

|  | B | SE B | B | P |
|---|---|---|---|---|
| *Peer support* | 0.11 (−0.06, 0.29) | 0.09 | 0.09 | $P = 0.214$ |
| *Peer sex communication* | −0.09 (−0.25, 0.07) | 0.08 | -0.09 | $P = 0.259$ |
| *Peer sex attitudes* | −0.04 (−0.25, 0.17) | 0.11 | -0.04 | $P = 0.651$ |
| *Parental support* | 0.11 (−0.19, 0.15) | 0.08 | -0.02 | $P = 0.797$ |
| *Parental sex communication* | −0.09 (−0.10, 0.18) | 0.07 | 0.03 | $P = 0.620$ |
| *Parental sex attitudes* | −0.04 (−0.26, 0.18) | 0.11 | -0.02 | $P = 0.722$ |
| *Sex knowledge* | −0.09 (−0.15, 0.20) | 0.06 | 0.11 | $P = 0.091$ |
| *Safe sex in media* | −0.22 (−0.69, 0.25) | 0.24 | -0.06 | $P = 0.362$ |
| *pornography* | −0.63 (0.08, 1.17) | 0.28 | 0.15 | $P = 0.024$[a] |
| *sex information* | −0.50 (−0.32, 1.33) | 0.42 | 0.07 | $P = 0.232$ |
| *School performance* | −0.14 (−0.08, 0.36) | 0.11 | 0.09 | $P = 0.210$ |

[a] $P < .05$.
[b] $P < .001$.

communication, parental sex attitudes, sexual health knowledge, safe sex in media, pornography, sexual information and school performance. Age was added as a control variable.

Using the enter method it was found that the predictors did not explain a significant amount of the variance of intention to have safe sex in the next year $F(17, 300) = 2.072$, $P < 0.381$ ($R^2 = 0.05$, $R^2_{Adjusted} = 0.04$) (Table 7.8).

**TABLE 7.8**
**Summary of Results.**

|  | Predictors that Explain a Significant Amount of the Variance |
|---|---|
| Sex before age 16 years | Higher sensation seeking and higher high quality sexual health information. Early sex decreases with higher self-esteem, higher delayed gratification, and higher sex knowledge. |
| Intention to have sex in the next year | Higher peer pressure and higher pornography |
| Intention to have safe sex in the next year | None of the predictors could predict intention to have safe sex in the next year |

## Discussion

The analysis has shown that higher *sensation seeking* and more *high-quality sexual health information, lower self-esteem, lower delayed gratification,* and *lower sexual health knowledge* significantly predicts early sex before age 16 years. Throughout our previous studies, *self-esteem* has qualitatively been identified as a highly important factor, and in this study has now been identified quantitatively as a predictor to early sex before age 16 years. This statistically significant finding of self-esteem is in contrast to previous literature (Salazar & Crosby, 2005). However, this may be due to the complex nature of self-esteem development, which is known to interact with SES background, family, and individual characteristics (Boden & Horwood, 2006). Research that has included these factors in the analyses has found self-esteem impacts on risk-taking behaviors (Laflin, Wang, & Barry, 2008). This current study included parental support and attitudes, peer influences, and other self-characteristics and this may help explain the reason for the statistically significant finding. Therefore, for low SES female teenagers' self-esteem with the interplay of sensation seeking, sexual health information, sexual health knowledge, and delayed gratification can predict early sex before age 16 years.

The finding that sensation seeking and delayed gratification are predictors of early sex is consistent with previous research. Other studies have shown links with sensation seeking and earlier initiation (Hoyle,

Fejfat & Miller, 2000) and higher delayed gratification predicting less unprotected sex (Reyna & Wilhelms, 2016). The present study has extended the delayed gratification findings and shown that this factor is also significantly related to early sexual intercourse. These findings also support the problem behaviors theory discussed in chapter 2 (Donovan, Jessor & Costa, 1988), as self-regulatory deficits often manifest themselves in a cluster of problem behaviors, linking with higher engagement in risky sex (Skinner et al., 2015).

The findings with respect to sexual health information present a more mixed and inconsistent picture. The finding that lower sexual health knowledge but higher quality sexual health information significantly predicts early sex may reflect an issue with the self-report nature of the sexual health information question. Teenagers may have reported that they have received a sexual health talk, and therefore, were categorized as receiving high-quality sexual health information. Yet, due to the outdated nature of Sex and Relationship Education focusing on the biological aspects of sexual health, such as periods (OfSTED, 2002), teenagers may still have little sexual health knowledge when it comes to other areas of sexual health, such as consent, pregnancy, and STIs. For that reason, methodological issues with the sexual health information self-report questions may mean that this finding needs to be interpreted with caution.

The analysis shows that higher peer pressure and higher pornography use significantly predicts intention to have sex in the next year. Whereas, none of the predictors could significantly predict intention to have safe sex in the next year. Peer pressure has been highlighted throughout our previous studies (Chapters 4 and 6), and the existing literature, as an important predictor of teenage sexual risk-taking. Peer pressure has been associated with earlier sexual initiation and higher number of sexual partners (Lagus, Bernat, Bearinger, Resnick, & Eisenberg, 2011; Santelli, Abma, et al., 2004). However, this present study has highlighted that while peer pressure is associated with intention to have sex in the next year, peer pressure does not significantly predict earlier sexual initiation. This is consistent with Gillmore et al. (2002) who found that social norms and peer pressure are important, as believing peers have had sex is associated with intention to have sex. Peer pressure also links with the findings in Table 7.6 of delayed gratification; higher delayed gratification has been protective against peer pressure (Reyna & Wilhelms, 2016). This is in line with the theory of planned behavior (Ajzen, 1991) discussed in chapter 2, as a model of cognitive processes underlies teenagers'

decisions to have sex, subjective norms and attitudes influence teenagers' sexual intentions (Gillmore et al., 2002; Morrison, Baker, & Gillmore, 1998). Therefore, as Table 7.6 shows that lower delayed gratification is a statistically significant predictor of early sex before age 16 years, and Table 7.7 shows peer pressure is a significant predictor of intention to have sex, the two may be interactive together in predicting sex before age 16 years.

Also, Table 7.7 highlights that pornography is important in determining intention to have sex in the next year. Previous research has found teenagers who access pornography tend to have higher permissive sexual attitudes, more casual sex, and greater occurrence of sexual intercourse (Peter & Valkenburg, 2016). However, in this study even though pornography does not significantly predict earlier intercourse, it is linked with intention to have sex in the next year. Sensation seekers are more likely to access pornography, and more likely to have early sex, and therefore, the influence of sensation seeking and pornography may also be interactive in predicting sex before age 16 years (Peter & Valkenburg, 2016).

## Limitations and Strengths

The reliance on self-report means of assessment is a serious limitation given the highly sensitive nature of sexual behavior (Schaeffer, 2000). Although the anonymity of this method tends to increase the validity of sexual health surveys for teenagers, especially when compared to face-to-face interviews (Alexander & Fisher, 2003) and previous research has demonstrated that adolescent girls can reliably report sexual behavior and contraceptive use as long as reliable scale is administrated (Sieving et al., 2005), relying solely on the use of self-report measures as means of assessment remains a limiting factor. Also, the testing environment varied for teenagers recruited externally versus teenagers recruited through schools. Teenagers recruited through schools completed the online questionnaire in a classroom setting and were asked to concentrate on the task and not discuss the questions with anyone in the room. However, there was no control over the testing environment for teenagers recruited externally, and they may have discussed the questions with someone. An online questionnaire was administered because for highly sensitive topics, online surveys elicit less social desirability bias (Booth-Kewley, Larson, & Miyoshi, 2007). However, those teenagers completing the questionnaire in a classroom setting with the researcher present may not have perceived the questionnaire to be as anonymous and confidential as teenagers completing

## Implications

Self-esteem has been identified as a statistically significant predictor of early sexual initiation in this study of low SES female teenagers. This is consistent with the findings of our previous study described in Chapter 4 in which sexual health professionals identified self-esteem as a highly important predictor to risky sexual behaviors in female teenagers. Corresponding with our study with teenagers (described in Chapter 6) it was found that lower sexual health knowledge is also an important predictor of early sexual behaviors. Female teenagers who report higher levels of peer pressure and are exposed to greater pornography in the media have higher intentions to have sex in the next year, hence, information about pornography and minimizing peer pressure should also be included in sexual health information sources.

Understanding the predictors of risky sexual behaviors provides a strong basis for a sexual health intervention program. Consequently, the following chapter describes teenagers' views of current digital sexual health education websites and mobile apps, given the evidence that teenagers prefer anonymous and confidential ways of acquiring sexual health information and remain reluctant to discuss the issue face to face.

# CHAPTER 8

# Teenagers' Views of Sexual Health Education Websites and Apps

## CHAPTER OUTLINE

Introduction ...................................................... 99
Method ............................................................. 100
    Participants ................................................. 100
    Materials...................................................... 101
        *Websites and apps*................................. **101**
        *Focus group* ......................................... **102**
    Procedure.................................................... 103
    First Discussion .......................................... 103
    Viewing and Interacting with Websites and
    Apps ............................................................ 103
    Return to Website/App and Final Discussion... 104
    Analysis Procedure...................................... 104

Results ............................................................. 104
    Drivers for Seeking Sexual Health Information
    Online ......................................................... 105
    Design of Website and Apps......................... 105
    Website and App Content............................. 107
    Trusting and Using Websites and Apps ........... 108
    Return to Favorite Website/App..................... 110
Discussion ....................................................... 110
    Limitations................................................... 112
    Implications ................................................. 112
    Chapter Summary........................................ 112

## ABSTRACT

This chapter aims to consider teenagers' views of using existing mobile apps and websites for sexual health information. The chapter is divided into four sections. Section Introduction provides a brief overview of the literature on current sexual health websites and apps. Section Methods describes the method used in this study, and subsequently Results section discusses the main qualitative findings. Finally, the results and implications of using sexual health websites and apps with teenagers are discussed in Discussion section.

## KEYWORDS

Digital health interventions; Focus groups; Online sexual health interventions; Qualitative research; School-based sexual health education; Sexual health; Sexual health education; Sexual health interventions; Sexual health mobile apps; Sexual health websites; Teenagers.

## INTRODUCTION

As previously discussed in Chapter 3, the Internet plays an important role in teenagers' everyday lives, and 95% of teenagers have access to a smartphone with 45% of

teenagers reporting that they are online constantly (Anderson & Jiang, 2018). It is also well reported that teenagers use the Internet to search for sexual health advice (Gray & Klein, 2006). Teenagers do still regard healthcare providers as the most reliable source for sexual health information, but in a society that considers discussing sexual health a taboo, it can be embarrassing to discuss sex face to face (Eisenberg, Bernat, & Bearinger, 2008). As school-based sexual health education programs are inconsistent, the Internet is becoming a more important resource for private sexual health information (Lindberg, Maddow-Zimet, & Boonstra, 2016).

Recently, some sexual health websites have developed interventions to improve teenagers' knowledge of sexual health (Simon & Daneback, 2013). Four of the main ways interventions are delivered online are through sexual health websites (Buhi, Daley, Oberne, & Smith, 2010), social networking sites (SNSs) (Gold & Pedrana, 2011), text messaging (Selkie, 2011), and mobile apps (Muessig, Pike, & LeGrand, 2013). However, SNSs are more useful as a signpost to other health websites because SNSs are restrictive in the amount and type of information that can be presented (Gold & Pedrana, 2011). Teenagers also worry that because their names are associated with SNSs, they may not be

Teenagers, Sexual Health Information and the Digital Age. https://doi.org/10.1016/B978-0-12-816969-8.00008-4
Copyright © 2020 Elsevier Inc. All rights reserved.

private and anonymous (Divecha, Divney, & Ickovics, 2012). Text messages are perceived as more private, as phones feel personal to teenagers (Cole-Lewis & Kershaw, 2010). However, it is time consuming to collect teenagers' phone numbers and someone unauthorized could gain access to this personal information; consequently, there could be serious issues with confidentiality. Due to the limited character length of text messages, and the decline in teenagers using text messaging services (OfCom, 2014), it may be more appropriate to target teenagers through more up-to-date services such as mobile apps.

Mobile apps facilitate interaction in a quick, efficient way and can be constantly accessed and updated (Apps & Krebs, 2016). However, we need to know whether (1) teenagers are currently using mobile apps to access sexual health information, (2) what content teenagers consider to be important on sexual health apps, and (3) what features teenagers perceive as important for determining credibility and privacy when using health apps.

In comparison to mobile apps, websites have been extensively researched. Evaluations of current sexual health sites reveal issues around the quality of the information they provide. The information provided on more technically complex websites is often inaccurate (Buhi et al., 2010) and outdated (Harris, Byrd, Engel, & Weeks, 2016). From a user perspective, the literature also suggests a preference for sexual health websites that present clear information, free from technical or complex language. Websites should cover a wide range of sexual health topics, including sexual pleasure, relationships, and STIs. Also, websites should include videos that teenagers can relate to (McCarthy, Carswell, Murray, & Free, 2012), and resources should be accessible, trustworthy, private, and safe (Selkie & Benson, 2011).

We know what design features teenagers like in sexual health websites; however, we do not know if these are the same for mobile apps. Therefore, this study aimed to build upon existing research concerning sexual health websites by exploring the preferences of female teenagers with respect to accessing sexual health information via websites and mobile apps. We investigated trust and privacy issues associated with the two formats. The research also aimed to explore if female teenagers currently use sexual health websites and mobile apps to seek sexual health information and if so, whether these resources are currently meeting their sexual health needs (Table 8.1).

## METHOD

This was a qualitative study in which female teenagers engaged with a number of sexual health websites and sexual health apps and then took part in a follow-up focus group to discuss their reactions to these different resources. The study is explained in detail in the following section.

## Participants

Twenty-three female participants aged 13–16 years (M = 14.3, SD = 0.91) took part in the study. Participants were recruited from five schools in the North East of England. The delivery, content, and amount of formal sexual health education received differed between schools. The existing sexual health sessions ranged from 1 hour of sexual health education (which just covered menstruation for girls) in Year 7 to regular sexual health classes run by an external health center. See Table 8.2 for a full overview of existing sexual health knowledge.

Participants were low SES based on parental educational background and parental income; 12 participants' parents' highest educational attainment was primary school, 8 secondary school, and 3 sixth form or college. Five participants were on free or reduced price school lunches, which meant their parents have an annual income of less than £16,190. Twenty participants identified as White British, two as Black or Black British African, and one as Other Mixed Background.

---

**TABLE 8.1**
**Overview of Existing Research on Sexual Health Websites and Mobile Apps.**

**Summary Points**

- The Internet remains an increasingly important resource for obtaining sexual health information.
- Websites have been extensively researched, and teenagers want websites that provide simple sexual health advice.
- It is important to target teenagers with up-to-date technology that they are familiar with; however, it is unclear what design features of sexual health mobile apps are important to teenagers.
- It is important that teenagers perceive sexual health websites as private and credible sources of information.

CHAPTER 8 Teenagers' Views of Sexual Health Education Websites and Apps **101**

**TABLE 8.2**
**Overview of Schools' Existing Sexual Health Sessions.**

| School | Participants | Existing Sexual Health Sessions |
|--------|-------------|--------------------------------|
| School 1 | Year groups 9–10, ages 14–15 years. (N = 4) | 1 hour of sexual health education in Year 7. Session focused on reproductive talks and menstruation; teacher had no previous sexual health education or experience. No drop-in services available. |
| School 2 | Year group 10, ages 14–15 years. (N = 5) | 1 hour of sexual health education in Year 8. Session focused on menstruation; teacher had no previous sexual health education or experience. No drop-in services available. |
| School 3 | Year groups 10–12, ages 15–16 years. (N = 5) | Regular sexual health enrichment classes run by experienced sexual health professionals from an external health center. Also, drop-in services twice a week at dedicated youth center in school. |
| School 4 | Year group 9, ages 15–16 years. (N = 5) | 1 hour of sexual health education in Year 7. Session focused on reproduction and menstruation. Previously had nurses running a drop-in service with the c-card scheme. |
| School 5 | Year group 9, ages 13–14 years. (N = 4) | 1 hour of sexual health education in Year 8. Session focused on reproduction and menstruation. No drop-in services available at school, but local ones advertised to pupils. |

See Table 8.3 for a full overview of participant's demographic background.

## Materials

### Websites and apps

Google was used to search for sexual health websites between June 20 and July 20, 2016. The websites on the first three pages of the Google search were then examined; this is because previous research has found that teenager searches that return a large number of results are often resolved by confining their interest to the first few results (Hansen, Derry, & Resnick, 2003a). Inclusion criteria included the website addressed one or more aspects of sexual health/safe sex advice, specifically aimed at and suitable for female teenagers, contained accurate sexual health information, and was written in English. Exclusion criteria included the following: specifically stated that it was not suitable for teenagers, stated that it was not regarded as a source for health-related information, websites for healthcare professionals, absence of original content (links to secondary sources), focused solely on HIV/AIDS, and websites that did not provide a holistic coverage of sexual health. Websites deemed suitable from these criteria were categorized as charity websites, US websites, independent websites, websites by teens for teens, UK health provider websites, and discussion forums. One website

**TABLE 8.3**
**Summary of Participants' Demographic Background.**

| Demographic Background | | Number (percentage) |
|-----------------------|--------------------------------|----------------------|
| | Free or reduced price lunches | 5 (21.7%) |
| Ethnicity | White British | 20 (86.9%) |
| | Black or Black British African | 2 (8.7%) |
| | Other mixed background | 1 (4.4%) |
| Living with parents | Living with mother | 8 (34.8%) |
| | Live with both parents | 12 (52.2%) |
| | Living in care | 3 (13.1%) |
| Parents' education background | Primary school | 12 (52.2%) |
| | Secondary school | 8 (34.8%) |
| | Sixth form or college | 3 (13.1%) |

from each category was then chosen for the study (see Table 8.4 for full details of websites and apps).

Search terms included the following: *can you have sex on your period? how do you get an STI? sexual health advice UK, sexual health advice, girl's sexual health, sex education, teen sex education, teen sexual health, safe sex, safer sex, teen safe sex, condoms.*

**TABLE 8.4**
**Summary of Chosen Websites and Apps.**

| | Provider | Category |
|---|---|---|
| **WEBSITES** | | |
| Brook website | Brook—UK charity providing sexual health services for young people under 25 years | Charity website |
| Girls health | Office of women's health as part of US department of health and human services | US website |
| Young lovers guide | Independent website providing sex education for teens | Independent website |
| Sex etc. | Written by teens for teens but published by ANSWER, a national organization | By teens for teens |
| NHS | NHS—National health service in the United Kingdom | UK health provider |
| Health talk | Healthtalk.org provides free, reliable information about health issues, by sharing people's real-life experiences | Discussion forum |
| **MOBILE APPS** | | |
| Condom Craze | Free app that promotes a social media dialogue on safe sex | Interactive game |
| My teen mind | Gaia Technologies—research work carried out by a UK school. Covering all areas of sexual health | School-based sexual education app |
| Girl empowered | Developed by Medical Services Pacific (MSP), a charity that provides free holistic healthcare to women and youth in need | Information provider |

IPads were used to view the sexual health mobile apps; therefore the researchers searched for sexual health apps on the Apple App Store, using the same search terms as the websites. Inclusion criteria included the app addressed one of more aspects of sexual health promotion/safe sex advice, app rated as suitable for under 16s, accurate sexual health information, relevant to female teenagers, and written in English. Exclusion criteria included the following: specifically stated that it was not suitable for under 16s, stated that it was not regarded as a source for health-related information, apps for healthcare professionals, apps categorized as "Entertainment", "Games", "Casual", or "Puzzle"; focused solely on HIV, sexual positions, sexual performance, technique or sex trivia, sexual dysfunction, fertility and ovulation checker, contraception, or condom size; apps that could not be downloaded because of country restrictions that prevented access in the United Kingdom; technical problems with the app, sexual health clinic/condom locators outside the United Kingdom; paid apps that were a paid version of a free app ("lite" version). The apps deemed suitable from these criteria were then categorized as school-based sexual education apps, interactive game apps, and information provider apps. One app from each category was chosen. Six websites but only three mobile apps were chosen, due to there being limited appropriate mobile apps, whereas there were hundreds of suitable websites.

### Focus group

A focus group schedule was developed using open-ended and semi-structured questions in order to keep on topic but allowing participants to provide further explanations and discuss their own experiences. Example questions on the focus group schedule included: *"How have you previously searched for sexual health information?"* and *"Which website did you find most useful, any reasons why?"*

Teenagers were also provided with a worksheet to write down any thoughts about the websites or apps while they were viewing them. The website/app name was on the top of the page, with four statements; *"I like this website because ..."*; *"I dislike this website because ..."*; *"The information I find useful is ..."*; and *"any other comments"*. A large box was provided after each statement for participants' answers. Participants were told that these answers would help them during the focus group and that the researcher would be collecting the worksheets when the focus group had finished (Fig. 8.1).

CHAPTER 8 Teenagers' Views of Sexual Health Education Websites and Apps 103

FIG. 8.1 Girls health website.

## Procedure

The study was granted ethical approval from Northumbria University's Faculty of Health and Life Sciences Ethical Committee. The study took place in a school setting, and parental consent was sought using an opt-out procedure. Parental letters were posted home by the school, explaining the study and parents informed the schools within 2 weeks if they did not want their daughters taking part in the research. The testing day took place 2 weeks after the last parental letter had been posted. An information sheet was given to the participant and the researcher verbally explained the procedure. Participants gave their informed consent to take part in the research on the testing day.

## First Discussion

Participants took part in focus groups in groups of either four or five. The focus groups took place in a quiet location within their school. The researcher and a teacher were present during the focus groups. The researcher kept the focus group on track using the focus group schedule. In the first discussion, participants discussed their previous experiences of sexual health education and experiences of searching for sexual health information. Participants were asked to think about the ways in which they have previously searched for sexual health information, and if they had not searched for sexual health information before to think about how they might do this. If participants had not mentioned the Internet, this was prompted and participants were asked to think about the positives and negatives of using the Internet for searching for sexual health information.

## Viewing and Interacting with Websites and Apps

Participants viewed either the six sexual health websites or the three sexual health mobile apps for 5 minutes and the researcher let the participants know when to move onto the next website/app. Participants were asked to write notes about each of the websites and apps to use as prompts in the next discussion. They were then instructed to concentrate on what they liked and disliked about the website/app and whether the information provided on the website/app was useful. Participants then took part in another group discussion, using their written prompts, in which their thoughts on each of the websites and mobile apps were discussed.

### Return to Website/App and Final Discussion

Participants then had 15 minutes to revisit their favorite app or website. They also wrote notes on why they visited that particular website or mobile app. Participants then took part in a final group discussion to discuss their "favorite" app or website. The entire session lasted approximately 1 hour. These sessions were audio recorded using an Olympus dictaphone and transcribed verbatim. At the end of the study, participants were fully debriefed and thanked for their time. For an overview of the procedure see Fig. 8.2.

### Analysis Procedure

The written comments on the worksheets were added to the verbatim transcripts. The transcripts were analyzed using thematic analysis (Braun & Clarke, 2006) for emerging themes based on the markers used by the participants to assess their preferences and selection patterns (See Chapter 4, section 2 for an overview of thematic analysis). A coding scheme was developed and a first pass through the transcripts revealed a number of themes relating to the first impressions of the websites and mobile apps and participants' reasons for liking and disliking the websites and mobile apps. These themes were then checked with the original coding scheme to ensure that all areas were covered; reasons for liking the websites/apps, reasons for disliking the websites/apps, reasons for trusting the websites/apps and favorite website/apps. The themes were then appropriately named and defined. The final stage involved producing the report and choosing examples of quotes from the worksheets and transcripts to illustrate each theme and to give a good explanation of the point being made.

### RESULTS

The full qualitative results are displayed below, with summary tables of each theme presented. The analysis sought to clarify participants' current practice with regard to seeking sexual health information and to understand the context in which websites and mobile apps may or may not be used for sexual health information. Firstly, findings are presented on teenagers' current sexual health information seeking practices and then the key factors in terms of shaping

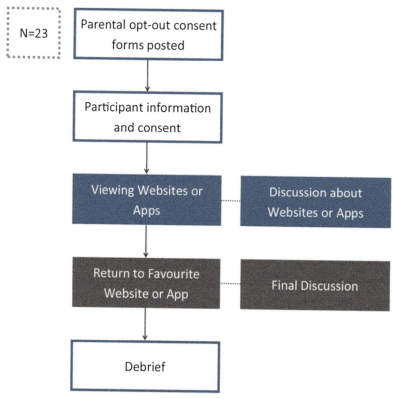

FIG. 8.2 Overview of procedure.

## CHAPTER 8 Teenagers' Views of Sexual Health Education Websites and Apps

**TABLE 8.5**
**Snapshot of Drivers for Seeking Sexual Health Information Online.**

| Drivers for Seeking Sexual Health Information Online |
| --- |
| Feel too embarrassed to attend a sexual health information center. |
| Mobile phones are preferred for accessing sexual health information because of the ease of access and privacy they afford. |
| Not a single participant had heard of a sexual health mobile app. |

preferences for web-based and mobile app–based sexual health information are discussed. There are five themes: *"Drivers for seeking sexual health information online"*; *"Design of websites and apps"*; *"Website and app content"*; *"Trusting and using websites and apps"*; and *"Return to favorite website/app."* The themes are illustrated by quotes from the focus groups and written comments on the worksheet.

### Drivers for Seeking Sexual Health Information Online

Teenagers were aware that speaking to healthcare professionals would be the most reliable way to receive sexual health information, and they were wary of the information that they find on sexual health websites. Despite this, they regularly searched for sexual health information online, and preferred this way of obtaining information. This was because the Internet was considered a private and anonymous way to receive sexual health information. Teenagers were embarrassed at the idea of visiting a sexual health center, and did not feel comfortable attending one, even though they knew where they were located.

*P7: Like they [healthcare providers] look at you funny (Starts laughing)* (School 2)

*P5: Like it's embarrassing.* (School 2)

Teenagers typically used their mobile phones to access sexual health information online. They discussed mobile phones as personal devices, which were individual and personalized to them, unlike computers which may be shared with other family members. Teenagers were worried that parents may see their Internet search history, and speak to them about why they were accessing sexual health websites. Therefore, their mobile phones afforded them privacy and ease of access to websites. Surprisingly, although all the teenagers used their phones for accessing the Internet and sexual health information, not a single participant had previously used a sexual health mobile app, in fact none of the

participants had even heard of a sexual health app (Table 8.5).

*P5: I haven't seen a sexual health app before*

*I: OK, has anyone seen a sexual health app?*

*All: No* (School 2)

### Design of Website and Apps

Teenagers discussed their preferred design features on sexual health websites and mobile apps. Teenagers wanted websites and mobile apps that looked professional, rather than childish, but preferred bold and colorful websites. Teenagers would not use websites if they contained images of people who appeared significantly younger than themselves. Our participants agreed that it was important that websites included pictures of people that they could relate to, people similar to themselves.

*P13: Well, it is because like it talks about sexual health and well-being but like it looks like, with the children there, it's like for children.* (School 5; Brook)

It was important that websites and mobile apps were easy to use and worked well. Teenagers would very quickly close the website and not use it again if it contained a broken link, or would not allow them to access parts of the website. Participants did not want to have to spend time searching for information and preferred websites that were simple to access. Participants liked websites and apps that were easy to use with a clear layout (see Fig. 8.3).

*P21: Yeah, like it's better a bit simpler, to like read* (School 3, Brook)

One concern that participants had about the mobile apps was the app icon design and name. Participants mentioned they would be nervous about downloading an app that looked embarrassing or was obviously about sexual health, as it would be displayed on their phone. It was likely that their friends or parents would

**106**   Teenagers, Sexual Health Information and the Digital Age

FIG. 8.3 Participants believed the Brook website was easy to use and had a clear layout.

see the app on their phone, and so it needed to have a neutral name and icon. Apps need to avoid names and icons that overtly referenced sexual health as privacy and discreetness were key concerns (Table 8.6) (Fig. 8.4).

> P23: *I'm not, my mam will be like, what's this doing on your phone* (School 5, condom craze)

## Website and App Content

Participants also discussed the website features that they enjoyed. The teenagers particularly liked the videos that were on the websites, especially if they contained relevant information. Teenagers preferred videos that were short and covered different sexual health topics, and they liked videos that included personal experiences from other teenagers. It was key that teenagers could relate to the videos and participants lost interest if the videos were outdated or too long.

> P18: *The condom video was useful because it shows you how to work it* (School 4, Girls health)

Teenagers were also quick to switch off from information-only websites and preferred websites and apps that contained some kind of interaction, or at least a link to another website or service. Some of the websites contained quizzes and games and these helped to aid discussion around sexual health, and allowed participants to discuss the topic in a light-hearted way. The elements of humor in the games and videos was something that appealed to teenagers.

> P3: *I think a quiz is better than like that.* (School 1, Brook)

In terms of the written information on the websites and apps, teenagers liked bullet-pointed information, rather than those containing blocks of complex information. A key difference between the websites and apps related to the depth and breadth of information participants perceived them to contain. Teenagers believed the information on the apps was too basic, and further information would be beneficial. Participants wanted to see information that covered a wide range of sexual health topics, including relationships and gender. They liked information that contained positive language, clear advice, and guidance on common problems. Websites and apps that used negative language, had a narrow view, or concentrated on abstinence or STI prevention were ignored.

> P15: *Yeah. But like it also says about abstinence on the videos. I don't like that.*
>
> I: *No?*
>
> P15: *It's like Christian god stuff, like all that crap.* (School 4, Health talk).

**TABLE 8.6**
**Snapshot of Design of Websites and Apps.**

| Design of Websites and Apps |
| --- |
| Teenagers want bold, colorful, but professional-looking websites and mobile apps |
| Easy to use with a clear layout (see Fig. 1.3) |
| Discreet names and icons (for example, My Teen Mind, rather than Condom Craze) |

FIG. 8.4 The My teen mind app icon, condom craze icon and girls health icon. Participants believed icons should be discreet, whereas the condom craze app was overtly about sexual health.

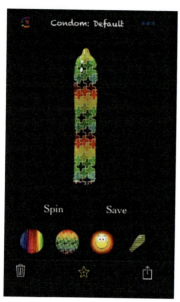

FIG. 8.5 Condom Craze interactive game app.

TABLE 8.7
Snapshot of Website and App Content.

**Website and App and Content**

Like videos and interactive features

Bullet-pointed, easy-to-read information

Combination of games and accurate sexual health information

They were mixed views of the interactive content present in the apps. Some participants enjoyed a condom game (see Fig. 8.5) on the Condom Craze app, and believed that it appealed to teenagers. Participants found it light-hearted and generated easy discussion around the topic.

*P11: It makes me lose interest, too much reading.*

*P10: Yeah, I like the condom one, I'm going to design a condom now. I'm going to do a white one*

*P11: I don't like white, I'm going to put an emoji on mine*

*P10: (Laughing) Can you do that? Miss is it ok if we design a condom? (School 3, Condom craze)*

On the other hand, some participants believed the game was childish and lacked trustworthy information. Participants believed the game would be better if it allowed them to access further, practical information about condoms and where to obtain them. Therefore, a key issue with the apps was that they were either purely information based or purely interactive, whereas the teenagers expressed a preference for a combination of information and interactive elements (Table 8.7).

*P14: This bit is funny but like the rest is like really like plain*

*I: Yeah, so not as much on the other parts of it.*

*P14: No. But it's definitely more interactive here but it needs more information? (School 3, Condom craze)*

## Trusting and Using Websites and Apps

Participants struggled with whether they would trust sexual health websites and apps. Apps and websites that were game-based were viewed as less trustworthy, even though they enjoyed these interactive elements. In terms of website providers, teenagers were happier to trust websites when they recognized the provider. Teenagers stated, for example, that they did not trust the information on any of the websites they viewed in this study with the exception of the NHS site. The NHS website was already familiar to them, and the reputation and familiarity of the site acted as key trust indicators. This was regardless of whether they had previously viewed sexual health information on this site (Fig. 8.6).

*P4: yeah, like when you see the NHS logo, I would trust that. (School 1)*

Participants knew that it was important to identify who had developed the website or app when determining its credibility. However, participants found that it was easier to determine who had developed the websites compared to the apps. This made it more difficult for participants to be able to trust the sexual health apps. Participants thought the apps that contained contact details of the organization who had developed it were more trustworthy. In checking the credibility of the app, participants suggested they would check the ratings and reviews on the app store. If an app had more positive ratings and reviews, then it would be considered more trustworthy.

*I: Do you prefer the apps over the websites?*

*P10: the websites are more informative*

*I: Yeah, and do you trust the information on these apps?*

*P11: It depends like what reviews and stuff they had (School 3)*

If participants were unsure whether they could trust an unknown website or app, then they agreed that it

# CHAPTER 8  Teenagers' Views of Sexual Health Education Websites and Apps

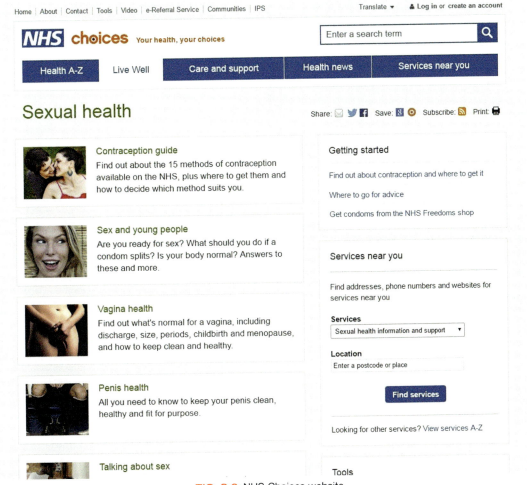

FIG. 8.6 NHS Choices website.

needed to be endorsed or promoted through a trusted source, for example, their school.

*I: Yeah, so you are worried about what you find online?*

*P23: Yeah*

*I: So what would make you trust something online?*

*P20: Advertised through the school (School 5)*

However, sexual health apps are not regularly advertised through their school in the same way as websites. In addition, it was easier for the participants to identify the information provider on websites (for example, NHS or Brook); however, participants found it difficult to determine the information provider on the sexual health apps.

*I: Ok, and compared to the websites did you trust them [apps] more or less than the websites?*

*P1: Less*

*I: Ok, any reasons for that?*

*P1: Erm, not sure who put the apps there*

Participants were asked to reflect on whether they would consider using a sexual health mobile app in the future. Participants valued the convenience of using apps and thought alongside the improvements they would like to see to their design, content, and branding; this would drive them to use this kind of app in the future (Table 8.8).

*I: Ok, and after having a look at them do you think you would ever use a sexual health app in the future?*

**110** Teenagers, Sexual Health Information and the Digital Age

| TABLE 8.8 |
|---|
| **Snapshot of Trusting and Using Websites and Apps.** |
| **Trusting and Using Websites and Apps** |
| Trust known website providers (for example, if their school endorsed it) |
| Difficult to know if they could trust the information on apps |
| Would use an app or website in the future for sexual health information |

*P13: Yeah, if they had more information on I would*

*P12: If the NHS or someone wrote it.*

*P11: It is easier on phones*

### Return to Favorite Website/App

In the second part of the focus group, participants were asked to return to their favorite website and app. For websites, the majority of participants commented that they would return to the *Brook* website. This was because they believed it contained a lot of useful information especially about STIs. Participants believed that it explained what they could do in certain situations to provide them with the confidence to discuss STIs. It was also interactive and allowed participants to make appointments offline.

*P3: I like it because: It lets you ask questions and shows you more information*

*The information I find useful: it gives you confidence when talking about STIs (School 1, Brook)*

*P10: It tells you how to make appointments, it contains a wide range of information and it explains what to do in several situations. (School 3, Brook)*

*P12: It looks professional, it's clear a charity has provided the information (School 3; Brook)*

Participants would also recommend the Brook website to their peers, if they needed sexual health information, because of how useful they perceived the information to be. The other website that participants returned to was *health talk*. Participants enjoyed the videos, believed the information was useful, and the design of the website appealed to their age group. Therefore, in terms of websites, participants were most likely to return to the website that contained the most relevant and useful information, but also those that were suitable for their age group.

*P20: It gives you useful information and if you are struggling I would 100% advice [Sic] you look at this (School 5, Brook).*

*P12: loved it, appeals to the young generation, Health talk, liked the videos, example info (School 3, Health talk).*

Similarly, participants returned to apps that contained the most relevant information. The majority of participants returned to *Girl Empowered*. This was because they believed it covered all areas of sexual health and topics that they were interested in such as STIs. Even though in comparison to other apps, this one was not as colorful or as interactive, they were more likely to return to the app that had the most relevant information.

*P9: Girl empowered because it has the most information and lots of different options about everything you would need to know and how to keep yourself safe against things like diseases and what to do if you have one. (school 4)*

Participants also returned to *My Teen Mind*. This app also had a lot of information; participants also believed that the information was reliable and easy to understand. Only three of the participants returned to *Condom Craze*, even though they enjoyed the gaming aspect (See Table 8.9). More participants returned to apps that had reliable information (Table 8.10).

*P5: My teen mind because it has more information and looks reliable and easier to understand (School 2, My Teen Mind)*

### DISCUSSION

This study has highlighted the design features teenagers want to see in sexual health websites and sexual health mobile apps. There are a number of similarities and differences in what teenagers believe should be on a sexual health website compared to a sexual health app. Similar to previous findings, teenagers want websites that are clear and easy to read and that present information on a wide range of sexual health issues (McCarthy et al., 2012; Selkie & Benson, 2011). Teenagers also believe mobile apps should have the same level of quality but there are also new issues here for designers to consider. It is vital that app names and icons are

# CHAPTER 8 Teenagers' Views of Sexual Health Education Websites and Apps 111

**TABLE 8.9**
**Table Detailing the Frequency and (Percentages) of Teenagers Who Returned to Each Website and App.**

|  | Frequency and (Percentage) |
|---|---|
| **WEBSITES** | |
| Brook | 7 (30.43%) |
| Girls health | 4 (17.39%) |
| Young lovers guide | 0 (−%) |
| Sex etc. | 2 (8.69%) |
| NHS | 4 (17.39%) |
| Health talk | 6 (26.08%) |
| **MOBILE APPS** | |
| Condom Craze | 3 (13.04) |
| My teen mind | 12 (52.17) |
| Girl empowered | 8 (34.78) |

**TABLE 8.10**
**Snapshot of Return to Favorite Website and Mobile App.**

| Return to Favorite Website and App |
|---|
| Most likely to return to websites and apps that featured interactive elements as well as accurate sexual health information. |

discreet. The privacy afforded by mobile devices is in danger of being undermined by poorly designed icons and inappropriate names for sexual health apps. As the app name and icon are displayed overtly on the home screen of the phone, it is important that it is not embarrassing or too overt an indicator of sexual health content. A key finding, consistent across both platforms, was that participants wanted videos and images that they can identify with. According to social learning theory, modeling by significant others can be highly influential to teenagers in behavior change (Bandura & Walters, 1977). Models that have shown to be effective in other health-related domains are peers whose behavior they see as being rewarded and who are of the same age or slightly older (Laureati, Bergamaschi, & Pagliarini, 2014). Thus, if websites or apps are using images of teenagers, then they should consider teenagers who are a similar age or older than their intended audience, this will increase the likelihood of teenagers relating to the information.

Teenagers believed that the sexual health information provided on apps lacked range and depth compared to the sexual health information provided on the websites. While this narrower focus may be intentional on the part of the developer, the teenage target audience of these apps reported that they expect much richer information. This supports general reviews of sexual health apps that have found they tend to take a one-size-fits-all approach to sexual health (Singh, Gibbs, Estcourt, & Sonnenberg, 2017). Therefore, app designers should aim to cover a wide range of sexual health information, even if they are looking to target a specific area (for example, pregnancy) in detail, it should still include information on all areas of sexual health. Teenagers also felt that they understood trust cues better on websites compared to apps. Teenagers believed that they could trust known websites, for example, the NHS site when promoted by their school. However, there was no such guidance concerning mobile apps. Without the presence of a "known provider" teenagers' confidence in being able to distinguish between trustworthy and untrustworthy sources diminished rapidly. Related literature looking at health apps more broadly suggests that people are willing to use other peoples' experiences of the app as a trust indicator and rely on the apps' ratings and reviews especially where "paid for" apps are concerned (Sillence, Briggs, & Harris, 2017). Therefore, designers need to think carefully about how they will make sure their app is deemed as trustworthy by teenagers, or teenagers may not feel comfortable downloading the app and believing the information it contains. Teenagers suggested that would trust unknown apps if they were recommended through a known source, for example, their school.

All of the teenagers in this study had smartphones, and used their mobiles every day. However, none of the participants in this sample had previously used or heard of a sexual health app. When teenagers used the apps, they enjoyed using them and could see the value in sexual health apps; however, they are currently not well advertised to teenagers. Our findings suggest that a redesign of content alongside careful design of icons and names will be important in terms of increasing uptake but that designers will also need to be creative in terms of thinking through their advertising and marketing campaigns. For this age group at least, trust transference is going to be important with content endorsed by familiar, well-known "brands" and a campaign strategy that sees schools lending their support to the use of such apps. Based on the findings of this study some

## TABLE 8.11
## Summary and Recommendations.

| | Websites | Mobile Apps |
|---|---|---|
| Design | Clear layout, easy to use, bold vibrant colors, and age-appropriate images. | Appropriate app icon/name, easy to use, simple clear layout, bold vibrant colors, and age-appropriate images. |
| Content | Short videos featuring "people like me", interactive quizzes and games, external links. Bullet-pointed and age-appropriate information that covers all sexual health topics. | Appropriate interactive game or quiz combined with accurate sexual health information that covers all topics. References to sources of information—link to known sources. |
| Trust | Professional design and advertised through a known source. | Professional design, advertised through a known source, positive reviews and ratings and contains external contact details. |

guidelines are presented for the development of future sexual health websites and mobile apps (see Table 8.11).

## Limitations

During the "return to favorite website and app" we could only use websites and apps that we had showed participants during the study; we were not able to also include a "free search". It would be interesting to allow teenagers to search freely and see which sexual health websites or apps teenagers would choose themselves. However, a free search was not possible within the constraints of a school-based study because of the number of websites and apps blocked on the schools computers. We had to get the websites and apps used approved by schools in advanced, and unblocked on the schools' Internet servers during the study.

Participants discussed that they perceive their phones as more private when searching for sexual health information than on a computer; however, the mobile apps were shown to teenagers on iPads. Research has shown individuals perceive smaller screens as more private than larger screens (Little & Briggs, 2006), therefore it would be interesting to

compare teenagers' initial views of the apps if they were shown on a smaller screen. Teenagers believed that the condom game was not discreet and believed the name displayed on a phone would be embarrassing; however, teenagers may have perceived this game as more private if it was displayed on a smaller screen. This should be taken into account in future research investigating mobile apps.

## Implications

Teenagers currently use websites to seek sexual health information, yet they prefer to use their phones to find this information. Teenagers would prefer to use a sexual health app for information because of the privacy and convenience that they associate with a mobile app. However, current mobile apps are not well advertised to teenagers and do not comprise sufficient interactive features and helpful information. If teenagers are going to continue to search for sexual health information online, then it is vital that the future development of sexual health websites and mobile apps consider incorporating quality information, exciting features, and identifiable trust cues.

## Chapter Summary

This chapter has presented a qualitative study investigating female teenagers' views of current sexual health websites and mobile apps. Participants either viewed six existing sexual health websites or three existing sexual health mobile apps chosen to be representative of the range and variety currently available. Participants then took part in focus groups evaluating each of the websites and mobile apps. The findings indicate that teenagers currently use their phones to access sexual health information due to ease of access and privacy. However, teenagers were not aware of sexual health apps. Participants believed apps should have similar design features to websites but apps should contain an appropriate interactive element paired with accurate sexual health information. At the moment, female teenagers are not using sexual health mobile apps; they believe they are more convenient and private compared to websites, yet they trust sexual health websites more than mobile apps.

The following chapter presents current literature and a small case study of older teenagers' and young adult's views of sexual health apps. Gaining information on younger and older teenager's views and preferences of sexual health information websites and apps allows practitioners to design websites and apps that are age-appropriate and targeting teenagers with information that is relevant to them and their age group.

# CHAPTER 9

# Students' Views of Sexual Health Apps

## CHAPTER OUTLINE

Background ................................................................. 113
   Why Is the Menstrual Cycle Important to Sexual
   Health? ..................................................................... 113
   Apps to Track the Menstrual Cycle ................... 114
   Reviewing Menstrual Tracking Apps: Accuracy and
   Motivations for Use ............................................. 114
   Summary ................................................................ 117
Small-Scale App Case Study Interviews ........... 117
   Participants ........................................................... 117
Materials and Procedure ..................................... 117
Results ........................................................................ 118
   Reliable Information ............................................ 118
   Ease of Use ............................................................ 119
   Trust and Privacy ................................................. 119
Small-Scale Study Discussion ............................... 120
   Chapter Summary ................................................ 121

## ABSTRACT

This chapter aims to consider students' views of menstrual tracking apps. The chapter is divided into four sections. Section Background provides a background to the menstrual cycle and previous literature on menstrual tracking apps. It also situates this work within the context of sexual health. Small-scale App Case Study Interviews describes a small-scale study of students' views of menstrual tracking apps. The results of this study are discussed in Results section, and reflections presented in the Small-scale Study Discussion section.

## KEYWORDS

Digital health interventions; Menstrual tracking apps; Online sexual health interventions; Qualitative research; School-based sexual health education; Sexual health; Sexual health education; Sexual health interventions; Teenagers.

## BACKGROUND

### Why Is the Menstrual Cycle Important to Sexual Health?

The menstrual cycle is the time from the first day of a female's period to the day before their next period, the length of a menstrual cycle varies but on average is 28 days and consists of four stages; the menstrual phase, follicular phase, ovulation phase, and luteal phase (see Fig. 9.1 for details). Females typically reach puberty and start experiencing menstrual periods when they are 11–14 years old. The menstrual cycle is important as it is a primary contributor to female mood and behavior (Pierson, Althoff, Thomas, Hillard, & Leskovec, 2019). The premenstrual phase of a cycle

FIG. 9.1 Illustration of the menstrual cycle.

has long been linked with low mood, and large quantitative reviews have found 26% greater risks of suicide deaths, attempts (17%), and psychiatric admissions (20%) at premenstruation (Jang & Elfenbein, 2018). In adolescents, menstruation is often described as a *vital sign* of health (Hilalrd et al., 2017). Understanding one's own menstrual cycle is thus important for women and especially adolescents. Technology may help teenagers appreciate not only why it is important for them to understand their own menstrual cycle but also provide them with the modality to track their menstrual cycle on a mobile app. Health tracking has captured a lot of attention in recent years, although there has been less of a focus on women's health tracking specifically (Almedia, Robb & Balaam, 2016). The menstrual cycle is important to sexual health, as tracking the menstrual cycle and being aware of fertile days can be used as a contraceptive method and as a way to plan conception.

## Apps to Track the Menstrual Cycle

In addition to the information-based sexual health apps described in Chapters 3 and 8, there are also a number of apps that are aimed at self-monitoring and self-quantification of sexual and reproductive activities. These usually have specific functions, for example, the ability to track certain phases of the cycle or to monitor mood or other physical symptoms. Tracking health behavior using mobile apps helps users gain self-knowledge for monitoring or even changing behavior. Health-related self-tracking is becoming increasingly popular with a range of different sexual health self-tracking apps now available to download.

Initially, these apps were developed with the aim of helping women track their cycle in order to understand their fertility and to manage family planning. Recently, there has been increased demand for apps that can also help prevent pregnancy (Johnson, Marriot and Zinaman, 2018). Sexual health apps that allow fertility tracking usually allow users to record the dates of their menstrual cycles, as well as additional information, such as mood, symptoms, sexual activity, and pill reminders. Many of these apps claim to predict fertility windows based on menstrual cycle data. Therefore, they can be useful to females who are trying to conceive or prevent conception. These types of apps are a relatively new concept, yet fertility tracking itself is not; many females have previously used pen-and-paper methods to record their menstrual cycle. Apps make it possible to track the menstrual cycle more easily, and provide women with reminders that may help them plan around their periods. Furthermore, women often track their menstrual cycles without an explicit goal in

| TABLE 9.1<br>Summary of Menstrual Tracking Apps. | |
|---|---|
| | **Menstrual Tracking Apps** |
| What are they? | Apps that allow users to track their menstrual cycle, and insert data such as mood, symptoms, and length. |
| Why use one? | These apps allow users to understand their menstrual cycle, and predict their fertile days as well predict when their period will start. |

mind but rather to maintain an awareness of where they are within their menstrual cycle, and to reflect on mood and overall well-being. This function of an app is especially useful for adolescents and teenagers who may still be learning to recognize the rhythm of their own bodies and the hormonal changes that are taking place (Table 9.1).

## Reviewing Menstrual Tracking Apps: Accuracy and Motivations for Use

Moglia, Ngugen, Chyjek, Chen and Catano (2016) evaluated menstrual tracking apps that were available for free on smartphones; the original review found 116 apps, after removing duplicates, non-English apps, apps with inaccurate information, and paid-for apps they had 20 free apps. Very few cited medical literature (5%) or any health professional involvement (5%). Table 9.2 lists the 20 apps reviewed, and Table 9.3 details some of the common features and functionality of the apps. Clue was the most accurate and well-reviewed app (See Fig. 9.2 below).

The accuracy of these apps is important to users and is a key evaluation point. Mogolia et al. (2016) also examined the reviews left on the apps; 302 app reviews mentioned how accurately the app predicted their cycle, with 65 reviewers describing apps as unhelpful due to inaccuracy. Most apps supported tracking factors beyond the timing of a woman's menstrual cycle, including information about the period itself, factors predictive of period onset (e.g., cramping, mood), and other health-related factors (e.g., exercise, sleep). Users appreciated these tracking factors and believed it made the apps more accurate.

If apps are predicting menstrual cycles, then it is also important that they are biologically accurate. Johnson, Marriot and Zinaman (2018) examined 949 adult females' ovulation day using urine samples, looking for luteinizing hormone, and then tracked this against

**CHAPTER 9** Students' Views of Sexual Health Apps

**TABLE 9.2**
**The 20 Apps Identified (Mogolia et al., 2016).**

| App Name | Main Function of App | Developer |
| --- | --- | --- |
| Clue | Helps predict menstrual cycle, PMS, ovulation, and fertility. | BioWink GmbH |
| Day after | Period tracker, personal diary, and calendar. Track periods and daily life. | Elliptikal, LLC |
| FemCal lite | Record and chart menstrual cycle, body temperature, and possible fertile days | Watmough Software |
| Fertility cycle | Period and ovulation tracker | 74 Monkeys |
| The flow | Period and fertility tracking | Lucia LUKANOVA |
| Free Girl Cal | Period calendar | Dionisie Nagy |
| Glow | Fertility tracker | Glow |
| Groove | Period predictor | Groove |
| iPeriod Period tracker free | Period tracker | Winkpass Creations, Inc |
| It's a girl thing | Period tracker, reminders for smear tests, and breast examinations | It's a Girl Thing Sanitary Products |
| Lily | Fertility tracker and sexual health information | Whimsical Inc |
| LoveCycles Menstrual, ovulation & Period Tracker | Period tracker | Plackal Tech |
| Menstrual Calendar | Period tracker and reminders | Witiz |
| Menstrual period Tracker | Period tracker | EFRAC |
| Period Tracker | Period tracker and reminders | Symetric Productions, Inc |
| GP Apps | Fertility information and period tracker | Coesius Ltd |
| Period Tracker Free Menstrual Calendar | Period tracker and reminders | Sevenlogics, Inc |
| GP Apps | Period tracker | GP Intl |
| Period Tracker, Free menstrual Calendar | Period tracker and reminders | Tamtris Web Services Inc |
| Pink Pad Period & Fertility Tracker Pro | Fertility trackers and menstrual predictor | Alt12 Apps, LLC |

menstrual tracking apps. It was found that accuracy of ovulation prediction was no better than 21% of the apps. Ovulation day varies greatly for any menstrual cycle, and so it is not possible for apps that use cycle-length information alone to accurately predict the day of ovulation. Most of these types of apps use the average length of a cycle which is 28 days; however, this varies greatly between women. If a user wants to use the app as a contraception method to prevent pregnancy, then the app needs to have more sophisticated science features for predicting ovulation and menses.

Unsurprisingly, women's clear preferences are for evidence, assurances, and medical accuracy when deciding to trust an app as users report that they want scientifically valid mobile apps (Starling, Kandel, Haile, & Simmons, 2018).

Quality and accuracy of information appear to be a concern with menstrual tracking apps (and apps offering contraception advice more broadly—see for example a recent systematic review Lunde, Perry, Sridhar, & Chen, 2017). Currently, however, little is known about the extent to which students are evaluating the

## TABLE 9.3
### Common App Features.

| App Feature | Percentage of Apps That Included This |
|---|---|
| Conception information | 80% |
| Contraception information | 50% |
| Password protection | 55% |
| No requirement for Internet connectivity | 80% |
| No advertisements | 65% |
| In-applications technical support | 70% |
| Medical disclaimers | 65% |
| Health information | 55% |
| Menstrual flow tracking | 70% |
| Symptoms | 70% |
| Intercourse | 75% |
| Next menses | 65% |
| Fertility | 55% |
| Cycle length information | 75% |

## TABLE 9.4
### Accuracy of Menstrual Tracking Apps.

| | Accuracy of menstrual tracking apps |
|---|---|
| Users' opinions | Users report that they want scientifically accurate apps |
| Information accuracy | Previous research has found that a very small amount of the apps available actually provide up-to-date medically accurate information. |
| Biological accuracy | Apps that predict ovulation on cycle length alone are not very accurate. |

accuracy of these apps, when choosing which one to download and use (Table 9.4).

In addition to measuring and predicting mood (Lee & Kim, 2019), there are five main reasons women use menstrual tracking apps; to be aware of how their body is doing, to understand their body's reactions to different phases of their cycle, to be prepared, to become pregnant, and to inform conversations with healthcare providers (Epstein et al., 2017). More recently, Gambier-Ross, McLernon, and Morgan (2018) also examined why people use menstrual tracking apps and found similar reasons. Four main

FIG. 9.2 Example of the menstrual tracking app (clue).

uses were identified: (1) to observe; (2) to conceive; (3) to inform fertility treatment; and (4) as contraception. Therefore, previous research investigating adult women's reasons for using menstrual tracking apps are mainly for fertility reasons or for contraception. Thus, menstrual tracking is important to sexual health.

## Summary

Menstrual tracking apps are the fourth most popular health app among adults (Pew Research, 2012) and are the second most popular among adolescent females (Teens, Health & Technology, 2015). We know that adults are using menstrual tracking apps to track their fertility and as a means of contraception by understanding their ovulation days. Users judge these apps on their perceived accuracy. It is also known that students are using menstrual tracking apps; however, less is known about why this group are using these apps and what they think to them. Currently, we know little about the perceived use of these apps to students and how they evaluate and judge the perceived accuracy and reliability of these apps.

## SMALL-SCALE APP CASE STUDY INTERVIEWS

We conducted a small-scale study to gain some qualitative feedback on menstrual tracking apps. We specifically wanted to explore students' experience with menstrual tracking apps, and if they believe they are accurate at predicting their menstrual cycle and mood. We wanted to investigate why students might use these types of apps and if they think they would be suitable for a younger population as well. As we wanted to explore users' personal experiences of apps, we asked participants to download and use a menstrual tracking app (moody month, detailed below) for 8 weeks prior to taking part in the study. We know from the previous chapter that teenagers had not heard of sexual health information apps, but liked the idea of using a sexual health information app; however, within that study users were only shown the app and did not have a chance to interact with the app in their own time. This study extends the previous study (described in Chapter 8) by allowing users to interact with the app for 8 weeks before taking part in the interviews. This allowed us to gain users real views of the apps and explore their motivations for using the app.

## Participants

We recruited three students from a University in the North East of England, using a purposeful sampling method. Participants were all required to be female, as assigned at birth and experience regular menstruation. Participants were also required to download a menstrual tracking app and use the app for 8 weeks prior to taking part in the interviews. This ensured a sample of women who could provide their views and personal experiences in using a menstrual tracking app. See Table 9.5 for an overview of each participant's demographic background.

## Materials and Procedure

The study received ethical approval from Northumbria University's Faculty of Health and Life Sciences Ethics Committee prior to the interviews taking place.

An interview schedule was formulated by creating open-ended and semi-structured questions on topic but allowing participants to provide further explanations and discuss their own experiences. Example questions on the interview schedule included "How did you find using the app generally to track your cycle?" *and* "Do you think the app is accessible to all ages?"

Participants were recruited through social media advertisements. Participants were asked to download the app Moody Month (described in Table 9.6) onto their phone, and use the app for 8 weeks prior to taking part in the study.

All of the interviews were carried out either at the University or a quiet location at the participants' home. Participants took part on a voluntary basis. Participants were informed about the confidentiality procedures in place, how their data were to be used, and

---

**TABLE 9.5**
**Demographic Background of Participants.**

| | Demographic Background |
|---|---|
| P1 | Age 30, graduate student who had recently had a baby. Currently in a heterosexual relationship. Experiencing regular menstruation and using a nonhormonal contraceptive. |
| P2 | Age 19, first-year undergraduate student. Not in a relationship and no children. Experiencing regular menstruation and using a hormonal contraceptive. |
| P3 | Age 22, undergraduate student. Not in a relationship and no children. Experiencing regular menstruation and using a nonhormonal contraceptive. |

## TABLE 9.6
## Moody Month.

| Moody Month | |
|---|---|
| Features | Tracks menstrual cycle to notice changes in mood and well-being. Users can log information on mood, body and world |
| Information | Information on four phases of the cycle and the hormonal, biological, and environmental changes that can affect mood. |
| Design | Bright, colorful, and easy to use. |

that they were free to withdraw from the study at any time without explanation. All participants were provided with an information sheet, signed an informed consent form, and fully debriefed at the end of the session.

Questions were open-ended and semi-structured, allowing for flexibility and elaboration by the researcher or the participant. This achieved a two-way dialogue allowing exploration of key themes. We were expecting to find similar themes as in the previous study (described in Chapter 8), therefore, when analyzing the data we looked for similar codes, describing the design and app content, trust and privacy and their views on why they would use a menstrual tracking app. Interviews lasted between 30 and 60 minutes and were audio-recorded and later transcribed.

## RESULTS

Thematic analysis was used to analyze the data (see Chapter 4, Section 2 for a full overview of thematic analysis). The full qualitative themes are described below, and then a summary snapshot of each theme. We report on three key themes that explained users' experiences of the app; reliable information, ease of use; trust; and privacy.

### Reliable Information

Participants enjoyed having access to what they perceived to be reliable information in an easy and convenient way. Participants realized that there was a lot about the menstrual cycle that they had not realized before they started using the app. Participants discovered that they did not know a lot about their menstrual cycle; however, before using the app, they would never think to search for this information. Having this information accessible and available to them was very useful.

I just like reading the little advice articles about periods *Participant 3*

More in depth about how the cycle actually works and to be honest I'm not really, I don't really know enough about things like that so that was really informative to know a bit more about what's going on in your body at the time. *Participant 1*

Participants also liked that they could match their mood to the stage of their cycle. Participants had not realized how much their mood was affected by their cycle. In particular, participants liked that they could track their mood symptoms themselves and over time, the app would notify them about how they might typically feel the next day. This would allow them to be more organized and get the most out of their day, for example, if they were likely to have less energy 1 day, they could aim to be more productive the day before.

Yeah, I've tried to do that when I'm ovulating I have so much energy and I'm like oh this is the week I'm going to do like everything. *Participant 3*

In addition, by tracking their mood, it allowed them to feel better about themselves. For example, if they were feeling really fed up, seeing on the app that they were likely to feel tired because of the stage they were at in their cycle, it allowed them to take a break without feeling guilty. Participants believed that they were more accepting of how they were feeling by understanding that there was a scientific reason for it.

Before I used it, I found I wasn't understanding my hormones, why I was up and down. *Participant 2*

Just being aware of your mood and how it changes throughout your cycle so knowing that your... whatever you're feeling is probably because of your cycle *Participant 3*

Participants also believed that this type of information on the menstrual cycle is needed at a younger age, as they had not learned about this in any sex education at school. Participants believed this information would be useful when first starting periods, as they had not realized how much the stage of their cycle affected all aspects of their lives (Table 9.7).

Girls have to pick up this information from somewhere or other ... And our parents grew up in a different era and they. I don't know about your parents, but some other peoples parents might not know as much. And school doesn't tell you much they just say oh its part of like ... They teach it as part of like... Reproduction rather than women's health specifically ... So I think they're useful for teaching people sort of thing *Participant 3*

## CHAPTER 9 Students' Views of Sexual Health Apps    **119**

---

> **TABLE 9.7**
> **Snapshot of Reliable Information.**
>
> **Theme One: Reliable Information**
>
> - Participants did not know a lot about their menstrual cycle but it is not something they would think to search information on.
> - Convenient having reliable information in an accessible way.
> - Participants benefited from understanding that their mood changes may be due to the stage of their menstrual cycle.

### Ease of Use

One of the main appeals of the app was how easy it was to use. Users found that the app felt modern and had more features than other apps. A lot of menstrual tracking apps are just a calendar app but this app had interactive features. It had both interactive and information features, while not being overly complicated. It had daily tips that would come through as a push notification. Participants liked the combination of reliable information and interactive features.

> What I really liked about the moody app was the little tip things … I thought that was good. *Participant 3*

The app also had an attractive design, it had bright colors and looked attractive, and this made users happier to use the app. Bright colors, participants described as uplifting that matched in with the app promoting understanding mood and positivity.

> And also as well this is going to sound stupid but I like the fact that it's pretty *Participant 2*

Participants had previously tried tracking their cycles but found it difficult to track through traditional pen and paper methods. With the app, users found that they did not have to think about tracking, so it was a lot easier to keep on top of. When using pen and paper methods participants would often forget to write it down, whereas with the app because it is automatic it is a lot easier to keep track of. It also had push reminders. Participants would worry as in the past they had missed a period or their period had been late and they had not realized because their tracking was not up to date. Therefore, the app reduced their anxiety.

> I wasn't very good … I used to put it in my diary, but I would forget. *Participant 1*

Participants were able to be more organized for their period as their tracking was more accurate with the app than when they were using pen-and-paper methods. Even if participants were regularly tracking their menstrual cycle, they would often forget to look in their diary to see if they were approaching a bleeding day; however, the app would send them a reminder. Therefore, it allowed them to be more prepared (Table 9.8).

> Just knowing in advance I think that's it is better to be prepared. *Participant 1*

> it's with you all the time… It's always with you, also I feel like … If you write it down on like if your like oh I'll write it down when I get home … Periods and stuff … People … I never did that it just went straight over my head id always forget and like that could be for some people … Could mean that they end up getting like pregnant without noticing for a while because they'll be like oh it's near the end of the month *Participant 2*

### Trust and Privacy

One of the main appeals of the app was the perceived privacy of the app. Participants believed that the app was very discreet and they did not feel awkward using it. Participants believed that it was secure enough for them to record their daily mood, etc. and that their data would be kept private and safe. Participants believed no one would be interested in gaining information from a menstrual tracking app.

> I feel like with these companies I trust, I trust those companies with my data. *Participant 3*

> I don't really care cause if you think about it in the general scheme of things they're getting far much more data from other places than they would from a period tracking app. *Participant 1*

Participants noted that there is still a lot of stigma around periods and menstrual cycles, and that there is also a lot of shaming for girls. Being able to record information privately on the app made them feel more comfortable about periods. Participants noted that

---

> **TABLE 9.8**
> **Snapshot of "Ease of Use" Theme.**
>
> **Theme Two: Ease of Use**
>
> Participants liked how easy the app was to use.
> It was easier to keep track of their menstrual cycle than through pen-and-paper methods
>
> The app would send reminders, therefore participants could be prepared.

they would feel embarrassed if they had to get a tampon out of their bag in front of people, especially when they were younger at school, and so it would be beneficial for younger adolescents to know that periods are not anything to feel ashamed of.

> I used to take my bag to the toilets in school, so people wouldn't see me holding a tampon, I felt embarrassed *(Participant 3)*

> There was no like proper education on the cycle and there was almost like a stigma a shame and there still is a little bit with having a period so this sort of thing... Is kind of promoting positivity around it *Participant 2*

Also, the app made them realize what was normal about periods, since it is not something that is discussed, knowing that different parts of their cycle was normal made them feel better about it. Again, it expressed that it would be useful for younger adolescents, especially as apps like this have recently been used by influencers on websites such as YouTube, which are aimed at a younger audience. All of the participants in this study had previously heard of menstrual tracking apps, either through friends or on social media. Therefore, apps like this help break down the shame and stigma often felt by taboo topics such as periods. This may help adolescents feel that they can discuss periods more openly (Table 9.9).

> *[where had you heard of these apps]* guess like just online like I watch a lot of you tubers *Participant 2*

## SMALL-SCALE STUDY DISCUSSION

The participants in this study had all previously heard of menstrual tracking apps, usually through friends. This is unsurprising as previous research has found that menstrual tracking apps are the fourth most popular health app among adults (Pew Research, 2012) and are the second most popular among adolescent females (Teens,

Health & Technology, 2015). However, in comparison to the previous study (Chapter 8), none of the teenagers in that study had previously heard of a sexual health information app. It would be interesting to explore whether teenagers have heard of, or used a menstrual tracking app. Participants enjoyed using the menstrual tracking app because of how easy it was to use. Participants thought trying to keep track of periods through traditional pen-and-paper methods is difficult, and it is very easy to forget to track, this was a particular worry if participants were late or missed a period and they had not realized. This could potentially be useful for younger adolescents who may be first learning about periods and unfamiliar with the cycle. Therefore, having access to reliable information in a private and convenient way would be beneficial. Especially as teens like using the Internet and particularly novel ways of learning about health (Gray & Klein, 2006; Lenhart, 2015). Even though teenagers in the previous study had not heard of a sexual health information app, they were enthusiastic about using a sexual health app in the future; therefore, it would be interesting to explore teenagers' views of menstrual tracking apps and whether they would be useful and beneficial for them.

Periods are still seen as a taboo topic to openly discuss and so there is a lot of shame and stigma surrounding periods. Menstrual tracking apps that promote positivity around periods and menstruation could be beneficial in breaking down this stigma and helping women and adolescents to feel comfortable discussing periods. It is important younger adolescents understand their cycle—especially if they want to use nonhormonal contraceptive methods; sexual health education should not just focus on not getting pregnant but also girls understanding their own bodies; these types of apps could contribute to this. This fits in with the new RSE guidelines that have a focus on different types of relationships, including strangers, friends, intimate relationships, consent and healthy relationships, well-being and mental health, safety online, sex and sexuality, sexual health in the context of relationships, healthy bodies, healthy minds, self-esteem, mental health resilience, and economic well-being (Long, 2017). Understanding their own bodies, self-esteem and mood would help cover some of these topics. An app with reliable information could potentially help with this.

Even though, in this study, using this a menstrual tracking app as a contraception method did not come up in interviews, previous research has found that women can use these for contraception (Epstein et al.,

| TABLE 9.9 |
| --- |
| Snapshot of Trust and Privacy. |
| **Theme Three: Trust and Privacy** |
| • Participants believe their information is safe on a menstrual tracking app, as no one would be interested in that data. |
| • Apps were perceived as private, and participants felt comfortable using the app—especially as periods can be a taboo topic. |

2017). This could be useful for adolescents to be able to understand their own bodies and help them choose a suitable contraception method, and whether a hormonal or nonhormonal method would be more appropriate for them. One of the reasons it was not mentioned in the interviews could have been because the participants were directed to use the app. Future research might explore app users across a range of different menstrual tracking apps to understand more about their use of the technology in relation to decisions about contraception. More research is needed to explore how women use these types of apps for contraception methods, and if they are reliable and appropriate.

## Chapter Summary

This chapter has presented a qualitative study investigating female students' views of menstrual tracking apps. As well as current literature on why people download and use menstrual tracking apps and the benefits of menstrual tracking apps. Participants were all aware of menstrual tracking apps, and enjoyed using the menstrual tracking app over the 8 weeks. They also believed that they would be beneficial for younger adolescents.

The following chapter presents a brief online intervention study, aimed at increasing teenagers' self-esteem in order to increase their intentions to have safe sex and increase their sexual health knowledge.

# CHAPTER 10

# A Brief Online Self-affirmation Intervention to Promote Safe sex Intentions

## CHAPTER OUTLINE

Introduction ............................................................ 123
The Study ............................................................... 124
    Design ................................................................ 124
    Participants ........................................................ 125
    Materials ............................................................ 125
    Baseline Measures ............................................. 125
    The Intervention ................................................ 127
    Sexual Health Website ....................................... 127
    PostManipulation Measures .............................. 127
    Procedure .......................................................... 127
    Session 1 ........................................................... 128
    Session 2 ........................................................... 128

Results .................................................................. 129
    *Treatment of data* ............................................. 129
    *Baseline measures and manipulation*
    *check* .............................................................. 129
    *Self-esteem* ..................................................... 129
    *Website check* .................................................. 130
    *Sexual health knowledge and*
      *intention to have sex* ..................................... 130
Discussion .............................................................. 132
    *Strengths and Limitations* .................................. 133
    *Implications* ..................................................... 133

## ABSTRACT

This chapter aims to consider if a brief online sexual health and self-affirmation intervention would be appropriate for female teenagers. The chapter is divided into four sections. Section Introduction provides an overview of the literature on current online self-affirmation interventions. Section The Study describes the method used in this current study, and subsequently Results section discusses the main results of the self-affirmation intervention. The results and implications of using a sexual health and self-affirmation intervention for female teenagers are then discussed in Discussion section.

## KEYWORDS

Digital health interventions; School-based sexual health education; Self-affirmation; Self-affirmation intervention; Self-esteem; Sexual health; Sexual health education; Sexual health interventions; Teenagers.

## INTRODUCTION

Self-esteem has previously been identified as a highly important predictor of risky sexual behaviors for low SES female teenagers (see Chapter 7 for more detail). However, self-esteem is difficult to increase (Dalgas-Pelish, 2006; LeCroy, 2005). Most self-esteem programs are long-lasting (6 weeks or longer) with two 60 min sessions per week; these programs use a range of tasks, including talks and working through self-esteem worksheets (Dalgas-Pelish, 2006). These programs have had mixed results and may not be effective for all teenagers (LeCroy, 2005). Another way self-esteem can be enhanced is through self-affirmation. Indeed, self-esteem is often studied alongside self-affirmation. Self-affirmation techniques may boost self-esteem which in turn may facilitate adaptive message processing (Schuz, Cooke, Schuz, & Koningsbruggen, 2017). Those with low self-esteem may also gain more from self-affirmation techniques on attitudes and intentions than those with high self-esteem (Düring & Jessop,

---

Teenagers, Sexual Health Information and the Digital Age. https://doi.org/10.1016/B978-0-12-816969-8.00010-2
Copyright © 2020 Elsevier Inc. All rights reserved.

2015). Therefore, there are clear links between self-esteem and self-affirmation techniques, and self-affirmation can be used as an easier and faster way to increase self-esteem levels.

Self-affirmation theory (Steele, 1988) proposes that people respond in a defensive manner to material that they find threatening (Epton & Harris, 2008). This is because people are motivated to protect the view of themselves as being morally adequate. In response to self-defense, people are primarily concerned about their global sense of self-worth (Steele, 1988). Therefore, when an individual self-affirms in one domain that is important to them (for example, kindness), they will be more open to potentially threatening information about another source (for example, risky sexual behaviors).

Self-affirmation techniques have been used with a wide range of health behaviors, including alcohol and caffeine consumption (Armitage, Harris, & Arden, 2011; Reed & Aspinwall, 1998), smoking (Armitage, Harris, & Hepton, 2008; Memish, Schüz, & Frandsen, 2016), physical activity (Charlson, Wells, & Peterson, 2014; Falk, O'Donnell, & Cascio, 2015), diet (Fielden, Sillence, Little & Harris, 2016; Pietersma & Dijkstra, 2011), sun protection (Jessop, Simmonds, & Sparks, 2009; Schüz, Schüz, & Eid, 2013), diagnostic tests (Klein, Lipkus, & Scholl, 2010; Koningsbruggen & Das, 2009), and self-management tests (Logel & Cohen, 2012; Wileman, Farrington, & Chilcot, 2014). However, there is limited research on self-affirmation and safe sex or risky sexual behaviors.

Sherman and Nelson (2000) recruited sexually active undergraduate students who were randomly allocated to a self-affirmation or control condition and watched an AIDS educational video. The self-affirmed participants saw themselves at a greater risk for HIV and purchased more condoms than the non-affirmed group. In addition, Ko and Kim (2010) recruited both male and female undergraduate students and found that participants in the self-affirmed group picked up more STI brochures following the intervention than the nonaffirmed group. Blanton, Gerrard, and McClive-Reed (2013) also recruited male and female undergraduate students and found that the self-affirmed group had increased intentions to use condoms compared to the nonaffirmed group. Therefore, in undergraduate populations, self-affirmation techniques have improved intentions to use contraception and increased the positive behaviors, including picking up STI brochures and condoms. However, there have been no sexual health

and self-affirmation interventions with younger teenage populations. It is also not known if self-affirmation techniques can increase sexual health knowledge.

Self-affirmation theory has been effective in promoting positive intentions and behaviors and attitudes (Epton & Harris, 2008; Harris & Napper, 2005; Schuz et al., 2017; Sherman & Nelson, 2000), and we know that female teenagers are seeking sexual health knowledge. In this context, it is therefore noteworthy that self-affirmation can improve information seeking and knowledge (Demetriades & Walter, 2016) although whether this extends to a sexual health context is unknown. In the remainder of this chapter we outline our use of self-affirmation techniques to increase self-esteem levels and sexual health knowledge in low SES female teenagers.

We tested a brief intervention delivered online as the Internet provides a basis for low-cost, far-reaching, and timely interventions making them suitable for low SES teenagers (Griffiths, Lindenmeyer, & Powell, 2006). The sexual health information was delivered through a sexual health website. Overall, the research aimed to evaluate whether self-esteem, intentions, and knowledge were increased post intervention and at a 1-week follow-up to evaluate the sustainability of these effects over a 1-week period. Based on previous research three hypotheses were proposed:

Hypothesis 1: Female teenagers who have self-affirmed (self-affirmation group) will have significantly higher self-esteem post intervention than those who have not (control group).

Hypothesis 2: The self-affirmation group will have significantly higher intentions to have safe sex post intervention than the control group.

Hypothesis 3: The self-affirmation group will have significantly higher sexual health knowledge post intervention than the control group.

## THE STUDY
### Design

The study employed a 2 (condition) x 3 (time) experimental design. The between participants factor was conditioned with two levels: self-affirmation and control. The within-participants factor was time with three levels: baseline, postintervention, and 1 week follow-up. The dependent variables were self-esteem, sexual health knowledge, intentions to have sex in the next year, and intention to have safe sex in the next year. See Fig. 10.1 for overview.

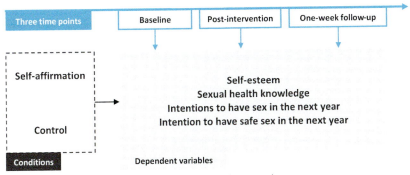

FIG. 10.1 Study design overview.

## Participants

A total of 107 participants were recruited, comprising low SES female teenagers. Teenagers were recruited from five schools in the North East of England; teenagers were approached by their teacher and asked if they would like to take part in the research. Participants were categorized as low SES based on parental educational background and parental income. Participants were considered low SES if their parents' highest educational attainment was primary school or secondary school, or if they were on free or reduced price school lunches, which meant their parents have an annual income of less than £16,190. Participants were also categorized as low SES if their parents were unemployed or had working-class jobs. See Table 8.1 for an overview of participants' demographic background. Complete data were available for 102 participants, n = 50 in the self-affirmation condition age range 13–16 years (Mean = 14.0, SD = 0.90) and n = 52 in the control condition age range of 13–16 years (Mean = 13.9, SD = 0.72). Two participants were identified as high SES, one participant failed to log complete data online, and two participants dropped out before the 7-day follow-up (Table 10.1).

Participants' previous sexual behaviors were also examined. In the self-affirmation group, 21 participants reported that they were in a heterosexual romantic relationship, with one partner, and had been with their partners between 1 and 12 months. All participants were the same age or within 3 years older than the participants. Eight participants reported previously having sex with a condom under the age of 16 years, and six participants reported having sex without a condom under the age of 16 years. In the control group, 13 participants reported that they were in a heterosexual romantic relationship, with one partner, and had been with their partners between 2 and 11 months, all partners were the same age or 2 years older than participants

were. Two participants reported previously having sex with condom under the age of 16 years and three participants reported having sex without a condom under the age of 16 years. A Chi-square test revealed that there were no significant differences between the self-affirmation and control group in terms of having sex before age 16 years ($\chi(2) = 4.873$, $P = .087$). See Table 10.2 for full overview of previous sexual behaviors.

## Materials

Participants accessed an online questionnaire to take part in the study.

## Baseline Measures

Three questionnaires measuring self-esteem, previous sexual behaviors, and intentions to have sex that were previously described in Chapter 7 (questionnaire study with teenagers) were utilized. These questionnaires were used as they were deemed age appropriate and reliable from our previous study.

*Self-esteem* was measured using the amended 10-item self-esteem scale (Rosenberg, 1965), for example, "I take a positive attitude toward myself." Items are scored from *Strongly Disagree* (0) to *Strongly Agree* (3), five questions are reversed scored. The scale ranges from 0 to 30, higher scores indicate higher self-esteem.

*Previous sexual behaviors* were measured using the Raine previous sexual behaviors scale (Skinner, Robinson, Smith, Chenoa, & Robbins, 2015). Four questions measured relationship status, partner gender, age, and length of relationship. Early sex before 16 years was measured using two self-developed questions. Participants were asked what age measured from *Haven't yet* to *16 years* they had vaginal sex with and without a condom.

*Intentions to have sex* was measured using three questions. For example, "During the next year I expect to have

126     Teenagers, Sexual Health Information and the Digital Age

**TABLE 10.1**

Number and Percentage (%) of Participant Demographic Information Between the Self-affirmation and Control Group.

| | | Self-affirmation N (%) | Control N (%) |
|---|---|---|---|
| | Free or reduced price lunches | 20 (40%) | 19 (36%) |
| Ethnicity | White British | 46 (92%) | 47 (94%) |
| | Asian or Asian British Pakistani | 1 (2%) | 2 (3.8%) |
| | Other mixed background | 2 (4%) | 1 (2%) |
| | Other white background | 1 (2%) | |
| Living with parents | Living with mother | 25 (50%) | 24 (48%) |
| | Living with father | 1 (2%) | 2 (3.8%) |
| | Live with both parents | 20 (40%) | 12 (34%) |
| | Living in care | 1 (2%) | 1 (2%) |
| | Living with another relative | 2 (6%) | 5 (9.6%) |
| | Other | | 1 (2%) |
| Parents' education background | Primary school | 1 (2%) | 4 (7.7%) |
| | Secondary school | 19 (38%) | 22 (42.3%) |
| | Sixth form or college | 2 (4%) | 2 (3.8%) |
| | University (undergraduate) | 1 (2%) | 1 (1.9%) |
| | Don't know | 27 (54%) | 23 (44.2%) |

**TABLE 10.2**

Number and Percentage (%) of Reported Previous Sexual Behaviors for Self-affirmation (SA) Group and Control (C) Group.

| Age | HAVEN'T YET N (%) | | UNDER 13 YEARS N (%) | | 13 YEARS N (%) | | 14 YEARS N (%) | | 15 YEARS N (%) | |
|---|---|---|---|---|---|---|---|---|---|---|
| | Sa | C | Sa | C | Sa | C | Sa | C | Sa | C |
| Kissing | 5 (10) | 9 (17) | 32 (64) | 39 (75) | 7 (14) | 3 (5.8) | 6 (12) | 1 (1.9) | - | — |
| Touching a partner's genitals | 41 (82) | 43 (82.7) | 1 (2) | 1 (1.9) | 1 (2) | 5 (9.6) | 6 (12) | 3 (5.8) | 1 (2) | — |
| Being touched on genitals | 39 (78) | 39 (76.5) | 2 (4) | 2 (3.8) | — | 7 (13.5) | 7 (14) | 3 (5.8) | 2 (4) | — |
| Giving oral sex | 38 (76) | 44 (84.6) | 4 (8) | — | — | 6 (11.5) | 3 (6) | 2 (3.8) | 5 (10) | — |
| Receiving oral sex | 43 (86) | 47 (90.4) | 2 (4) | — | — | 3 (5.8) | 2 (4) | 2 (3.8) | 3 (6) | — |
| Sex with a condom | 41 (82) | 50 (96.2) | 4 (8) | — | — | — | 3 (6) | 2 (3.8) | 2 (4) | — |
| Sex without a condom | 44 (88) | 49 (94.2) | 2 (4) | — | — | 1 (1.9) | 3 (6) | 2 (3.8) | 1 (2) | — |

*sex." Intentions to have safe sex was measured using three questions. For example, "During the next year if I have sex it is likely I will use contraception." Items are scored from Strongly Disagree (0) to Strongly Agree (7). The scale ranges from 0 to 21, higher scores indicate higher intentions to have sex and higher intentions to have safe sex.*

## The Intervention

In the self-affirmation condition participants were asked to write a 5-minute essay about an event in their life they are proud of, as this has previously been identified as an appropriate self-affirmation task for young teenagers (Klein, Blier, & Janze, 2001). Any self-reflective writing can lead to participants self-affirming, therefore in the control task participants were asked to list everything they had eaten or drunk in the past 48 h (Harvey & Oswald, 2000). Both groups were asked to spend 5 minute on this task. The online questionnaire system timed the page and participants could not move onto the next stage until they had spent at least 5 minute on the essay. These essays were checked to ensure that all participants had engaged appropriately with the task (see Fig. 10.2 for an example essay). During the task participants in the self-affirmation group completed essays on times they had won awards, been on holiday, their pets, or received good grades. Within the control group all participants provided a list of food and drinks they had consumed in the past 48 h.

## Sexual Health Website

In our previous studies, we had identified that teenagers preferred the sexual health information available on the Brook website (https://www.brook.org.uk/). Therefore, we used the Brook website for this study to deliver the sexual health information. This website covered all areas of sexual health, including contraception, STIs, relationships, sex, gender, sexuality, pregnancy, health and well-being, abuse and violence, staying safe online, bodies, and pornography. All information was bullet pointed and age appropriate. It included a range of information services as well as interactive tools, videos, and games, which were identified in Chapter 8 (Teenagers' views of websites and apps) as important to female teenagers. It also had a bright, bold, and clear layout, therefore it was easy to use and navigate. The website had a professional design and was linked to known UK charities which were identified by teenagers as an important trust cue. See Fig. 10.3 for an example.

## PostManipulation Measures

Three questions were utilized after teenagers had viewed the sexual health website, to ensure they had trusted and believed the information. These were *"I trusted the sexual health information on the website"*; *"I believed the sexual health information on the website"*; and *"I learnt something about sexual health from the website."* These were scored from Strongly Agree (5) to Strongly Disagree (1). These questions ensured that the sexual health website used to deliver the information was perceived as trustworthy, credible, and appropriate. Questions were also utilized to measure post self-esteem and post intentions to have sex and post intentions to have safe sex in the next year.

## Procedure

All the testing took place within school settings. Before the study day itself, participants took part in a 30-minute session where the study procedure and ethical

**Please write an essay on a positive experience in your life.**
**For example, an event in your life that made you feel proud (Please be as detailed as you can, write the event, what happened and how you felt)**

*I won a dance award for the hardest worker in 2018. This made me feel proud of myself as I was chosen and stood out to my dance teacher even out of ALL the other people there. It was a massive shock to be even nominated, as I felt that there were many people who were better and more skilled than me. It felt great to make my mam proud of me, and see how happy she was for me. Especially as I never win anything. I was only supposed to be going to a party that night and the awards were unexpected, but my mam picked me up we went to her best friend's house and we celebrated, it was a wonderful and memorable day.*

FIG. 10.2 Self-affirmation essay example.

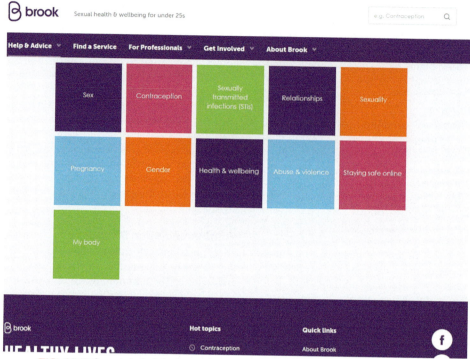

FIG. 10.3 Screenshot of the brook website, showing a bright, clear, and bold layout.

considerations were verbally explained. It was emphasized to participants that the study was voluntary and they did not have to take part if they did not want to. Participants were also given paper-based information sheets. Any teenager who was interested in taking part in the study informed their teacher that week (in private, if they wanted) and parental letters and opt-out consent forms were posted home to their parents.

## Session 1

The study day took place 2 weeks after the last parental consent form had been posted home. On the study day, teenagers were given another paper-based information sheet and the researcher verbally explained the study and again emphasized that the study was voluntary to ensure that each participant was happy to take part. Written consent was then sought from participants. Participants were randomized to either the self-affirmation or control condition. Two separate links were given out on pieces of paper for the self-affirmation and control task. These were randomly passed to participants and they were allocated to condition based on the link they received. Participants were asked to create a 5-character code word and enter this into the online questionnaire. Participants were asked to remember this code for the second session 1 week later. They were then told to write this code down and keep it safe, if they needed to.

Participants then started the study and completed the four online baseline questionnaires; self-esteem, sexual health knowledge, sexual intentions, and previous sexual behaviors. They then took part in the 5-minute self-affirmation or control task. Participants were then asked to view a sexual health website for 15 min (https://www.brook.org.uk/). After 15 min, the self-esteem questionnaire and a website quality questionnaire were then used as manipulation checks. Participants then completed a post manipulation sexual health knowledge and intentions questionnaire. This whole session lasted approximately 1 h.

## Session 2

One week later participants were asked to log back onto Qualtrics and enter their 5-character code word. Participants were then asked to complete the sexual behaviors, intentions, self-esteem, and knowledge questionnaires. At the end of the session, participants were fully debriefed and thanked for their time. This second session lasted approximately 15 min. See Fig. 10.4 for overview of the study procedure.

### CHAPTER 10 A Brief Online Self-affirmation Intervention

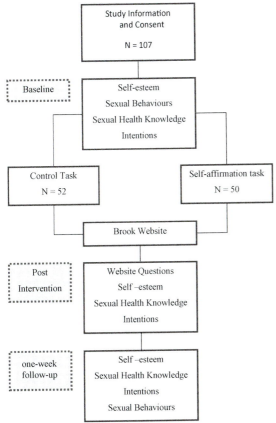

FIG. 10.4 Overview of study procedure for Study.

## Results
The full statistical results are presented below, followed by a snapshot of the results in Table 10.6.

## Treatment of data
All questionnaires were scored and the data were entered into SPSS for analysis. Descriptive statistics were calculated, including means, standard deviations, and mean standard errors for each scale. T-tests were conducted to establish if there were any differences between groups at baseline. 2 x 3 ANOVAs were conducted to determine if there were any differences between the conditions for self-esteem and sexual health knowledge. Due to differences at baseline, ANCOVAs were conducted for intentions to have sex and intentions to have safe sex.

## Baseline measures and manipulation check
Baseline measures were used to establish that there were no differences between the groups at baseline. T-tests revealed no significant difference between the conditions at baseline with respect to self-esteem levels or sexual health knowledge (See Table 10.3). However, there were significant differences between the groups at baseline with respect to levels of intention to have sex and intention to have safe sex. The control group reported significantly higher intention to have sex and significantly higher intention to have safe sex than the self-affirmation group (See Table 10.3).

Therefore, randomization to condition was only partially successful. Due to these differences at baseline, baseline intention to have sex and baseline intention to have safe sex were controlled statistically.

## Self-esteem
Self-affirmation techniques were used to increase participant's self-esteem. Self-esteem was measured at baseline, post, and 1 week to evaluate if the manipulation had been successful. Due to there being no differences in self-esteem levels at baseline, a 2 × 3 ANOVA was conducted.

The ANOVA determined there was a significant main effect of time for self-esteem levels $F(1.6, 164) = 11.401$, $P < .001$, $\eta p2 = 0.140$. Pairwise comparisons revealed there was a significant difference between baseline and post self-esteem levels ($P = .010$) and baseline

TABLE 10.3
Comparison of Baseline Measures Between the Conditions for Each of the Dependent Variables.

|  | Self-affirmation Mean (SD) | Control Mean (SD) | t (df) | P |
|---|---|---|---|---|
| Self-esteem | 15.0 (4.42) | 16.1 (4.20) | −1.256 (100) | .212 |
| Sexual health knowledge | 12.4 (5.24) | 11.98 (3.47) | 0.568 (100) | .575 |
| Intention to have sex | 6.9 (3.82) | 9.1 (4.66) | −2.625 (100) | .010[a] |
| Intention to have safe sex | 15.8 (3.72) | 17.7 (4.58) | −2.289 (100) | .024[a] |

[a] Significant P-values at alpha level .05.

and 1-week self-esteem levels ($P < .001$). However, there was no significant differences between post and 1-week self-esteem levels ($P = .114$).

There was a significant main effect of condition between the self-affirmation and control groups $F (1, 100) = 7.337, P < .001, \eta p2 = 0.180$. The self-affirmation group (Mean $= 17.72$) had significantly higher self-esteem levels than the control group (Mean $= 16.41$).

There was also a significant interaction between time x condition $F (1.6, 164) = 5.958, P = .006, \eta p2 = 0.077$. The self-affirmation group did not have significantly higher self-esteem post intervention ($P = .064$), but did have significantly higher self-esteem at the 1-week ($P = .039$) follow-up compared to the control group. The interaction shows that self-esteem levels continued to increase for the self-affirmed group, whereas self-esteem levels in the control group stayed the same (see Fig. 10.5).

### Website check

The sexual health website was checked to ensure participants trusted, believed, and learned from the sexual health website. A one sample t-test against the neutral point (3) was conducted. The t-tests showed significant differences between participant responses and the neutral point (see Table 10.4). Therefore, the website was successful as participants reported trusting, believing, and learning from the sexual health website.

TABLE 10.4
Trust, Learn and Belief Means and (SD) and

|  | Mean (SD) | t (df) | P |
| --- | --- | --- | --- |
| Trust | 4.09 (0.07) | 14.005 (101) | <.001[a] |
| Learn | 3.83 (0.08) | 9.663 (101) | <.001[a] |
| Believe | 3.87 (0.09) | 9.028 (101) | <.001[a] |

[a] Significant P-values at alpha level .05.

### Sexual health knowledge and intention to have sex

As there were no differences in sexual health knowledge at baseline, a 2 × 3 ANOVA was conducted to assess changes in knowledge over the course of the study. There were no significant main effects between the three time points ($F (1.82, 200) = 1.580, P = .210 \eta p2 = 0.16$) and no significant main effects of condition ($F (1, 100) = 3.872, P = .52 \eta p2 = 0.37$). There was also no significant interaction effect between time x condition ($F (1.82, 200) = 1.229, P = .293 \eta p2 = 0.12$) (Table 10.5).

Due to the baseline differences between the self-affirmation and control group on intention to have sex and intention to have safe sex, two analyses of covariance (ANCOVAs) were conducted. Intention to

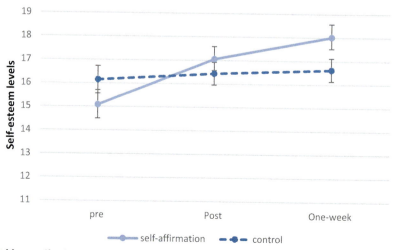

FIG. 10.5 Mean self-esteem scores at baseline, post intervention, and 1 week later. Error bars represent standard error.

## TABLE 10.5
Knowledge, Intentions to Have Sex, and Intentions to Have Safe Sex Means and (SD) Between Self-affirmation and Control Group for Baseline, Post, and One-week Intervention.

|  |  | Self-affirmation Mean (SD) | Control Mean (SD) |
|---|---|---|---|
| *Knowledge* | Baseline | 12.5 (5.24) | 11.9 (3.47) |
|  | Postmanipulation | 14.0 (3.59) | 12.0 (2.67) |
|  | One week | 13.4 (4.43) | 12.5 (3.65) |
| *Intentions to have sex* | Baseline | 6.9 (3.82) | 9.1 (4.66) |
|  | Postmanipulation | 11.1 (5.50) | 9.05 (4.16) |
|  | One week | 8.5 (4.69) | 9.0 (4.51) |
| *Intentions to have safe sex* | Baseline | 15.8 (3.72) | 17.7 (4.58) |
|  | Postmanipulation | 19.16 (3.59) | 16.34 (3.67) |
|  | One week | 18.80 (4.43) | 16.76 (3.65) |

have sex and intention to have safe sex at baseline were added as the covariates.

The homogeneity of regression assumption was tested. There were no significant differences between post intervention baseline sex intention x condition (F(1,98) = 0.269, P = .605) nor any differences at 1-week baseline sex intention x condition (F(1,98) = 0.000, P = .993). Therefore, it was assumed the homogeneity of regression assumption had not been violated and the ANCOVA was conducted.

There were no significant main effects of time between post and 1 week F(1,99) = <0.001, P = .985 ηp2 = <0.001. However, there was a significant main effect of condition F(1,99) = 4.551, P = .035, ηp2 = 0.016. The self-affirmation condition had higher intention to have sex (Mean = 10.08) than the control condition (Mean = 8.75).

There was a significant interaction between time x condition F(1,99) = 6.802, P = .011, ηp2 = 0.064 (see Fig. 10.6). The self-affirmation group had

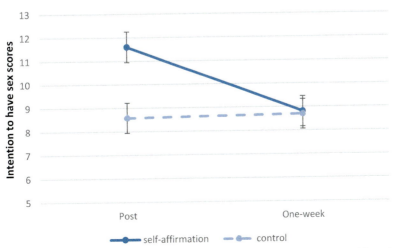

FIG. 10.6 Marginal mean intention to have sex scores at baseline, post intervention, and 1 week later. Error bars represent standard error.

significantly higher intentions to have sex post intervention than the control group t(100) = 2.120, P = .036. There were no significant differences between the self-affirmation and control groups 1 week later t(100) = 0.549, P = .585.

A second ANCOVA was conducted, the dependant variables were intention to have safe sex post intervention and 1-week post intervention, and the covariate was baseline intention to have safe sex. The homogeneity of regression assumption was tested. There were no significant differences between post baseline intention x condition (F(1,98) = 0.053, P = .819) nor any differences at 1-week baseline intention x condition (F(1,98) = 0.683, P = .411). Therefore, it was assumed the homogeneity of regression assumption had not been violated and the ANCOVA was conducted.

There were no significant main effects of time F(1,99) = 0.322 P = .572 $\eta p2$ = 0.003. There was a significant main effect of condition F(1,99) = 26.160, P = <.001, $\eta p2$ = 0.209. The self-affirmation group (Mean = 19.00) had significantly higher intentions to have safe sex than the control group (Mean = 16.53). There were no significant interaction effects between time x condition F(1,99) = 0.842, P = .361, $\eta p2$ = 0.008. See Fig. 10.7.

## Discussion

The self-affirmation manipulation was successful, as the self-affirmation group had significantly higher self-esteem post manipulation and at 1 week after the intervention than the control group. Therefore, hypothesis 1 as stated in the introduction was supported. This supports previous research findings that there are links between self-affirmation techniques and self-esteem (Schuz et al., 2017). Hypothesis 2 was also supported as the self-affirmation group had significantly higher intentions to have safe sex post intervention and at a 1-week follow-up than the control group. The self-affirmation group also had significantly higher intention to have sex than the control group post

**TABLE 10.6
Snapshot of Results.**

|  | Online Sexual Health and Self-affirmation Intervention |
|---|---|
| Self-esteem | The self-affirmation group had significantly higher self-esteem post at 1 week after the intervention than the control group. |
| Sexual health knowledge | No significant differences in sexual health knowledge |
| Intention to have sex | The self-affirmation group had significantly higher intentions to have sex post intervention than the control group. |
| Intention to have safe sex | The self-affirmation group had significantly higher intentions to have safe sex post intervention and 1 week later than the control group. |

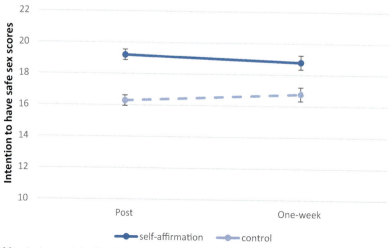

FIG. 10.7 Marginal mean intention to have safe sex scores at baseline, post intervention, and 1 week later. Error bars represent standard error.

intervention; however, there were no significant differences 1 week later. Hypothesis 3 was not supported, as there were no significant differences post intervention or at a 1-week follow-up in sexual health knowledge between the self-affirmation and control group.

The findings support previous research that has found self-affirmation techniques paired with sexual health information can increase intentions to have safe sex (Blanton et al., 2013). However, research by Blanton et al. (2013) was conducted with undergraduate populations, with a mean age of 19.9 years, therefore this current study has extended these findings and showed that safe sex intentions are also increased in a younger teenage population. Safe sex intentions were also significantly higher in the self-affirmation group at a 1-week follow-up than the control group, showing that intentions to have safe sex are sustainable over a 1-week period. Also, intentions to have sex were significantly higher in the self-affirmation group compared to the control group post intervention, yet there were no significant differences at a 1-week follow-up. It is known from previous literature and our previous studies that peer pressure significantly increases intention to have sex (Gillmore et al., 2002). As this brief intervention was conducted in a group classroom setting, it may have facilitated the higher intentions to have sex, therefore it is not known if there would be different trends in intention to have sex if the intervention was conducted in an individual setting.

The self-affirmation and sexual health website had no significant effect on sexual health knowledge. This is in contrast to Demetriades and Walter (2016) who found that self-affirmation techniques could increase information seeking behaviors and knowledge. However, this may be due to the way that adolescents use the Internet to search for information. Adolescents process information differently on the Internet compared to traditional reading. Sutherland-Smith (2002) and Gilbert (2017) proposed that teenagers are instantly gratified by rapid search and just adopt a "snatch and grab" approach to information on the Internet, without evaluating and reading the information. This then leads to shallow and passive interactions with the text and does not facilitate learning (Coiro, 2003). In this study, participants were instructed to read the website rather than perform a specific task, for example, find information on how to use a condom. Providing more signposting for teenagers about interacting with the information may have encouraged teenagers to actively search and read the sexual health information.

## Strengths and Limitations

The restrictions involved in conducting a school-based study meant that it was not possible to measure behavioral outcomes. We know from previous research with undergraduate students that self-affirmed participants are more likely to take condoms and HIV brochures (Ko & Kim, 2010; Sherman & Nelson, 2000). It is not known whether self-affirmation has a positive effect on behavioral outcomes for younger teenagers. The relatively short follow-up period made it impossible to measure longitudinally sexual behaviors and early sexual initiation. Research has demonstrated that self-affirmation manipulations may have effects over longer periods in other health domains. For example, in relation to fruit and vegetable consumption, effects have been demonstrated at 3 month and 6 months follow-ups (Wileman et al., 2014).

## Implications

This study is one of the first to investigate a brief self-affirmation and sexual health intervention for low SES female teenagers. Self-affirmation techniques paired with reliable sexual health information can successfully increase safe sex intentions in low SES female teenagers. These safe sex intentions are sustainable over a 1-week period. However, self-affirmation has no significant effects on sexual health knowledge; this may be due to issues in the way that teenagers interact with digital and online information. We know from previous studies that sexual health knowledge is a significant predictor of early sexual behaviors. This study has highlighted how important it is that websites incorporate design features that actively encourage teenagers to engage with the information. This study could have far-reaching potential implications for sexual health education, using an online self-affirmation task with online sexual health information is an easy, low-cost way to deliver a sexual health intervention. It could potentially be used in classrooms to deliver sexual health education. However, research around online self-affirmation and sexual health interventions is still at an early stage; this study has highlighted the value of administrating a low-cost online intervention to bolster self-esteem and promote safe sex intentions in low SES female teenagers.

The final chapter moves onto some final reflections and conclusions. It provides a summary and conclusion based on each of our studies presented throughout the book and an overview and summary of the main research literature. Finally, future research ideas and design implications for moving forward with online self-esteem and sexual health intervention programs are reflected on and discussed.

# CHAPTER 11

# Reflections

## CHAPTER OUTLINE

Reflections: Key Messages ................................. 135
Reflections: Methodology ................................... 135
   Including Stakeholders and Teens when
   Developing Interventions ................................. 135
   Types of Research ............................................ 137

Ethical Considerations ........................................ 137
Policy .................................................................... 137
Society ................................................................. 139
Future Directions ................................................. 139

## ABSTRACT

This final chapter moves onto some final reflections and conclusions. It provides a summary of the ideas presented throughout this book, and a summary of our studies. Finally, future research ideas and design implications for digital sexual health interventions programs with teenagers are considered.

## KEYWORDS

Digital health interventions; Online sexual health interventions; School-based sexual health education; Sexual health; Sexual health education; Sexual health interventions; Teenagers.

## REFLECTIONS: KEY MESSAGES

Throughout this book, we have presented six of our own studies, along with a review of the current literature around sexual health, sexual health interventions, and digital sexual health interventions. In the following sections we provide a summary of the previous chapters. Table 11.1 described our own previous studies that we have presented throughout the book. Our own studies were all conducted in the North East of England in the United Kingdom, with low SES female teenagers, apart from the study described in Chapter 9, where older University students from the North East of England were interviewed.

In Chapter 2 we explored previous literature that has investigated sexual health in the modern world. We found a plethora of predictors of teenagers' risky sexual behaviors described in previous literature. We also looked at sexual health in the digital world and explored the literature around teenagers' use of pornography and sexting (Table 11.2).

In Chapter 3, we explored current offline sexual health intervention programs that are available for teenagers. We found that sexual health intervention programs are mainly based in schools for teenagers, and discussed UK-based school sexual health education and how this varies globally. We also provided a summary of sexual health interventions that are available externally outside of schools (Table 11.3).

We also explored digital sexual health interventions, as teenagers are known for their early adoption of the Internet and mobile technology, and it is known that teenagers are enthusiastic about the idea of using technology and the Internet for health advice. The Internet provides an anonymous platform for seeking sexual health information. Four main digital interventions and the pros and cons were explored; sexual health websites, sexual health mobile apps, text messaging, and social networking sites (Table 11.4).

## REFLECTIONS: METHODOLOGY
### Including Stakeholders and Teens when Developing Interventions

Our previous studies have demonstrated how important it is to include key stakeholders' perceptions, experiences, and beliefs before tailoring the intervention to a target group. For example, the literature around self-esteem was mixed, and large systematic reviews had concluded that it was not a statistically significant predictor of risky sexual behaviors for teenagers (Buhi & Goodson, 2007). However, in our first qualitative study it was identified by sexual health professionals as the most important predictor of risky sexual behavior for female teenagers, and a barrier to teenagers seeking sexual health information. This was an important finding and one that we carried forward into our following studies.

Teenagers, Sexual Health Information and the Digital Age. https://doi.org/10.1016/B978-0-12-816969-8.00011-4
Copyright © 2020 Elsevier Inc. All rights reserved.

**TABLE 11.1**
**Summary of Our Own Previous Studies Discussed in Previous Chapters.**

| Our Research Study | Summary |
|---|---|
| Sexual health professionals (Chapter 4) | We interviewed sexual health professionals and found self-esteem, society, family, and peers were barriers to teens seeking sexual health advice. |
| Teens' diary study (Chapter 6) | Teens kept a diary for 4 weeks and recorded their sexual health thoughts. Teens had a severe lack of sexual health knowledge and no strategies for seeking sexual health information. |
| Teens' questionnaire study (Chapter 7) | A large questionnaire study with teenagers found lower self-esteem and sexual health knowledge predicts earlier sex before age 16 years. |
| Teens' apps and website study (Chapter 8) | Teen's views of current sexual health apps and websites; teens want to use sexual health apps that have interactive features and reliable information. |
| Student app study (Chapter 9) | Student's views of a menstrual tracking app, enjoyed using one and found that it was easy to use and provided them with reliable information. |
| Online intervention (Chapter 10) | An online intervention aimed at increasing self-esteem was piloted with teenagers and found that higher self-esteem promotes higher intention to have safe sex. |

**TABLE 11.2**
**Summary of Sexual Health in the Modern World.**

| Sexual Health in the Modern World | Summary |
|---|---|
| Predictors | There are many predictors of teens risky sexual behaviors; peers, parents, self, personality, situational factors, and external factors. |
| Pornography | Pornography is easily accessible, and previous research has found it is having an effect on teens' attitudes toward sex. |
| Sexting | Sending explicit messages, photos, and videos are becoming more common for teens; there are mixed findings on what effect this is having on teens' sexual behaviors and attitudes. |

**TABLE 11.3**
**Summary of Offline Sexual Health Intervention Programs.**

| Interventions | Summary |
|---|---|
| School-based | School-based sex education is very varied and not all programs cover inclusive information about sexual health. |
| Outside of schools | External sexual health interventions are more reliable and have appropriate information but tend to be too costly and not accessible for lower socioeconomic areas. |

Self-esteem may not have been included in the questionnaire (described in Chapter 7), without this insight from sexual health professionals (described in Chapter 4). We found that self-esteem was a predictor of risky sexual behaviors for female teenagers with the interplay of other factors. Therefore, this finding highlights the importance of including key stakeholders in the early stages of intervention design, especially if they have extensive knowledge of the target group.

It is also important to understand the experiences, attitudes, and beliefs of the target audience before developing an intervention. Sexual health professionals highlighted the taboo in society of discussing sexual health, which is a barrier to teenagers seeking sexual health information. In addition, the double standards of the mass media, that pornography is easily accessible, but safe sex is rarely displayed, can cause confusion for teenagers in relation to sexual health. This was then confirmed by teenagers, who reported that they speak

## CHAPTER 11 Reflections

**TABLE 11.4**
**Summary of Digital Sexual Health Intervention Programs.**

| Digital Interventions | Summary |
|---|---|
| Overall | Teens are comfortable using the Internet for health advice and like the anonymity and privacy it affords. |
| Sexual health websites | Websites act as interventions and provide sexual health information. However, a lot of websites contain inaccurate information. |
| Sexual health mobile apps | Sexual health apps allow for interaction but it is difficult to identify if they have reliable information and to determine their credibility. |
| Text messages | Text messaging is fast and convenient but allows for only limited information and works better alongside another intervention. |
| Social networking sites | Social networking sites allow for high collaboration and multilevel interaction between users and can be effective for sexual health promotion. May work better alongside an external intervention, as teens are wary of using them for health information. |

to their friends about sexual health, described in Chapter 6, but are worried about the "shaming" associated with peers who have had sex. This leads to confusion for teenagers, as they do not know which aspects of sexual health are acceptable to discuss, and worry that they might be shamed themselves. Teenagers want sexual health information although they are reluctant to actively search for it. This may change with the UK 2019/2020 Relationships and Sex Education guidelines; as sexual health hopefully becomes less of a taboo topic. It is important to consider how to advertise sexual health interventions, as developing an intervention and not effectively targeting it to teenagers may render it "invisible." There are many sexual health websites, apps, and online information sources available online, yet over a 4-week period teenagers did not access any of

these resources. Interventions need to be targeted and advertised to teenagers in creative ways as they are unlikely to actively search for sexual health information.

### Types of Research

We also found it valuable to use a mixed methods approach. Most previous health studies investigating the predictors of risky sexual behaviors for teenagers have either taken a quantitative approach (Buhi & Goodson, 2009) or a solely qualitative approach (Marston & King, 2006). While both of these approaches have contributed to the literature, approaching the topic from a combined perspective has proved very useful.

Previous research has found that teenagers are enthusiastic about using novel sources for sexual health information (Selkie, Benson, & Moreno, 2011), and teenagers report that they want confidential and private sources of health information. The development of sexual health apps builds upon these findings. However, there were previously no studies exploring teenagers' views of existing sexual health apps. We addressed this in Chapter 8 and noted that despite the growth in such apps, teenagers had not heard of any sexual health apps. Teenagers like using their phone, but they would not download a sexual health app as those currently available do not have reliable information paired with practical interactive content, which is what teenagers want from a sexual health app. Also, teenagers do not trust the information on sexual health apps and worry their parents may see the sexual health app on their phone. We took these findings forward when considering how best to present sexual health information during an intervention, and chose to use a website rather than an app.

### Ethical Considerations

Research ethics provides guidelines for the responsible conduct of research to ensure all research is conducted at a high ethical standard. It is vital to consider ethical considerations when conducting sexual health research with teenagers; and this is discussed in full in Chapter 5. Teenagers under the age of 18 years are deemed as vulnerable members of society and special considerations of consent, understanding of the research, and anonymity are often legal, as well as moral, requirements. Below we have summarized three of the main ethical points to consider when recruiting teenagers for sexual health research (Table 11.5).

### Policy

Currently in UK schools, sex and relationship education is compulsory in local authority maintained schools,

## TABLE 11.5
## Ethical Considerations When Conducting Sexual Health Research With Teenagers.

| | Why is This Important | Best Practice |
|---|---|---|
| Recruiting teenagers | An appropriate number of participants need to be recruited to ensure studies have sufficient power. Teenagers may feel embarrassed over volunteering to take part in a sexual health study, especially in front of people. | Leave written information sheets with teachers or in the back of a classroom for participants to collect in their own time. Provide participants a sufficient amount of time to let their teacher know discreetly if they would like to take part. |
| Explaining ethics and gaining consent | It is vital teens understand the research before they provide consent to take part. They should understand if the research may cause them any embarrassment. If participants do not believe that the research is anonymous and confidential, then they may not give honest answers. | Written information should not be too long, be bullet pointed, and the key information should be highlighted. The researcher should also give verbal information and provide teens the chance to ask questions. It is important to explain confidentiality, anonymity, and safeguarding information in a clear way. The researcher should explain their own qualifications. For example, if you are not an expert in sexual health and unable to answer teenagers' sexual health questions, then this should be explained to the teenagers at the start of the project. |
| Parental consent | It is vital to gain parental consent for any research project involving teens under the age of 18 years. It is important parents understand that their child has not been targeted to take part in the research. The benefits and any potential downsides of their child taking part should also be fully explained. | There are two main ways of gaining parental consent: Opt-in consent: Parents provide their informed consent for their child to take part in the research, before the research day. Opt-out consent: The parent is informed of the research and contacts the researcher in a given time if they do not want their child to take part in the study. |

but it is not assessed and therefore, is also inconsistent in these schools (see Chapter 3) The only information that schools are required to teach is basic sex education such as puberty, reproduction, and the menstrual cycle (UK Department of Education and Employment, 2000, pp. 1–34). This information does not reflect the complex and broad array of sexual health issues. There are guidelines on content, although as the term suggests these are not compulsory to include. The current guidelines are *to teach about responsibilities of parenthood as well as sexual intercourse, to focus on boys and girls, to build self-esteem, to discuss responsibility and consequences of ones actions in relation to sex and parenthood, to include information about different contraception methods, to use teenage mothers and fathers as educators, to provide a clear argument for delaying sex and resisting peer pressure, to link sex education with other risky behaviors such as drugs, alcohol,* *smoking, and lastly to ensure young people understand the law and consent* (UK Department of Education and Employment, 2000).

This current system is due to change for the 2019/2020 academic year. It has been proposed that all secondary schools, including academies and maintained schools, will have to teach relationships and sex education (RSE) (Gov UK Legislation, 2017). This will be age-appropriate information that will start in primary schools (4–11 year olds). Primary schools will focus on relationships and move to relationships and sex education in secondary schools. The details of this proposed change are not confirmed; however, it is known that all schools will have to have a written policy on sex education, and make this freely available to parents (Long, 2017). This will encourage parents to discuss sex education with their children. In addition, it will be compulsory to cover different types of relationships (including strangers, friends, and intimate relationships), consent and healthy relationships, well-being and mental health, safety online, sex and sexuality, sexual health in the context of relationships, healthy bodies, healthy minds, self-esteem, mental health resilience, and economic well-being (Long, 2017). Also, there will be a push for RSE in the modern world, which will include information on meeting strangers online and sexting (Gov UK, 2017). All schools will be inspected to ensure schools are providing the full statutory curriculum.

One of the issues identified with current Sex and Relationship Education is that teachers conducting these sessions do not usually have the correct training and have insufficient knowledge about STIs and emergency contraception to effectively deliver these sessions (Westwood & Mullan, 2007). Sexual health professionals are ideally placed to provide SRE but are not easily accessible in the eyes of teenagers and so are viewed in a less positive light than other potential sources of information (Westwood & Mullan, 2009). Even though some schools have a school nurse, most low SES schools are underresourced and teenagers are not able to access the school nurse for sexual health questions (France, 2014). However, using the Internet would be a cost-effective way to cover all areas of sexual health. Sexual health websites can be updated by sexual health professionals and can easily cover all areas in the new RSE guidelines. This would be an easy method for low resourced schools to add up-to-date and relevant sexual health information to their existing sexual health education programs, and sexual health websites could provide teachers with essential sexual health information.

While the sexual health intervention we developed in Chapter 10 would be difficult to implement at a distance, it could have potential in a classroom setting. It would be easy and low-cost to add an online self-affirmation task before showing sexual health information to teenagers. Self-affirmation tasks can be completed in a relatively short time, for example, a 5-min essay as used in the study described in Chapter 10. There are also a range of self-affirmation tasks available to maintain teenagers' interest over time. These include value scales, inserting values into sentence stems, value essays, and positive feedback (McQueen & Klein, 2006). Thus, there are easy ways of heightening self-esteem online through self-affirmation techniques.

This type of online intervention would be appropriate in a classroom setting and would meet the new RSE guidelines. It has been proposed that building

self-esteem is likely to be on the new curriculum (Long, 2017), and current self-esteem interventions are long-term (6 weeks or longer) and difficult to administer (Dalgas-Pelish, 2006; LeCroy, 2005). Therefore, self-affirmation techniques can provide an easier and short-term way to increase self-esteem and, when paired with reliable sexual health information, ultimately improve intentions to have safe sex.

## Society

While most intervention programs are based on the individual, it is important to acknowledge that there is a broader societal element to sexual health. In our research, sexual health professionals highlighted the taboo in society of discussing sexual health, which is a barrier to teenagers seeking sexual health information. In addition, the double standards of the mass media, that pornography is easily accessible, but safe sex is rarely displayed, can cause confusion for teenagers, and a reluctance to seek and discuss sexual health information. This may change with the 2019/2020 Relationships and Sex Education guidelines, as sexual health may become less of a taboo to discuss. In contrast to other countries, sex is much more openly talked about in the Netherlands, and sex education is taught at a much earlier age, incorporating a more holistic view of sex in general (Fine & McClelland, 2006). Also, the Netherlands have some of the lowest rates of STIs and teenage pregnancy, and research suggests that teenagers are more likely to delay sexual initiation than those in the United Kingdom (Lewis & Knijn, 2003). Therefore, while the brief intervention discussed in Chapter 10 focused solely on the individual, there is a need to address societal issues around the open discussion of sex and sexual health before we witness any real change.

## Future Directions

It has been emphasized that a sexual health website could work in a classroom setting; however, there is still the potential for the development of sexual health apps to address sexual health. Especially as students in Chapter 9 were enthusiastic about menstrual tracking apps as a way of having an interactive app that also includes reliable information. In Chapter 6 teenagers emphasized that they prefer to use their phones to access sexual health information because of the privacy phones afford. While, as described above, a sexual health website would be more appropriate in a classroom setting, an app could be used for additional information away from the classroom. A sexual health app could be far-reaching and provide timely up-to-date information to teenagers. Teenagers need formal sexual health education in a classroom setting, where they can seek further face-to-face advice and clarification, but a sexual health app could be appropriate to use at home to complement the Relationships and Sex Education. However, currently teenagers have not heard of sexual health apps, and when we showed them the sexual health apps, they perceived apps to be lacking in detail and were wary of trusting the information. Despite their current reservations, teenagers did believe they would be convenient compared to websites, and with the recommendations they described, teenagers would be likely to use a sexual health app in the future. Teenagers want sexual health apps that are easy to use with a clear layout and host age-appropriate information and images. The content should include appropriate videos and interactive features as well as information that covers all areas of sexual health. However, current sexual health apps are lacking identifiable trust cues, and teenagers are unsure how to identify a trustable app.

Previous research has identified that sexually active teenagers are more likely to seek sexual health information than nonsexually active teenagers (Jones & Biddlecom, 2011). However, our use of anonymous methods (for example, diary methods), meant that we could not directly compare sexually active and nonactive teenagers in regard to their sexual health information seeking behaviors. Understanding this difference would provide insight into the most effective ways to target teenagers with sexual health information. Future research could seek to understand whether and why differences exist between sexually active and nonactive teenagers in information seeking practices, and this could be incorporated into future intervention programs, so teenagers feel comfortable accessing sexual health information.

The previous chapter demonstrated that self-affirmation techniques can increase self-esteem, and that this is sustainable over a 1-week period. However, it is not known if self-esteem can be heightened over a longer period through self-affirmation techniques. One session of self-affirmation may not be enough to heighten self-esteem for longer periods of time. Self-esteem is complex to heighten, and most sessions are longer term, 6 weeks or longer, before there are any long-term effects of self-esteem enhancement (Dalgas-Pelish, 2006). Going forward, there is scope for future research to investigate self-affirmation on sexual behaviors further.

Previous research has demonstrated that it is important to tailor interventions to the target group (Kreuter, Lukwago, Bucholtz, Clark, & Sanders-Thompson, 2003). Our research has focused on low SES female teenagers because previous research has identified particular factors in their lives that make it more likely for them to engage in earlier sexual intercourse (Kellam, 2014). Sexual health information earlier on can help prevent against earlier intercourse (Finer, 2013). It was beyond the scope of our research to include both males and females. However, the guidelines for Relationship and Sex Education highlight that both males and females should receive equal attention. In addition, previous research has highlighted that it is important that males and females are both included in sexual health interventions, so that together they can make informed decisions about sex (Harden, Brunton, Fletcher, & Oakley, 2009; Milburn, 1995). Therefore, more work is needed with teenage males to investigate if a similar self-esteem approach would be effective in promoting sexual health knowledge and safe sex intentions.

# References

Abma, J., Driscoll, A., & Moore, K. (1998). Young women's degree of control over first intercourse: An exploratory analysis. *Family Planning Perspectives*, 12–18.

Abraham, C., & Michie, S. (2008). A taxonomy of behavior change techniques used in interventions. *Health Psychology*, 27(3), 379.

Aiken, K. D., & Boush, D. M. (2006). Trustmarks, objective-source ratings, and implied investments in advertising: Investigating online trust and the context-specific nature of internet signals. *Journal of the Academy of Marketing Science*, 34(3), 308–323.

Ajilore, O. (2015). Identifying peer effects using spatial analysis: The role of peers on risky sexual behavior. *Review of Economics of the Household*, 13(3), 635–652.

Ajzen, I. (1991). The theory of planned behavior. *Organizational Behavior and Human Decision Processes*, 50(2), 179–211.

Alderson, P., & Morrow, V. (2004). Ethics, social research and consulting with children and young people. *Bulletin of Medical Ethics*, 139, 5–7.

Alex Mason, W., Hitch, J. E., Kosterman, R., McCarty, C. A., Herrenkohl, T. I., & David Hawkins, J. (2010). Growth in adolescent delinquency and alcohol use in relation to young adult crime, alcohol use disorders, and risky sex: A comparison of youth from low-versus middle-income backgrounds. *Journal of Child Psychology and Psychiatry*, 51(12), 1377–1385.

Alexander, M. G., & Fisher, T. D. (2003). Truth and consequences: Using the bogus pipeline to examine sex differences in self-reported sexuality. *Journal of Sex Research*, 40(1), 27–35.

Antheunis, M. L., Schouten, A. P., & Krahmer, E. (2016). The role of social networking sites in early adolescents' social lives. *The Journal of Early Adolescence*, 36(3), 348–371. Apps and Krebs, 2016.

Armitage, C. J., & Conner, M. (2001). Efficacy of the theory of planned behaviour: A meta-analytic review. *British Journal of Social Psychology*, 40(4), 471–499.

Armitage, C. J., Harris, P. R., & Arden, M. A. (2011). Evidence that self-affirmation reduces alcohol consumption: Randomized exploratory trial with a new, brief means of self-affirming. *Health Psychology*, 30(5), 633.

Armitage, C. J., Harris, P. R., Hepton, G., & Napper, L. (2008). Self-affirmation increases acceptance of health-risk information among UK adult smokers with low socioeconomic status. *Psychology of Addictive Behaviors*, 22(1), 88.

Armitage, C. J., Rowe, R., Arden, M. A., & Harris, P. R. (2014). A brief psychological intervention that reduces adolescent alcohol consumption. *Journal of Consulting and Clinical Psychology*, 82(3), 546.

Armour, S., & Haynie, D. L. (2007). Adolescent sexual debut and later delinquency. *Journal of Youth and Adolescence*, 36(2), 141–152.

Aronowitz, T., Rennells, R. E., & Todd, E. (2005). Heterosocial behaviors in early adolescent African American girls: The role of mother-daughter relationships. *Journal of Family Nursing*, 11(2), 122–139.

Baams, L., Overbeek, G., van de Bongardt, D., Reitz, E., Dubas, J. S., & van Aken, M. A. (2015). Adolescents' and their friends' sexual behavior and intention: Selection effects of personality dimensions. *Journal of Research in Personality*, 54, 2–12.

Baele, J., Dusseldorp, E., & Maes, S. (2001). Condom use self-efficacy: Effect on intended and actual condom use in adolescents. *Journal of Adolescent Health*, 28(5), 421–431.

Barter, C., & Stanley, N. (2016). Inter-personal violence and abuse in adolescent intimate relationships: Mental health impact and implications for practice. *International Review of Psychiatry*, 28(5), 485–503.

Baumer, E. P., & South, S. J. (2001). Community effects on youth sexual activity. *Journal of Marriage and Family*, 63(2), 540–554.

Belgrave, F. Z., Van Oss Marin, B., & Chambers, D. B. (2000). Culture, contextual, and intrapersonal predictors of risky sexual attitudes among urban African American girls in early adolescence. *Cultural Diversity and Ethnic Minority Psychology*, 6(3), 309.

Benda, B. B., & Corwyn, R. F. (1996). Testing a theoretical model of adolescent sexual behavior among rural families in poverty. *Child and Adolescent Social Work Journal*, 13(6), 469–494.

Bickmore, T. W., Utami, D., Matsuyama, R., & Paasche-Orlow, M. K. (2016). Improving access to online health information with conversational agents: A randomized controlled experiment. *Journal of Medical Internet Research*, 18(1), e1.

Bingham, C. R., & Crockett, L. J. (1996). Longitudinal adjustment patterns of boys and girls experiencing early, middle, and late sexual intercourse. *Developmental Psychology*, 32(4), 647.

Birndorf, S., Ryan, S., Auinger, P., & Aten, M. (2005). High self-esteem among adolescents: Longitudinal trends, sex differences, and protective factors. *Journal of Adolescent Health*, 37(3), 194–201.

Bissell, M. (2000). Socio-economic outcomes of teen pregnancy and parenthood: A review of the literature. *The Canadian Journal of Human Sexuality*, 9(3), 191.

Bogg, T., & Roberts, B. W. (2004). Conscientiousness and health-related behaviors: A meta-analysis of the leading behavioral contributors to mortality. *Psychological Bulletin*, 130(6), 887.

van de Bongardt, D., Reitz, E., Sandfort, T., & Deković, M. (2015). A meta-analysis of the relations between three types of peer norms and adolescent sexual behavior. *Personality and Social Psychology Review, 19*(3), 203–234.

Booth-Kewley, S., Larson, G. E., & Miyoshi, D. K. (2007). Social desirability effects on computerized and paper-and-pencil questionnaires. *Computers in Human Behavior, 23*(1), 463–477.

Borzekowski, D. L., & Rickert, V. I. (2001). Adolescent cyber-surfing for health information: A new resource that crosses barriers. *Archives of Pediatrics & Adolescent Medicine, 155*(7), 813–817.

Braun-Courville, D. K., & Rojas, M. (2009). Exposure to sexually explicit web sites and adolescent sexual attitudes and behaviors. *Journal of Adolescent Health, 45*(2), 156–162.

Brawner, B. M. (2012). Attitudes and beliefs regarding depression, HIV/AIDS, and HIV risk-related sexual behaviors among clinically depressed African American adolescent females. *Archives of Psychiatric Nursing, 26*(6), 464–476.

Brawner, B. M., Davis, Z. M., Fannin, E. F., & Alexander, K. A. (2012). Clinical depression and condom use attitudes and beliefs among African American adolescent females. *Journal of the Association of Nurses in AIDS Care, 23*(3), 184–194.

Brawner, B. M., Gomes, M. M., Jemmott, L. S., Deatrick, J. A., & Coleman, C. L. (2012). Clinical depression and HIV risk-related sexual behaviors among African-American adolescent females: Unmasking the numbers. *AIDS Care, 24*(5), 618–625.

Brechwald, W. A., & Prinstein, M. J. (2011). Beyond homophily: A decade of advances in understanding peer influence processes. *Journal of Research on Adolescence, 21*(1), 166–179.

Broadstock, M., & Michie, S. (2000). Processes of patient decision making: Theoretical and methodological issues. *Psychology and Health, 15*(2), 191–204.

Brown, J., Burton, D., Nikolin, S., Crooks, P. J., Hatfield, J., & Bilston, L. E. (2013). A qualitative approach using the integrative model of behaviour change to identify intervention strategies to increase optimal child restraint practices among culturally and linguistically diverse families in New South Wales. *Injury Prevention, 19*(1), 6–12.

Brown, L. K., DiClemente, R. J., & Reynolds, L. A. (1991). *HIV prevention for adolescents: utility of the health belief model.* AIDS Education and Prevention.

Brown, J. D., L'Engle, K. L., Pardun, C. J., Guo, G., Kenneavy, K., & Jackson, C. (2006). Sexy media matter: Exposure to sexual content in music, movies, television, and magazines predicts black and white adolescents' sexual behavior. *Pediatrics, 117*(4), 1018–1027.

Brown, J. L., & Vanable, P. A. (2007). Alcohol use, partner type, and risky sexual behavior among college students: Findings from an event-level study. *Addictive Behaviors, 32*(12), 2940–2952.

Brown, J. D., & Wissow, L. S. (2009). Discussion of sensitive health topics with youth during primary care visits: Relationship to youth perceptions of care. *Journal of Adolescent Health, 44*(1), 48–54.

Brown, J. D., & Wissow, L. S. (2009). Discussion of sensitive health topics with youth during primary care visits: Relationship to youth perceptions of care. *Journal of Adolescent Health, 44*(1), 48–54.

Bruess, C. E., & Schroeder, E. (2013). *Sexuality education theory and practice.* Jones & Bartlett Publishers.

Buchanan, T., Paine, C., Joinson, A. N., & Reips, U. D. (2007). Development of measures of online privacy concern and protection for use on the internet. *Journal of the American Society for Information Science and Technology, 58*(2), 157–165.

Buhi, E. R., Daley, E. M., Oberne, A., Smith, S. A., Schneider, T., & Fuhrmann, H. J. (2010). Quality and accuracy of sexual health information web sites visited by young people. *Journal of Adolescent Health, 47*(2), 206–208.

Buhi, E. R., Klinkenberger, N., Hughes, S., Blunt, H. D., & Rietmeijer, C. (2013). Teens' use of digital technologies and preferences for receiving STD prevention and sexual health promotion messages: Implications for the next generation of intervention initiatives. *Sexually Transmitted Diseases, 40*(1), 52–54.

Byron, P., Albury, K., & Evers, C. (2013). "It would be weird to have that on Facebook": Young people's use of social media and the risk of sharing sexual health information. *Reproductive Health Matters, 21*(41), 35–44.

Caminis, A., Henrich, C., Ruchkin, V., Schwab-Stone, M., & Martin, A. (2007). Psychosocial predictors of sexual initiation and high-risk sexual behaviors in early adolescence. *Child and Adolescent Psychiatry and Mental Health, 1*(1), 14.

Campbell, F. A., Ramey, C. T., Pungello, E., Sparling, J., & Miller-Johnson, S. (2002). Early childhood education: Young adult outcomes from the Abecedarian Project. *Applied Developmental Science, 6*(1), 42–57.

Carpenter, C. J. (2010). A meta-analysis of the effectiveness of health belief model variables in predicting behavior. *Health Communication, 25*(8), 661–669.

Casey, E. A., & Beadnell, B. (2010). The structure of male adolescent peer networks and risk for intimate partner violence perpetration: Findings from a national sample. *Journal of Youth and Adolescence, 39*(6), 620–633.

Catalano, R. F., Berglund, M. L., Ryan, J. A., Lonczak, H. S., & Hawkins, J. D. (2004). Positive youth development in the United States: Research findings on evaluations of positive youth development programs. *The Annals of the American Academy of Political and Social Science, 591*(1), 98–124.

Charlson, M. E., Wells, M. T., Peterson, J. C., Boutin-Foster, C., Ogedegbe, G. O., Mancuso, C. A., & Isen, A. M. (2013). Mediators and moderators of behavior change in patients with chronic cardiopulmonary disease: The impact of positive affect and self-affirmation. *Translational Behavioral Medicine, 4*(1), 7–17.

Chau, P. Y., Hu, P. J. H., Lee, B. L., & Au, A. K. (2007). Examining customers' trust in online vendors and their dropout decisions: An empirical study. *Electronic Commerce Research and Applications, 6*(2), 171–182.

Claassen, L., Henneman, L., Timmermans, D., Nijpels, G., Dekker, J., & Marteau, T. (2011). Peer reviewed: Causal beliefs and perceptions of risk for diabetes and cardiovascular disease, The Netherlands, 2007. *Preventing Chronic Disease, 8*(6).

Clark, L. F., Miller, K. S., Nagy, S. S., Avery, J., Roth, D. L., Liddon, N., & Mukherjee, S. (2005). Adult identity mentoring: Reducing sexual risk for African-American seventh grade students. *Journal of Adolescent Health, 37*(4). 337-e1.

Coiro, J. (2003). Exploring literacy on the internet: Reading comprehension on the internet: Expanding our understanding of reading comprehension to encompass new literacies. *The Reading Teacher, 56*(5), 458–464.

Cole, F. L. (1997). The role of self-esteem in safer sexual practices. *Journal of the Association of Nurses in AIDS Care, 8*(6), 64–70.

Cole-Lewis, H., & Kershaw, T. (2010). Text messaging as a tool for behavior change in disease prevention and management. *Epidemiologic Reviews, 32*(1), 56–69.

Conner, M., & Armitage, C. J. (1998). Extending the theory of planned behavior: A review and avenues for further research. *Journal of Applied Social Psychology, 28*(15), 1429–1464.

Copen, C. E., Dittus, P. J., & Leichliter, J. S. (2016). Confidentiality concerns and sexual and reproductive health care among adolescents and young adults aged 15–25. *Age, 15*(17), 18–19.

Cornelius, J. B., & Appiah, J. A. (2016). Using mobile technology to promote safe sex and sexual health in adolescents: Current practices and future recommendations. *Adolescent Health, Medicine and Therapeutics, 7*, 43.

Cranor, L. F., Durity, A. L., Marsh, A., & Ur, B. (2014). Parents' and teens' perspectives on privacy in a technology-filled world. In *10th Symposium On Useable Privacy and Security ({SOUPS} 2014)* (pp. 19–35).

Crocker, J., & Park, L. E. (2004). The costly pursuit of self-esteem. *Psychological Bulletin, 130*(3), 392.

Crockett, L. J., Bingham, C. R., Chopak, J. S., & Vicary, J. R. (1996). Timing of first sexual intercourse: The role of social control, social learning, and problem behavior. *Journal of Youth and Adolescence, 25*(1), 89–111.

Croyle, R. T., Sun, Y. C., & Hart, M. (1997). Processing risk factor information: Defensive biases in health-related judgments and memory. In *Perceptions of health and illness* (pp. 267–290).

Crutzen, R. (2010). Adding effect sizes to a systematic review on interventions for promoting physical activity among European teenagers. *International Journal of Behavioral Nutrition and Physical Activity, 7*(1), 29.

Dalgas-Pelish, P. (2006). Effects of a self-esteem intervention program on school-age children. *Pediatric Nursing, 32*(4).

Davis, T. M. (2002). An examination of repeat pregnancies using problem behavior theory: Is it really problematic? *Journal of Youth Studies, 5*(3), 337–351.

Day, R. D. (1992). The transition to first intercourse among racially and culturally diverse youth. *Journal of Marriage and Family*, 749–762.

De Genna, N. M., Larkby, C., & Cornelius, M. D. (2011). Pubertal timing and early sexual intercourse in the offspring of teenage mothers. *Journal of Youth and Adolescence, 40*(10), 1315–1328. https://doi.org/10.1007/s10964-010-9609-3.

de Sanjose, S., Cortés, X., Méndez, C., Puig-Tintore, L., Torné, A., Roura, E., & Castellsague, X. (2008). Age at sexual initiation and number of sexual partners in the female Spanish population: Results from the AFRODITA survey. *European Journal of Obstetrics & Gynecology and Reproductive Biology, 140*(2), 234–240.

Deardorff, J., Gonzales, N. A., Christopher, F. S., Roosa, M. W., & Millsap, R. E. (2005). Early puberty and adolescent pregnancy: The influence of alcohol use. *Pediatrics, 116*(6), 1451–1456.

Demetriades, S. Z., & Walter, N. (2016). You should know better: Can self-affirmation facilitate information-seeking behavior and interpersonal discussion? *Journal of Health Communication, 21*(11), 1131–1140.

Denzin, N. K. (1989). *Interpretive biography* (Vol. 17). Sage.

Devine, S., Bull, S., Dreisbach, S., & Shlay, J. (2014). Enhancing a teen pregnancy prevention program with text messaging: Engaging minority youth to develop TOP® plus text. *Journal of Adolescent Health, 54*(3), S78–S83.

Diamond, L. M. (2004). Emerging perspectives on distinctions between romantic love and sexual desire. *Current Directions in Psychological Science, 13*(3), 116–119.

Diamond, L. M., & Lucas, S. (2004). Sexual-minority and heterosexual youths' peer relationships: Experiences, expectations, and implications for well-being. *Journal of Research on Adolescence, 14*(3), 313–340.

DiClemente, C. C., Marinilli, A. S., Singh, M., & Bellino, L. E. (2001). The role of feedback in the process of health behavior change. *American Journal of Health Behavior, 25*(3), 217–227.

Divecha, Z., Divney, A., Ickovics, J., & Kershaw, T. (2012). Tweeting about testing: Do low-income, parenting adolescents and young adults use new media technologies to communicate about sexual health? *Perspectives on Sexual and Reproductive Health, 44*(3), 176–183.

Donnellan, M. B., Trzesniewski, K. H., Robins, R. W., Moffitt, T. E., & Caspi, A. (2005). Low self-esteem is related to aggression, antisocial behavior, and delinquency. *Psychological Science, 16*(4), 328–335.

Donovan, J. E., Jessor, R., & Costa, F. M. (1991). Adolescent health behavior and conventionality-unconventionality: An extension of problem-behavior therapy. *Health Psychology, 10*(1), 52.

Dube, S. R., Anda, R. F., Whitfield, C. L., Brown, D. W., Felitti, V. J., Dong, M., & Giles, W. H. (2005). Long-term consequences of childhood sexual abuse by gender of victim. *American Journal of Preventive Medicine, 28*(5), 430–438.

Duncan, S. C., Duncan, T. E., Biglan, A., & Ary, D. (1998). Contributions of the social context to the development of adolescent substance use: A multivariate latent growth modeling approach. *Drug and Alcohol Dependence, 50*(1), 57–71.

Düring, C., & Jessop, D. C. (2015). The moderating impact of self-esteem on self-affirmation effects. *British Journal of Health Psychology, 20*(2), 274–289.

Eisenberg, M. E., Bernat, D. H., Bearinger, L. H., & Resnick, M. D. (2008). Support for comprehensive sexuality education: Perspectives from parents of school-age youth. *Journal of Adolescent Health, 42*(4), 352–359.

Epton, T., & Harris, P. R. (2008). Self-affirmation promotes health behavior change. *Health Psychology, 27*(6), 746.

Eysenck, M. W. (1976). Arousal, learning, and memory. *Psychological Bulletin, 83*(3), 389.

Falk, E. B., O'Donnell, M. B., Cascio, C. N., Tinney, F., Kang, Y., Lieberman, M. D., & Strecher, V. J. (2015). Self-affirmation alters the brain's response to health messages and subsequent behavior change. *Proceedings of the National Academy of Sciences, 112*(7), 1977−1982.

Farmer, M. A., & Meston, C. M. (2006). Predictors of condom use self-efficacy in an ethnically diverse university sample. *Archives of Sexual Behavior, 35*(3), 313−326.

Ferrer, R. A., Klein, W. M., Persoskie, A., Avishai-Yitshak, A., & Sheeran, P. (2016). The tripartite model of risk perception (TRIRISK): Distinguishing deliberative, affective, and experiential components of perceived risk. *Annals of Behavioral Medicine, 50*(5), 653−663.

Fielden, A. L., Sillence, E., Little, L., & Harris, P. R. (2016). Online self-affirmation increases fruit and vegetable consumption in groups at high risk of low intake. *Applied Psychology: Health and Well-Being, 8*(1), 3−18.

Fine, M., & McClelland, S. (2006). Sexuality education and desire: Still missing after all these years. *Harvard Educational Review, 76*(3), 297−338.

Finer, L. B., & Philbin, J. M. (2013). Sexual initiation, contraceptive use, and pregnancy among young adolescents. *Pediatrics, 131*(5), 886−891.

Fisher, C. B. (2005). Deception research involving children: Ethical practices and paradoxes. *Ethics and Behavior, 15*(3), 271−287.

Flavián, C., & Guinalíu, M. (2006). Consumer trust, perceived security and privacy policy: Three basic elements of loyalty to a web site. *Industrial Management & Data Systems, 106*(5), 601−620.

Flavián, C., Guinalíu, M., & Gurrea, R. (2006). The role played by perceived usability, satisfaction and consumer trust on website loyalty. *Information & Management, 43*(1), 1−14.

Flay, B. R., Graumlich, S., Segawa, E., Burns, J. L., & Holliday, M. Y. (2004). Effects of 2 prevention programs on high-risk behaviors among African American youth: A randomized trial. *Archives of Pediatrics & Adolescent Medicine, 158*(4), 377−384.

Fogg, B. J., Marshall, J., Laraki, O., Osipovich, A., Varma, C., Fang, N., & Treinen, M. (2001). What makes web sites credible?: A report on a large quantitative study. In *Proceedings of the SIGCHI conference on human factors in computing systems* (pp. 61−68). ACM.

Fox, S. (2009). *The social life of health information. Pew internet & American life project 2009.* http://www.pewinternet.org/Reports/2009/8-The-Social-Life-of-Health-Information.aspx.

France, J. (2014). Using texts to increase access to school nurses. *Nursing Times, 110*(13), 18−19.

Gaskin, G. L., Bruce, J., & Anoshiravani, A. (2016). Understanding parent perspectives concerning adolescents' online access to personal health information. *Journal of Participatory Medicine, 8.*

Gerrard, M., Gibbons, F. X., & Bushman, B. J. (1996). Relation between perceived vulnerability to HIV and precautionary sexual behavior. *Psychological Bulletin, 119*(3), 390.

Gillmore, M. R., Archibald, M. E., Morrison, D. M., Wilsdon, A., Wells, E. A., Hoppe, M. J., &

Murowchick, E. (2002). Teen sexual behavior: Applicability of the theory of reasoned action. *Journal of Marriage and Family, 64*(4), 885−897.

Godin, G., Bélanger-Gravel, A., Vézina-Im, L. A., Amireault, S., & Bilodeau, A. (2012). Question−behaviour effect: A randomised controlled trial of asking intention in the interrogative or declarative form. *Psychology and Health, 27*(9), 1086−1099.

Godin, G., & Kok, G. (1996). The theory of planned behavior: A review of its applications to health-related behaviors. *American Journal of Health Promotion, 11*(2), 87−98.

Gold, J., Pedrana, A. E., Sacks-Davis, R., Hellard, M. E., Chang, S., Howard, S., & Stoove, M. A. (2011). A systematic examination of the use of online social networking sites for sexual health promotion. *BMC Public Health, 11*(1), 583.

Good, A., Harris, P. R., Jessop, D., & Abraham, C. (2015). Open-mindedness can decrease persuasion amongst adolescents: The role of self-affirmation. *British Journal of Health Psychology, 20*(2), 228−242.

Goodwin, N., Smith, J., Davies, A., Perry, C., Rosen, R., Dixon, A., & Ham, C. (2011). A report to the department of health and the NHS future forum. In *Integrated care for patients and populations: improving outcomes by working together.*

Gray, N. J., & Klein, J. D. (2006). Adolescents and the internet: Health and sexuality information. *Current Opinion in Obstetrics and Gynecology, 18*(5), 519−524.

Gray, N. J., Klein, J. D., Noyce, P. R., Sesselberg, T. S., & Cantrill, J. A. (2005). Health information-seeking behaviour in adolescence: The place of the internet. *Social Science & Medicine, 60*(7), 1467−1478.

Greenberg, J., Magder, L., & Aral, S. (1992). Age at first coitus. A marker for risky sexual behavior in women. *Sexually Transmitted Diseases, 19*(6), 331−334.

Griffiths, F., Lindenmeyer, A., Powell, J., Lowe, P., & Thorogood, M. (2006). Why are health care interventions delivered over the internet? A systematic review of the published literature. *Journal of Medical Internet Research, 8*(2), e10.

Guzmán, B. L., Schlehofer-Sutton, M. M., Villanueva, C. M., Stritto, M. E. D., Casad, B. J., & Feria, A. (2003). Let's talk about sex: How comfortable discussions about sex impact teen sexual behavior. *Journal of Health Communication, 8*(6), 583−598.

Halpern, C. T. (2010). Reframing research on adolescent sexuality: Healthy sexual development as part of the life course. *Perspectives on Sexual and Reproductive Health, 42*(1), 6−7.

Hammarlund, K., Lundgren, I., & Nyström, M. (2008). In the heat of the night, it is difficult to get it right—teenagers' attitudes and values towards sexual risk-taking. *International Journal of Qualitative Studies on Health and Well-Being, 3*(2), 103−112.

Hansen, D. L., Derry, H. A., Resnick, P. J., & Richardson, C. R. (2003). Adolescents searching for health information on the internet: An observational study. *Journal of Medical Internet Research, 5*(4), e25.

Harden, A., Brunton, G., Fletcher, A., & Oakley, A. (2009). Teenage pregnancy and social disadvantage: Systematic review integrating controlled trials and qualitative studies. *BMJ, 339,* b4254.

Harris, K., Byrd, K., Engel, M., Weeks, K., & Ahlers-Schmidt, C. R. (2016). Internet-based information on long-acting reversible contraception for adolescents. *Journal of Primary Care & Community Health, 7*(2), 76–80.

Harris, P. R., & Napper, L. (2005). Self-affirmation and the biased processing of threatening health-risk information. *Personality and Social Psychology Bulletin, 31*(9), 1250–1263.

Harter, S., & Whitesell, N. R. (2003). Beyond the debate: Why some adolescents report stable self-worth over time and situation, whereas others report changes in self-worth. *Journal of Personality, 71*(6), 1027–1058.

Harvey, R. D., & Oswald, D. L. (2000). Collective guilt and shame as motivation for white support of black programs 1. *Journal of Applied Social Psychology, 30*(9), 1790–1811.

Hendry, N. A., Brown, G., Dowsett, G. W., & Carman, M. (2017). Association between sexually transmissible infection testing, numbers of partners and talking to partners and friends about sexual health: Survey of young adults. *Sexual Health, 14*(4), 378–382.

Hensel, D. J., Nance, J., & Fortenberry, J. D. (2016). The association between sexual health and physical, mental, and social health in adolescent women. *Journal of Adolescent Health, 59*(4), 416–421.

Heywood, W., Patrick, K., Smith, A. M., & Pitts, M. K. (2015). Associations between early first sexual intercourse and later sexual and reproductive outcomes: A systematic review of population-based data. *Archives of Sexual Behavior, 44*(3), 531–569.

Holstrom, A. M. (2015). Sexuality education goes viral: What we know about online sexual health information. *American Journal of Sexuality Education, 10*(3), 277–294.

Hopkins, S., Lyons, F., Coleman, C., Courtney, G., Bergin, C., & Mulcahy, F. (2004). Resurgence in infectious syphilis in Ireland: An epidemiological study. *Sexually Transmitted Diseases, 31*(5), 317–321.

Horne, S., & Zimmer-Gembeck, M. J. (2005). Female sexual subjectivity and well-being: Comparing late adolescents with different sexual experiences. *Sexuality Research and Social Policy, 2*(3), 25–40.

Hoyle, R. H., Fejfar, M. C., & Miller, J. D. (2000). Personality and sexual risk taking: A quantitative review. *Journal of Personality, 68*(6), 1203–1231.

Hutchinson, M. K., Jemmott, J. B., III, Jemmott, L. S., Braverman, P., & Fong, G. T. (2003). The role of mother–daughter sexual risk communication in reducing sexual risk behaviors among urban adolescent females: A prospective study. *Journal of Adolescent Health, 33*(2), 98–107.

Jaccard, J., Dodge, T., & Dittus, P. (2002). Parent-adolescent communication about sex and birth control: A conceptual framework. *New Directions for Child and Adolescent Development, 2002*(97), 9–42.

Jackman, D. M., & MacPhee, D. (2017). Self-esteem and future orientation predict adolescents' risk engagement. *The Journal of Early Adolescence, 37*(3), 339–366.

Janz, N. K., & Becker, M. H. (1984). The health belief model: A decade later. *Health Education Quarterly, 11*(1), 1–47.

Jemmott, L. S., & Hacker, C. I. (1992). Predicting intentions to use condoms among African-American adolescents: The theory of planned behavior as a model of HIV risk-associated behavior. *Ethnicity & Disease, 2*(4), 371–380.

Jessop, D. C., Simmonds, L. V., & Sparks, P. (2009). Motivational and behavioural consequences of self-affirmation interventions: A study of sunscreen use among women. *Psychology and Health, 24*(5), 529–544.

Johnson, A. M., Mercer, C. H., Erens, B., Copas, A. J., McManus, S., Wellings, K., & Purdon, S. (2001). Sexual behaviour in Britain: Partnerships, practices, and HIV risk behaviours. *The Lancet, 358*(9296), 1835–1842.

Jolly, M. C., Sebire, N., Harris, J., Robinson, S., & Regan, L. (2000). Obstetric risks of pregnancy in women less than 18 years old. *Obstetrics & Gynecology, 96*(6), 962–966.

Jones, C. J., Smith, H., & Llewellyn, C. (2014). Evaluating the effectiveness of health belief model interventions in improving adherence: A systematic review. *Health Psychology Review, 8*(3), 253–269.

Kaestle, C. E., Halpern, C. T., Miller, W. C., & Ford, C. A. (2005). Young age at first sexual intercourse and sexually transmitted infections in adolescents and young adults. *American Journal of Epidemiology, 161*(8), 774–780.

Kanuga, M., & Rosenfeld, W. D. (2004). Adolescent sexuality and the internet: The good, the bad, and the URL. *Journal of Pediatric and Adolescent Gynecology, 17*(2), 117–124.

Kellam, S. G., Wang, W., Mackenzie, A. C., Brown, C. H., Ompad, D. C., Or, F., & Windham, A. (2014). The impact of the Good Behavior Game, a universal classroom-based preventive intervention in first and second grades, on high-risk sexual behaviors and drug abuse and dependence disorders into young adulthood. *Prevention Science, 15*(1), 6–18.

Keller, S. N., Labelle, H., Karimi, N., & Gupta, S. (2002). STD/HIV prevention for teenagers: A look at the internet universe. *Journal of Health Communication, 7*(4), 341–353.

Kim, Y. (2016). Trust in health information websites: A systematic literature review on the antecedents of trust. *Health Informatics Journal, 22*(2), 355–369.

Kinsman, S. B., Romer, D., Furstenberg, F. F., & Schwarz, D. F. (1998). Early sexual initiation: The role of peer norms. *Pediatrics, 102*(5), 1185–1192.

Kirby, D., & Laris, B. A. (2009). Effective curriculum-based sex and STD/HIV education programs for adolescents. *Child Development Perspectives, 3*(1), 21–29.

Klein, W. M., Blier, H. K., & Janze, A. M. (2001). Maintaining positive self-evaluations: Reducing attention to diagnostic but unfavorable social comparison information when general self-regard is salient. *Motivation and Emotion, 25*(1), 23–40.

Klein, W. M., Lipkus, I. M., Scholl, S. M., McQueen, A., Cerully, J. L., & Harris, P. R. (2010). Self-affirmation moderates effects of unrealistic optimism and pessimism on reactions to tailored risk feedback. *Psychology and Health, 25*(10), 1195–1208.

Ko, D. M., & Kim, H. S. (2010). Message framing and defensive processing: A cultural examination. *Health Communication, 25*(1), 61–68.

van Koningsbruggen, G., & Das, E. (2009). How self affirmation reduces defensive processing of threatening health information: Evidence at the implicit level. *Health Psychology*. Retrieved from: http://psycnet.apa.org/journals/hea/28/5/563/.

van Koningsbruggen, G. M., Das, E., & Roskos-Ewoldsen, D. R. (2009). How self-affirmation reduces defensive processing of threatening health information: Evidence at the implicit level. *Health Psychology, 28*(5), 563.

Laflin, M. T., Wang, J., & Barry, M. (2008). A longitudinal study of transition from virgin to nonvirgin status. *Journal of Adolescent Health, 42*(3), 228–236.

Lammers, C., Ireland, M., Resnick, M., & Blum, R. (2000). Influences on adolescents' decision to postpone onset of sexual intercourse: A survival analysis of virginity among youths aged 13 to 18 years. *Journal of Adolescent Health, 26*(1), 42–48.

Langille, D. B., Hughes, J., Murphy, G. T., & Rigby, J. A. (2005). Socio-economic factors and adolescent sexual activity and behaviour in Nova Scotia. *Canadian Journal of Public Health, 96*(4), 313–318.

Laraque, D., Mclean, D. E., Brown-Peterside, P., Ashton, D., & Diamond, B. (1997). Predictors of reported condom use in central Harlem youth as conceptualized by the health belief model. *Journal of Adolescent Health, 21*(5), 318–327.

Laureati, M., Bergamaschi, V., & Pagliarini, E. (2014). School-based intervention with children. Peer-modeling, reward and repeated exposure reduce food neophobia and increase liking of fruits and vegetables. *Appetite, 83*, 26–32.

Lawton, R., Conner, M., & McEachan, R. (2009). Desire or reason: Predicting health behaviors from affective and cognitive attitudes. *Health Psychology, 28*(1), 56.

LeCroy, C. W. (2005). Building an effective primary prevention program for adolescent girls: Empirically based design and evaluation. *Brief Treatment and Crisis Intervention, 5*(1).

Lee, J., & Kim, J. (2019). Can menstrual health apps selected based on users' needs change health-related factors? A double-blind randomized controlled trial. *Journal of the American Medical Informatics Association, 26*(7), 655–666.

Len-Ríos, M. E., Streit, C., Killoren, S., Deutsch, A., Cooper, M. L., & Carlo, G. (2016). US Latino adolescents' use of mass media and mediated communication in romantic relationships. *Journal of Children and Media, 10*(4), 395–410.

Levine, D. (2011). Using technology, new media, and mobile for sexual and reproductive health. *Sexuality Research and Social Policy, 8*(1), 18–26.

Lewis, J., & Knijn, T. (2003). Sex education materials in The Netherlands and in England and Wales: A comparison of content, use and teaching practice. *Oxford Review of Education, 29*(1), 113–150.

Lief, H. I., Fullard, W., & Devlin, S. J. (1990). A new measure of adolescent sexuality: SKAT-A. *Journal of Sex Education and Therapy, 16*(2), 79–91.

Lin, P., Simoni, J. M., & Zemon, V. (2005). The health belief model, sexual behaviors, and HIV risk among Taiwanese immigrants. *AIDS Education and Prevention, 17*(5), 469–483.

Lindberg, L. D., Maddow-Zimet, I., & Boonstra, H. (2016). Changes in adolescents' receipt of sex education, 2006–2013. *Journal of Adolescent Health, 58*(6), 621–627.

Lo, V. H., & Wei, R. (2005). Exposure to Internet pornography and Taiwanese adolescents' sexual attitudes and behavior. *Journal of Broadcasting & Electronic Media, 49*(2), 221–237.

Logel, C., & Cohen, G. L. (2012). The role of the self in physical health: Testing the effect of a values-affirmation intervention on weight loss. *Psychological Science, 23*(1), 53–55.

Ludwig, K. B., & Pittman, J. F. (1999). Adolescent prosocial values and self-efficacy in relation to delinquency, risky sexual behavior, and drug use. *Youth & Society, 30*(4), 461–482.

Manning, W. D., Longmore, M. A., & Giordano, P. C. (2000). The relationship context of contraceptive use at first intercourse. *Family Planning Perspectives*, 104–110.

Marino, J. L., Skinner, S. R., Doherty, D. A., Rosenthal, S. L., Robbins, S. C. C., Cannon, J., & Hickey, M. (2013). Age at menarche and age at first sexual intercourse: A prospective cohort study. *Pediatrics, 132*(6), 1028–1036.

Martino, S. C., Elliott, M. N., Corona, R., Kanouse, D. E., & Schuster, M. A. (2008). Beyond the "big talk": The roles of breadth and repetition in parent-adolescent communication about sexual topics. *Pediatrics, 121*(3), e612–e618.

Mazzaferro, K. E., Murray, P. J., Ness, R. B., Bass, D. C., Tyus, N., & Cook, R. L. (2006). Depression, stress, and social support as predictors of high-risk sexual behaviors and STIs in young women. *Journal of Adolescent Health, 39*(4), 601–603.

McBride, C. K., Paikoff, R. L., & Holmbeck, G. N. (2003). Individual and familial influences on the onset of sexual intercourse among urban African American adolescents. *Journal of Consulting and Clinical Psychology, 71*(1), 159.

McCarthy, O., Carswell, K., Murray, E., Free, C., Stevenson, F., & Bailey, J. V. (2012). What young people want from a sexual health website: Design and development of sexunzipped. *Journal of Medical Internet Research, 14*(5), e127.

McGee, R. O. B., & Williams, S. (2000). Does low self-esteem predict health compromising behaviours among adolescents? *Journal of Adolescence, 23*(5), 569–582.

McQueen, A., & Klein, W. M. (2006). Experimental manipulations of self-affirmation: A systematic review. *Self and Identity, 5*(4), 289–354.

Meier, A. M. (2007). Adolescent first sex and subsequent mental health. *American Journal of Sociology, 112*(6), 1811–1847.

Melchior, A. (1998). *National evaluation of Learn and Serve America school and community-based programs.*

Memish, K. E., Schüz, N., Frandsen, M., Ferguson, S. G., & Schüz, B. (2017). Using self-affirmation to increase the effects of emotive health warnings on smoking: A randomized exploratory trial. *Nicotine & Tobacco Research, 19*(10), 1238–1242.

Michael, M. C. C. J. B. C., & Cheuvront, C. C. J. B. (1998). Health communication on the internet: An effective channel for health behavior change? *Journal of Health Communication, 3*(1), 71–79.

Milburn, K. (1995). A critical review of peer education with young people with special reference to sexual health. *Health Education Research, 10*(4), 407–420.

Miller, J. D., & Lynam, D. R. (2003). Psychopathy and the five-factor model of personality: A replication and extension. *Journal of Personality Assessment, 81*(2), 168–178.

Miller, J. D., Lynam, D., Zimmerman, R. S., Logan, T. K., Leukefeld, C., & Clayton, R. (2004). The utility of the Five Factor Model in understanding risky sexual behavior. *Personality and Individual Differences, 36*(7), 1611–1626.

Montgomery, K. C. (2000). Children's media culture in the new millennium: Mapping the digital landscape. *The Future of Children*, 145–167.

Moore, S. G., Dahl, D. W., Gorn, G. J., & Weinberg, C. B. (2006). Coping with condom embarrassment. *Psychology, Health & Medicine, 11*(1), 70–79.

Moreno, M. A., & Kolb, J. (2012). Social networking sites and adolescent health. *Pediatric Clinics of North America, 59*(3), 601–612.

Moretti, R., Cremaschini, M., Brembilla, G., Fenili, F., Gambirasio, M. N., & Valoti, M. (2015). Is Facebook effective in preventing HIV/STDs in scholarized adolescents? A Cluster Rct. *Austin Journal of HIV/AIDS Research, 2*(2), 1016.

Muench, F., Weiss, R. A., Kuerbis, A., & Morgenstern, J. (2013). Developing a theory driven text messaging intervention for addiction care with user driven content. *Psychology of Addictive Behaviors, 27*(1), 315.

Muessig, K. E., Pike, E. C., LeGrand, S., & Hightow-Weidman, L. B. (2013). Mobile phone applications for the care and prevention of HIV and other sexually transmitted diseases: A review. *Journal of Medical Internet Research, 15*(1), e1.

Mulholland, E., & Van Wersch, A. (2007). Stigma, sexually transmitted infections and attendance at the GUM clinic: An exploratory study with implications for the theory of planned behaviour. *Journal of Health Psychology, 12*(1), 17–31.

Muris, P. (2001). A brief questionnaire for measuring self-efficacy in youths. *Journal of Psychopathology and Behavioral Assessment, 23*(3), 145–149.

Napolitano, M. A., Fotheringham, M., Tate, D., Sciamanna, C., Leslie, E., Owen, N., & Marcus, B. (2003). Evaluation of an internet-based physical activity intervention: A preliminary investigation. *Annals of Behavioral Medicine, 25*(2), 92–99.

Negriff, S., Fung, M. T., & Trickett, P. K. (2008). Self-rated pubertal development, depressive symptoms and delinquency: Measurement issues and moderation by gender and maltreatment. *Journal of Youth and Adolescence, 37*(6), 736–746.

Neppl, T. K., Dhalewadikar, J., & Lohman, B. J. (2016). Harsh parenting, deviant peers, adolescent risky behavior: Understanding the meditational effect of attitudes and intentions. *Journal of Research on Adolescence, 26*(3), 538–551.

Nguyen, P., Gold, J., Pedrana, A., Chang, S., Howard, S., Ilic, O., & Stoove, M. (2013). Sexual health promotion on social networking sites: A process evaluation of the FaceSpace project. *Journal of Adolescent Health, 53*(1), 98–104.

Noll, J. G., Haralson, K. J., Butler, E. M., & Shenk, C. E. (2011). Childhood maltreatment, psychological dysregulation, and risky sexual behaviors in female adolescents. *Journal of Pediatric Psychology, 36*(7), 743–752.

Norman, E., & Turner, S. (1993). Adolescent substance abuse prevention programs: Theories, models, and research in the encouraging 80's. *Journal of Primary Prevention, 14*(1), 3–20.

Norton, T. R., Bogart, L. M., Cecil, H., & Pinkerton, S. D. (2005). Primacy of affect over cognition in determining adult men's condom–use behavior: A review 1. *Journal of Applied Social Psychology, 35*(12), 2493–2534.

Parsons, J. T., Halkitis, P. N., Bimbi, D., & Borkowski, T. (2000). Perceptions of the benefits and costs associated with condom use and unprotected sex among late adolescent college students. *Journal of Adolescence, 23*(4), 377–391.

Patton, G. C., Sawyer, S. M., Santelli, J. S., Ross, D. A., Afifi, R., Allen, N. B., & Kakuma, R. (2016). Our future: A lancet commission on adolescent health and wellbeing. *The Lancet, 387*(10036), 2423–2478.

Perry, R. C., Braun, R., Cantu, M., Dudovitz, R. N., Sheoran, B., & Chung, P. J. (2014). Associations among text messaging, academic performance, and sexual behaviors of adolescents. *Journal of School Health, 84*(1), 33–39.

Philliber, S., Kaye, J. W., Herrling, S., & West, E. (2002). Preventing pregnancy and improving health care access among teenagers: An evaluation of the Children's Aid Society-Carrera Program. *Perspectives on Sexual and Reproductive Health*, 244–251.

Pietersma, S., & Dijkstra, A. (2011). Do behavioural health intentions engender health behaviour change? A study on the moderating role of self-affirmation on actual fruit intake versus vegetable intake. *British Journal of Health Psychology, 16*(4), 815–827.

Piper, D. L., Moberg, D. P., & King, M. J. (2000). The healthy for life project: Behavioral outcomes. *Journal of Primary Prevention, 21*(1), 47–73.

Potard, C., Courtois, R., & Rusch, E. (2008). The influence of peers on risky sexual behaviour during adolescence. *The European Journal of Contraception and Reproductive Health Care, 13*(3), 264–270.

Raynor, D. A., & Levine, H. (2009). Associations between the five-factor model of personality and health behaviors among college students. *Journal of American College Health, 58*(1), 73–82.

Reed, M. B., & Aspinwall, L. G. (1998). Self-affirmation reduces biased processing of health-risk information. *Motivation and Emotion, 22*(2), 99–132.

Reyna, V. F., & Wilhelms, E. A. (2017). The gist of delay of gratification: Understanding and predicting problem behaviors. *Journal of Behavioral Decision Making, 30*(2), 610–625.

Ritchwood, T. D., Ford, H., DeCoster, J., Sutton, M., & Lochman, J. E. (2015). Risky sexual behavior and substance use among adolescents: A meta-analysis. *Children and Youth Services Review, 52*, 74–88.

Rivis, A., & Sheeran, P. (2003). Descriptive norms as an additional predictor in the theory of planned behaviour: A meta-analysis. *Current Psychology, 22*(3), 218–233.

von Rosen, A. J., von Rosen, F. T., Tinnemann, P., & Müller-Riemenschneider, F. (2017). Sexual health and the internet: Cross-sectional study of online preferences among adolescents. *Journal of Medical Internet Research, 19*(11), e379.

Rosenberg, M., Schooler, C., Schoenbach, C., & Rosenberg, F. (1995). Global self-esteem and specific self-esteem: Different concepts, different outcomes. *American Sociological Review,* 141–156.

Rosenstock, I. M., Strecher, V. J., & Becker, M. H. (1988). Social learning theory and the health belief model. *Health Education Quarterly, 15*(2), 175–183.

Rowley, J., Johnson, F., & Sbaffi, L. (2015). Students' trust judgements in online health information seeking. *Health Informatics Journal, 21*(4), 316–327.

Russo, M. F., Stokes, G. S., Lahey, B. B., Christ, M. A. G., McBurnett, K., Loeber, R., & Green, S. M. (1993). A sensation seeking scale for children: Further refinement and psychometric development. *Journal of Psychopathology and Behavioral Assessment, 15*(2), 69–86.

Salazar, L. F., Crosby, R. A., DiClemente, R. J., Wingood, G. M., Lescano, C. M., Brown, L. K., & Davies, S. (2005). Self-esteem and theoretical mediators of safer sex among African American female adolescents: Implications for sexual risk reduction interventions. *Health Education & Behavior, 32*(3), 413–427.

Santelli, J. S., Lindberg, L. D., Finer, L. B., & Singh, S. (2007). Explaining recent declines in adolescent pregnancy in the United States: The contribution of abstinence and improved contraceptive use. *American Journal of Public Health, 97*(1), 150–156.

Santelli, J. S., Lowry, R., Brener, N. D., & Robin, L. (2000). The association of sexual behaviors with socioeconomic status, family structure, and race/ethnicity among US adolescents. *American Journal of Public Health, 90*(10), 1582.

Satterwhite, C. L., Torrone, E., Meites, E., Dunne, E. F., Mahajan, R., Ocfemia, M. C. B., & Weinstock, H. (2013). Sexually transmitted infections among US women and men: Prevalence and incidence estimates, 2008. *Sexually Transmitted Diseases, 40*(3), 187–193.

Saucier, G. (1994). Mini-markers: A brief version of Goldberg's unipolar big-five markers. *Journal of Personality Assessment, 63*(3), 506–516.

Schaeffer, N. C. (2000). Asking questions about threatening topics: A selective overview. In *The science of self-report: Implications for research and practice* (pp. 105–121).

Schmitt, D. P. (2004). The big five related to risky sexual behaviour across 10 world regions: Differential personality associations of sexual promiscuity and relationship infidelity. *European Journal of Personality, 18*(4), 301–319.

Schulman, S., & Davies, T. (2007). Evidence of the impact of the 'youth development'model on outcomes for young people-A literature review. In *Book evidence of the impact of the 'youth development'model on outcomes for young people-A literature review.*

Schüz, N., Schüz, B., & Eid, M. (2013). When risk communication backfires: Randomized controlled trial on self-affirmation and reactance to personalized risk feedback in high-risk individuals. *Health Psychology, 32*(5), 561.

Selkie, E. M., Benson, M., & Moreno, M. (2011). Adolescents' views regarding uses of social networking websites and text messaging for adolescent sexual health education. *American Journal of Health Education, 42*(4), 205–212.

Sherman, D. A., Nelson, L. D., & Steele, C. M. (2000). Do messages about health risks threaten the self? Increasing the acceptance of threatening health messages via self-affirmation. *Personality and Social Psychology Bulletin, 26*(9), 1046–1058.

Siebenbruner, J., Zimmer-Gembeck, M. J., & Egeland, B. (2007). Sexual partners and contraceptive use: A 16-year prospective study predicting abstinence and risk behavior. *Journal of Research on Adolescence, 17*(1), 179–206.

Sillence, E. (2010). Seeking out very like-minded others: Exploring trust and advice issues in an online health support group. *International Journal of Web Based Communities, 6*(4), 376–394.

Simmons, R. G., & Rosenberg, F. (1975). Sex, sex roles, and self-image. *Journal of Youth and Adolescence, 4*(3), 229–258.

Simon, L., & Daneback, K. (2013). Adolescents' use of the internet for sex education: A thematic and critical review of the literature. *International Journal of Sexual Health, 25*(4), 305–319.

Skinner, H., Biscope, S., Poland, B., & Goldberg, E. (2003). How adolescents use technology for health information: Implications for health professionals from focus group studies. *Journal of Medical Internet Research, 5*(4), e32.

Spencer, J. M., Zimet, G. D., Aalsma, M. C., & Orr, D. P. (2002). Self-esteem as a predictor of initiation of coitus in early adolescents. *Pediatrics, 109*(4), 581–584.

Steele, C. M. (1988). The psychology of self-affirmation: Sustaining the integrity of the self. In *Advances in experimental social psychology* (Vol. 21, pp. 261–302). Academic Press.

Steinberg, L. (2005). Cognitive and affective development in adolescence. *Trends in Cognitive Sciences, 9*(2), 69–74.

Stueve, A., & O'donnell, L. N. (2005). Early alcohol initiation and subsequent sexual and alcohol risk behaviors among urban youths. *American Journal of Public Health, 95*(5), 887–893.

Sutherland-Smith, W. (2002). Weaving the literacy web: Changes in reading from page to screen. *The Reading Teacher, 55*(7), 662–669.

Suzuki, L. K., & Calzo, J. P. (2004). The search for peer advice in cyberspace: An examination of online teen bulletin boards about health and sexuality. *Journal of Applied Developmental Psychology, 25*(6), 685–698.

Syred, J., Naidoo, C., Woodhall, S. C., & Baraitser, P. (2014). Would you tell everyone this? Facebook conversations as health promotion interventions. *Journal of Medical Internet Research, 16*(4), e108.

Takhteyev, Y., Gruzd, A., & Wellman, B. (2012). Geography of twitter networks. *Social Networks, 34*(1), 73–81.

Tapert, S. F., Aarons, G. A., Sedlar, G. R., & Brown, S. A. (2001). Adolescent substance use and sexual risk-taking behavior. *Journal of Adolescent Health, 28*(3), 181–189.

Tietz, A., Davies, S. C., & Moran, J. S. (2004). Guide to sexually transmitted disease resources on the internet. *Clinical Infectious Diseases, 38*(9), 1304–1310.

Turow, J. (2001). Family boundaries, commercialism, and the internet: A framework for research. *Journal of Applied Developmental Psychology, 22*(1), 73–86.

Tyson, M., Covey, J., & Rosenthal, H. E. (2014). Theory of planned behavior interventions for reducing heterosexual risk behaviors: A meta-analysis. *Health Psychology, 33*(12), 1454.

Vasilenko, S. A., Kugler, K. C., & Rice, C. E. (2016). Timing of first sexual intercourse and young adult health outcomes. *Journal of Adolescent Health, 59*(3), 291–297.

Ventola, C. L. (2014). Mobile devices and apps for health care professionals: Uses and benefits. *Pharmacy and Therapeutics, 39*(5), 356.

Wartella, E., Rideout, V., Montague, H., Beaudoin-Ryan, L., & Lauricella, A. (2016). Teens, health and technology: A national survey. *Media and Communication, 4*(3), 13–23.

Watson, L. B., Matheny, K. B., Gagné, P., Brack, G., & Ancis, J. R. (2013). A model linking diverse women's child sexual abuse history with sexual risk taking. *Psychology of Women Quarterly, 37*(1), 22–37.

Watts Sr, G. F., & Nagy, S. (2000). Attitude toward sexual intercourse and relationship with peer and parental communication. *American Journal of Health Studies, 16*(3), 156.

Webb, T., Joseph, J., & Yardley, L. (2010). Using the internet to promote health behavior change: A systematic review and meta-analysis of the impact of theoretical basis, use of behavior change. *Journal of Medical Internet Research.* Retrieved from: https://www.ncbi.nlm.nih.gov/pmc/articles/PMC2836773/.

Webb, T., Joseph, J., Yardley, L., & Michie, S. (2010). Using the internet to promote health behavior change: A systematic review and meta-analysis of the impact of theoretical basis, use of behavior change techniques, and mode of delivery on efficacy. *Journal of Medical Internet Research, 12*(1), e4.

Whitaker, D. J., & Miller, K. S. (n.d.). Parent-adolescent discussions about sex and condoms: Impact on peer influences of sexual risk behavior. Journal of Adolescent Research. 15. Retrieved from: http://journals.sagepub.com/doi/pdf/10.1177/0743558400152004.

Whitbeck, L. B., Yoder, K. A., Hoyt, D. R., & Conger, R. D. (1999). Early adolescent sexual activity: A developmental study. *Journal of Marriage and Family*, 934–946.

Wileman, V., Farrington, K., Chilcot, J., Norton, S., Wellsted, D. M., Almond, M. K., & Armitage, C. J. (2014). Evidence that self-affirmation improves phosphate control in hemodialysis patients: A pilot cluster randomized controlled trial. *Annals of Behavioral Medicine, 48*(2), 275–281.

Willoughby, J. F. (2015). Effectiveness of a social marketing campaign promoting use of a sexual health text service by teens. *Journal of Health Communication, 20*(10), 1206–1213.

Willoughby, J. F., & Jackson, K., Jr. (2013). 'Can you get pregnant when ur in the pool?': Young people's information seeking from a sexual health text line. *Sex Education, 13*(1), 96–106.

Wilson, H. W., & Widom, C. S. (2008). An examination of risky sexual behavior and HIV in victims of child abuse and neglect: A 30-year follow-up. *Health Psychology, 27*(2), 149.

Yager, A. M., & O'Keefe, C. (2012). Adolescent use of social networking to gain sexual health information. *The Journal for Nurse Practitioners, 8*(4), 294–298.

Yan, M. C. (2005). How cultural awareness works: An empirical examination of the interaction between social workers and their clients. *Canadian Social Work Review/Revue Canadienne de Service Social*, 5–29.

Yoost, J. L., Hertweck, S. P., & Barnett, S. N. (2014). The effect of an educational approach to pregnancy prevention among high-risk early and late adolescents. *Journal of Adolescent Health, 55*(2), 222–227.

Youn, S. (2005). Teenagers' perceptions of online privacy and coping behaviors: A risk–benefit appraisal approach. *Journal of Broadcasting & Electronic Media, 49*(1), 86–110.

Zeng, X., & Parmanto, B. (2004). Web content accessibility of consumer health information web sites for people with disabilities: A cross sectional evaluation. *Journal of Medical Internet Research, 6*(2), e19.

Ziebland, S. U. E., & Wyke, S. (2012). Health and illness in a connected world: How might sharing experiences on the internet affect people's health? *The Milbank Quarterly, 90*(2), 219–249.

Zimmer-Gembeck, M. J. (2011). *Sexual debut. Encyclopedia of adolescence* (pp. 2650–2657).

Zimmer-Gembeck, M. J., & Helfand, M. (2008). Ten years of longitudinal research on US adolescent sexual behavior: Developmental correlates of sexual intercourse, and the importance of age, gender and ethnic background. *Developmental Review, 28*(2), 153–224.

Zuckerman, M., Buchsbaum, M. S., & Murphy, D. L. (1980). Sensation seeking and its biological correlates. *Psychological Bulletin, 88*(1), 187.

Zytkoskee, A., Strickland, B. R., & Watson, J. (1971). Delay of gratification and internal versus external control among adolescents of low socioeconomic status. *Developmental Psychology, 4*(1, Pt.1), 93.

# Further reading

Gilbert, J. (2017). A study of ESL students' perceptions of their digital reading. *The Reading Matrix: An International Online Journal, 17*(2), 179–195.

# REFERENCES

Goodson, P., & Buhi, E. R. (2011). Abstinence education. *Encyclopedia of Adolescence*, 12–19.

Goodyear, M. D., Krleza-Jeric, K., & Lemmens, T. (2007). *The declaration of Helsinki*.

Hameed, T., & Swar, B. (2016). *Social value and information quality in online health information search*. arXiv preprint arXiv: 1606.03507.

Hillard, P. J. A., & Wheeler, M. V. (2017). Data from a menstrual cycle tracking app informs our knowledge of the menstrual cycle in adolescents and young adults. *Journal of Pediatric and Adolescent Gynecology*, 30(2), 269–270.

Jacobson, L., Richardson, G., Parry-Langdon, N., & Donovan, C. (2001). How do teenagers and primary healthcare providers view each other? An overview of key themes. *British Journal of General Practice*, 51(471), 811–816.

Jang, D., & Elfenbein, H. A. (2019). Menstrual cycle effects on mental health outcomes: A meta-analysis. *Archives of Suicide Research*, 23(2), 312–332.

Johnson, B., Harrison, L., Ollis, D., Flentje, J., Arnold, P., & Bartholomaeus, C. (2016). *'It is not all about sex': Young people's views about sexuality and relationships education*.

Kanfer, F. H. (1970). *Self-monitoring: Methodological limitations and clinical applications*.

Marston, C., King, E., & Ingham, R. (2006). Young people and condom use: Findings from qualitative research. In *Promoting young people's sexual health* (pp. 39–52). Routledge.

Marteau, T. M., Ogilvie, D., Roland, M., Suhrcke, M., & Kelly, M. P. (2011). Judging nudging: Can nudging improve population health? *BMJ*, 342, d228.

McCarthy, O., Ahamed, I., Kulaeva, F., Tokhirov, R., Saibov, S., Vandewiele, M., … Free, C. (2018). A randomized controlled trial of an intervention delivered by mobile phone app instant messaging to increase the acceptability of effective contraception among young people in Tajikistan. *Reproductive Health*, 15(1), 28.

McKellar, K., Little, L., Smith, M. A., & Sillence, E. (2017). Seeking sexual health information? Professionals' novel experiences of the barriers that prevent female adolescents seeking sexual health information. *International Journal of Adolescent Medicine and Health*.

Mercer, C. H., Prah, P., Field, N., Tanton, C., Macdowall, W., Clifton, S., … Sonnenberg, P. (2016). The health and well-being of men who have sex with men (MSM) in Britain: Evidence from the third National Survey of Sexual Attitudes and Lifestyles (Natsal-3). *BMC Public Health*, 16(1), 525.

Moreno, M. A., Standiford, M., & Cody, P. (2018). Social media and adolescent health. *Current Pediatrics Reports*, 6(2), 132–138.

Nilashi, M., Ibrahim, O., Mirabi, V. R., Ebrahimi, L., & Zare, M. (2015). The role of Security, Design and Content factors on customer trust in mobile commerce. *Journal of Retailing and Consumer Services*, 26, 57–69.

Norman, C., Moffatt, S., & Rankin, J. (2016). Young parents' views and experiences of interactions with health professionals. *Journal of Family Planning and Reproductive Health Care*, 42(3), 179–186.

Ott, M. A., & Santelli, J. S. (2007). Abstinence and abstinence-only education. *Current Opinion in Obstetrics & Gynecology*, 19(5), 446.

Pound, P. (2017). How should mandatory sex education be taught? *BMJ*, 357, j1768.

*Relationships and Sex Education in Schools (England)*.(2018). Retrieved from https://researchbriefings.parliament.uk/ResearchBriefing/Summary/SN06103.

Rice, M., & Broome, M. E. (2004). Incentives for children in research. *Journal of Nursing Scholarship*, 36(2), 167–172.

von Rosen, A. J., von Rosen, F. T., Tinnemann, P., & Müller-Riemenschneider, F. (2017). Sexual health and the internet: Cross-sectional study of online preferences among adolescents. *Journal of Medical Internet Research*, 19(11), e379.

Rosen-Palmowski, A. V. (2018). *Adolescent sexual health knowledge and preferences: What adolescents want from sexual health websites* (Doctoral dissertation).

Santa Maria, D., Markham, C., Bluethmann, S., & Mullen, P. D. (2015). Parent-based adolescent sexual health interventions and effect on communication outcomes: A systematic review and meta-analyses. *Perspectives on Sexual and Reproductive Health*, 47(1), 37–50.

Santelli, J. S., Kantor, L. M., Grilo, S. A., Speizer, I. S., Lindberg, L. D., Heitel, J., … Heck, C. J. (2017). Abstinence-only-until-marriage: An updated review of US policies and programs and their impact. *Journal of Adolescent Health*, 61(3), 273–280.

Scott-Jones, J., & Watt, S. (Eds.). (2010). *Ethnography in social science practice*. Routledge.

SRCD Governing Council. (2007). *Ethical standards for research with children*. Retrieved from https://www.srcd.org/about-us/ethical-standards-research-children.

Stone, N., & Ingham, R. (2003). When and why do young people in the United Kingdom first use sexual health services? *Perspectives on Sexual and Reproductive Health*, 35(3), 114–120.

Triandis, H. C. (1977). Subjective culture and interpersonal relations across cultures. *Annals of the New York Academy of Sciences*, 285(1), 418–434.

Walker, J. (2001). A qualitative study of parents experiences of providing sex education for their children: The implications for health education. *Health Education Journal*, 60(2), 132–146.

Walsh-Buhi, E. R., Marhefka, S. L., Wang, W., Debate, R., Perrin, K., Singleton, A., … Ziemba, R. (2016). The impact of the Teen Outreach Program on sexual intentions and behaviors. *Journal of Adolescent Health*, 59(3), 283–290.

Westwood, J., & Mullan, B. (2007). Knowledge and attitudes of secondary school teachers regarding sexual health education in England. *Sex Education*, 7(2), 143–159. https://doi.org/10.1080/14681810701264490.

World Health Organization. (2006). *The world health report 2006: Working together for health*. World Health Organization.

Youn, S. (2005). Teenagers' perceptions of online privacy and coping behaviors: A risk–benefit appraisal approach. *Journal of Broadcasting and Electronic Media*, 49(1), 86–110.

Retrieved from http://www.tandfonline.com/doi/abs/10.1207/s15506878jobem4901_6.

Gegenfurtner, A., & Gebhardt, M. (2017). Sexuality education including lesbian, gay, bisexual, and transgender (LGBT) issues in schools. *Educational Research Review, 22*, 215—222.

Steinberg, A., Griffin-Tomas, M., Abu-Odeh, D., & Whitten, A. (2018). Evaluation of a mobile phone app for providing adolescents with sexual and reproductive health information, New York City, 2013—2016. *Public Health Reports, 133*(3), 234—239.

# Index

## A
Abstinence-only programs, 27–28
Anonymity, 59t–62t
Attitudes, 7

## B
Brief Sensation Seeking Scale, 90–91
British Psychological Society's (BPS)
   ethical principles, 56
Brook website, 102t, 106f

## C
Competence, 57t–58t
Condom Craze interactive game app,
   102t, 108f
Condoms, 74
Confidentiality, 59t–62t
Conscientiousness, 16, 80
Conventional behaviors, 9–10

## D
Daily written diaries, 70
Deception, 59t–62t
Delay Gratification Scale, 90–91
Digital sexual health interventions
   internet and mobile technology
      appeals, 30
      behavior change techniques, 30
      benefits, 31t
      direct intervention, 34
      familiarization and time spent,
         33
      incentives-based approach, 30
      low SES teenagers, 30
      peer resources, 32–33
      Pew Research Center report, 30
      physical privacy, 34
      privacy, 33–34
      reputation, 32–33
      risk-reducing strategies, 34
      sex information online, 30
      social media sites, 34
      trust, 32–33
      trust factors, 32
      user-generated resources, 32–33
      website and content evaluation,
         32
   online health information, 31–32
   sexual health mobile apps, 39–40
   sexual health websites, 34–35
   social networking sites, 35–37
   text messaging, 37–38

## E
Environment and family, thematic
   approach, 45–46, 46t
Ethical issues. *See* Research ethics

## F
Facebook intervention, 36
Fertility tracking app, 114

## G
General Data Protection Regulation
   (GDPR), 63–64, 64t
Girl empowered app, 102t
Girls health website, 102t, 103f

## H
Health Belief Model (HBM)
   health adherence, 8–9
   individual perceptions, 8
   likelihood of action, 8
   meta-analysis, 8–9
   modifying factors, 8
   personal health behavior threat, 8
   schematic representation, 8, 9f
   sexual risk-taking behavior, 8
Health talk, 102t
Health tracking, 113–114
Heterosexual romantic relationship,
   125

## I
Incentives, 59t–62t
Informed consent, 59t–62t
Integrity, 57t–58t

## J
Jeopardy, 59t–62t

## L
Location-based sexual health apps, 39
Logistic Regression Model, 94t

## M
Menstrual tracking apps, 4
   accuracy, 114–115, 116t
   contraception method, 121
   example, 116f
   features and functionality, 115t–116t
   fertility tracking, 114
   function, 114
   menstrual cycle, 113–114, 113f
   ovulation prediction, 114–115

Menstrual tracking apps (*Continued*)
   pen-and-paper methods, 114, 120
   periods and menstruation, 120–121
   quality, 115–116
   reasons and uses, 116–117
   small-scale app case study interviews
      demographic background, 117t
      ease of use theme, 119, 119t
      materials and procedure, 117–118
      moody month app, 118f, 118t
      open-ended and semi-structured
         questions, 117
      participants, 117, 117t
      reliable information, 118–119,
         119t
      trust and privacy, 120, 120t
Mobile apps and websites, sexual
   health, 4, 137
   Condom Craze interactive game app,
      108, 108f
   design, 105–107, 107t
   information and interactive elements,
      108, 108t
   negative language, 107
   one-size-fits-all approach, 111
   positive language, 107
   qualitative study
      coding scheme, 104
      demographic background, 101t
      exclusion criteria, 101–102
      focus group, 102–103
      Google search, 101–102
      implications, 112
      inclusion criteria, 102
      IPads, 102
      limitations, 112
      participants, 100–101
      procedure, 103
      return to website/app, 104, 104f,
         110, 111t
      schools' existing sexual health
         sessions., 101t
      thematic analysis, 104
      websites and apps, 101–102, 102t
   quizzes and games, 107
   school-based sexual health
      education, 99
   sexual health information online
      drivers, 105
   sexual health websites, 100
   smartphone access, 99
   social learning theory, 110–111

*Note:* Page numbers followed by "f" indicate figures and "t" indicates tables.

## 154 INDEX

Mobile apps and websites, sexual health (*Continued*)
  social networking sites (SNSs), 99–100
  trusting and using, 108–110
  videos, 107
  viewing and interacting, 103
Multiple Regression Analysis, 94t–95t
Mutual responsibilities, 59t–62t
My teen mind app, 102t, 107f

### N

National health service (NHS) website, 102t, 108, 109f
National Sexual Attitudes and Lifestyles (NATSAL) survey, 6
Nonharmful procedures, 59t–62t
Nuremberg code, 55–56

### O

Offine consent
  debrief session, 66
  detailed summary, 66
  online information sheet, 65–66
  opt-out method, 65
  web-based questionnaire, 65
Online consent, 65–66
Online intervention, 136t

### P

Parental consent, 59t–62t, 67–68, 138t
Perceived behavioral control, 7
Personal misconduct, 59t–62t
Physical privacy, 34
Pornography, 18, 80, 96, 136t
Positive Youth Development (PYD) program, 29
Predictors, 136t
Predictors, risky sexual behaviors, 80t
  individual personality trait, 80
  questionnaire study, 136t
    descriptive statistics, 92
    early sex, 92
    intention to have sex, 92–95
    limitations and strengths, 96–97
    online questionnaire, 87, 87t–88t
    opt-in consent, 87t
    peers and parents, 91
    personality measures, 90–91
    pilot findings, 88–89
    procedure, 92, 93f, 94t
    professionals and parents, 86–87
    questionnaire construction, 86
    review, 81, 86
    revised findings, 88–89
    school performance, 91–92
    self-measures, 90
    sexual health, 91
    study design, 89, 89f
    survey materials, 81
    testing, 81
  self-esteem, 80
Premenstrual phase, 113–114, 113f

Problem behavior theory (PBT)
  alcohol use, 10–11
  conventional behaviors, 9–10
  demographic and socialization variables, 9
  psychosocial influences, 9
  schematic representation, 9–10, 10f
  self-esteem and cognition, 10–11
  unconventional behaviors, 9–10

### R

Raine previous sexual behaviors scale, 71
Rank order task, 44, 44f, 50
Research ethics, 3, 137, 138t
  doctor' trials, 55–56
  ethical guidelines
    British Psychological Society's (BPS) ethical principles, 56, 57t–62t
    child research, 56–63
    General Data Protection Regulation (GDPR), 63–64
  ethical standards, 55
  and gaining consent explaining, 67
  Helsinki declaration, 56
  legal guidance, 64–65
  Nuremberg code, 55–56
  offine consent, 65–67
  online consent, 65–66
  parental consent, 67–68
  recruiting teenagers, 67
  up-to-date research ethics, 55–56
Respect, 57t–58t
Responsibility, 57t–58t
Risky sexual behavior. *See also* Predictors, risky sexual behaviors
  age of puberty, 17
  body image and depression, 15–16
  delinquency and problem behaviors, 17
  Health Belief Model (HBM), 8–9
  mass media, 17
  parental and peer influences
    lack of communication, 14
    parental support, 13
    parent-teenagers communication, 13
    perceived peer attitudes, 14
    permissiveness, 14
    qualitative research, 13–14
    quantitative data, 13–14
    social norms and peer pressure, 14
  personality traits, 16
  predictors, 11t–13t
  problem behavior theory (PBT), 9–11
  school performance, 15–16
  self-efficacy, 15
  self-esteem
    and developmental stage, 14–15
    measurement, 14–15
    multivariate analysis, 15
    parents role, 15

Risky sexual behavior (*Continued*)
    sexual risk-taking, 15
  situational factors, 16–17
  theory of planned behavior (TPB), 7–11, 7f
Rosenberg Self-esteem Scale, 90

### S

Safe sex intentions, 133
School-based interventions, 3, 136t
  abstinence-only programs, 27–28
  Australian programs, 27–28
  in Germany, 27–28
  holistic approach, 27–28
  primary schools, 138–139
  in United Kingdom, 25–28, 27t
  in United States, 27–28
Scientific misconduct, 59t–62t
Self-affirmation intervention, 4, 139
  baseline measures
    intentions to have sex, 125–127
    and manipulation check, 129
    previous sexual behaviors, 125
    self-esteem, 125
  essay example, 127, 127f
  health behaviors, 124
  heterosexual romantic relationship, 125
  hypotheses, 124, 132–133
  implications, 133
  intention to have sex, 130–132
  low SES female teenagers, 125
  materials, 125
  online questionnaire system, 127
  participant demographic information, 125, 126t
  participants, 125
  postmanipulation measures, 127
  previous sexual behaviors, 126t
  safe sex intentions, 133
  self-affirmation theory, 124
  self-esteem programs, 123–124
  sexual health website, 127
  sexually active undergraduate students, 124
  "snatch and grab" approach, 133
  societal issues, 139
  strengths and limitations, 133
  study design, 124, 125f
  study procedure
    ANCOVAs, 129
    descriptive statistics, 129
    30-minute session, 127–128
    parental consent form, 128
    self-esteem, 129–130
    self-esteem questionnaire, 128
    T-tests, 129
    website check, 130, 130t
Self-affirmation theory, 124
Self-esteem, 129–130, 135–136
  ANOVA, 129–130
  baseline and post intervention, 130f
  depression and low self-esteem, 80
  longitudinal research, 80

## INDEX

**Self-esteem** (*Continued*)
  Rosenberg Self-esteem Scale, 90
  school performance, 80
  thematic approach, 48, 48t
**Self-regulation**, 16
**Sex and relationship education (SRE)**
  academies and free schools, 26, 26f
  basic sex education, 26−27
  issues, 139
  local authority maintained schools, 26−27
  secondary schools, 27
  sexual coercion, 26
  STIs and emergency contraception, 27
**Sex talk multiplayer game**, 39
**Sexting**, 136t
  age, 19
  American survey, 19
  best practices, 21
  definition, 18−19
  meta-analyses, 19
  prevalence, 18−19
  professional's views, 20−21
  and risky sexual behavior, 21
  self-report questionnaire studies, 18−19
  Sex and Tech survey, 19
  teenagers' views, 19−20, 20t
  United Kingdom, 19
**Sexual abuse**, 16−17
**Sexual health**, 2
  in digital world
    low SES female teenagers, 21−22
    negative sexual health outcomes, 21−22
    pornography, 18
    sexting. *See* Sexting
    teenage pregnancy consequences, 22
  risky sexual behavior. *See* Risky sexual behavior
**Sexual health education**
  professional views. *See* Sexual health professional views
  schools and digital interventions
    adolescent pregnancy prevention clinics, 28
    digital interventions. *See* Digital sexual health interventions
    "no worries clinics", 28
    outside of schools, 28−29
    parental communication, 29
    Positive Youth Development (PYD) program, 29

**Sexual health education** (*Continued*)
    school-based interventions, 25−28
    sexually active adolescents, 28−29
    Sex Worth Talking About (SWTA), 28−29
    stakeholders' perceptions, 28−29
    theory of planned behavior, 28−29
**Sexual health professional views**, 3, 136t
  genitourinary medicine (GUM) advice, 41−42
  qualitative method, 42
  thematic approach
    coding, 44−45
    environment and family theme, 45−46, 46t
    essentialism, 42
    high importance factors, 50t−51t
    implications, 53
    intervention programs, 48−49, 49t
    low importance factors, 52t
    materials and procedure, 43−44
    medium importance factors, 52t
    naming and defining, 44−45
    participants, 42−43, 43t
    peer influences, 47, 48t
    peer-to-peer resources, 53
    procedure, 44−45, 44f
    rank order task, 44, 44f
    self-esteem, 48, 48t, 53
    six-phase guide, 42
    society and media theme, 46−47, 47t
    transcribed data, 44−45
**Sex Worth Talking About (SWTA)**, 28−29
**Social networking sites (SNSs)**, 35−37, 99−100
**Society and media, thematic approach**, 46−47
**Student app study**, 136t
**Students' views, menstrual tracking apps**
**Subjective norms**, 7

### T

**Teenteenager's sexual health knowledge**, 3, 136t
  diary studies, 71t
    anal and oral sex, 74
    basic STI knowledge, 74
    coding, 73

**Teenteenager's sexual health knowledge** (*Continued*)
    contraception methods, 74
    daily written diaries, 70
    demographic information, 71, 71t
    diary entry, 72f
    future aspects, 77
    general sexual health questions, 74
    implications, 77
    information sources, 75−76, 76t
    lack of reproductive knowledge, 74
    participants, 70
    procedure, 72−73
    qualitative approach, 70
    social consequences of sex, 75
    socioeconomic status background, 70−71
    thematic analysis, 73
    4-week paper-based diary, 71−72
  low socioeconomic status (SES) backgrounds, 69−70
  sex and relationship education (SRE), 69
**Text messaging interventions**, 99−100
  advantages, 37
  face-to-face sessions, 38
  limitations, 38
  privacy and safeguarding issues, 38
  qualitative study, 37
  short daily text messages, 38
  smartphone technology, 37
  weekly text messaging intervention, 37−38
**Theory of planned behavior (TPB)**
  attitudes, 7
  cognitive mediators, 7−8
  condoms usage, 7−8
  criticism, 8
  perceived behavioral control, 7
  subjective norms, 7

### U

**Unconventional behaviors**, 9−10
**Unforeseen consequences**, 59t−62t

### W

**Web 2.0 framework**, 35−36
**4-week paper-based diary**, 71−72

### Y

**Young lovers guide website**, 102t